The Railways of Stourbridge

by
Clive Butcher

THE OAKWOOD PRESS

ISBN 0 85361 533 0

Typeset by Oakwood Graphics.
Repro by Ford Graphics, Ringwood, Hants.
Printed by Alpha Print (Oxford) Ltd, Witney, Oxon.

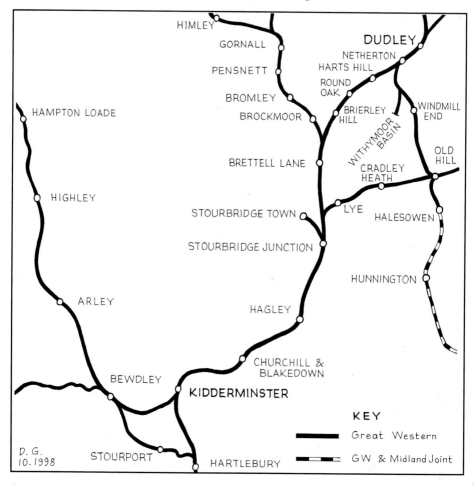

Title page: Stourbridge Junction clock, September 1997. An unusual feature of this clock is that the semaphore signals on the top, go up and down on the hour.   *Author*

Published by
The Oakwood Press (Usk)
P.O. Box 13, Usk, Mon., NP5 1YS.

Contents

Councillor H. Hardwick, Mayor of Stourbridge, seen at Stourbridge Junction, June 1964.
Birmingham Post & Mail

Acknowledgements

In the course of this work I have met, spoken and written to a large number of people. Whether it be large or small, their contributions have played a part and without them this book could not have provided the depth of information that I believe it has. Therefore, I gratefully acknowledge their assistance.

In particular I would like to thank former Stourbridge railwaymen Stan Lawrence, Ray Williams, Ray Kendrick and Dennis Harris; colleague John Heathcock, whose personal reminiscences and advice often opened up new avenues to investigate; Richard Woodley for patiently putting up with numerous enquiries and providing much useful data; Geoff Hingley and Trevor Lawrence for offering assistance and allowing access to books and documents; Patrick Evans of Shedmaster Archives; Richard Strange of Steam Archive Services; Steve Perkins for supplying data from his Archive Service; Norman Preedy for his lists of locomotives noted at the depot; Ned Williams for reading the manuscript; Eddie Lyons for permission to use shed drawings and help on track layout; George Bennett for lists of locomotives noted at Stourbridge; Tony Cooke for supplying much additional information on sidings and branches, correcting errors and allowing the use of track diagrams; Mark Rawlinson 'Freightmaster'; and valuable contributions from Fred Price, Geoff Pardoe, Giles Angell, Dave Hayes, Viv Morgan and also several members of the Engine Shed Society. To many of the above I was a total stranger, this though did not prevent them from giving me the benefit of their extensive knowledge.

I would also like to thank managers and staff at 'Collector's Corner'; Railfreight Distribution and Railtrack Midlands; as well as Roy Millership and several colleagues whose assistance was very much appreciated.

Thanks must also go to the staff of Dudley Archives and Local History Service; Kidderminster, Dudley, Stourbridge and Brierley Hill Libraries; Worcestershire County Records Office; Staffordshire Archive Service; the Public Record Office at Kew; the British Railways Board Records Centre; and the Planning and Leisure Department, Dudley MBC.

Thanks also to Express & Star Newspapers; Her Majesty's Stationery Office; *Birmingham Post & Mail*; the Black Country Museum; Lens of Sutton; Dudley Libraries; Kidderminster Railway Museum; Tom Cockeram, Roger Carpenter, W.F. Deebank, Trevor Lawrence, Keith Jones, John Dew, Richard Casserley, Norman Preedy, Ray Hinton, Dave Allen, Roger Walker, John Gibbs and Newsquest Media Group Ltd for permission to use photographs; Ordnance Survey who allowed extracts from maps to be reproduced and Miss D. Shelton.

Sadly, Stan Lawrence passed away during August 1996.

'57XX' class 0-6-0PT No. 3667 is seen at Stourbridge Junction on 9th February, 1957, whilst an unidentified Churchward Mogul heads a freight. *J.W. Gibbs*

Introduction

Mention of 'the Black Country', when speaking to those who live elsewhere, often leads to the question: 'That's Birmingham isn't it?' This vague association with the West Midlands' principal city though is rarely accepted gracefully by those who reside in the area, although the boundaries of the Black Country are themselves subject to local interpretation and often surrounded by controversy. One thing that most, if not all, local people would agree upon is that Birmingham is not part of it. Where then is 'the Black Country'? One definition of the region would include those towns that stood upon that part of the South Staffordshire coal measures (the 'thirty foot' or 'thick' coal seam) that had been easily workable, i.e. coal lying at shallow depths or as outcrops. These towns became the centre of a flourishing iron industry due to the abundance of good quality coal and the availability of ironstone. In the light of such a definition, then strictly speaking Stourbridge is not in the Black Country, but adjacent to its south-west periphery, lying as it does above coal seams which are much deeper than those exploited in nearby Brierley Hill, Cradley Heath and Dudley. However, to exclude Stourbridge from the Black Country this basis is to ignore the implications of a broader definition; one which emphasises the economic interdependence that inextricably bound Stourbridge to its Black Country neighbours. Consequently, in the context of this book at least, Stourbridge is as much a part of 'the Black Country' as those other towns located in easy reach of the 'thick' coal seam.

Originally known as 'Sturburg', the town was mentioned as early as 1255 AD in the Worcestershire assize role. Stourbridge clearly owes its name to an ancient bridge which lay across the River Stour, the old boundary between Staffordshire and Worcestershire. Along with most other towns in the Black Country, Stourbridge suffered from an inadequate transport system with roads, such as they were, being of little use as a means of moving large quantities of vital raw materials to the area and finished goods to the market. The situation improved slightly when the River Stour, between Stourbridge and Kidderminster, was made navigable by Andrew Yarranton in the mid-1660s although, this said, transport facilities between Stourbridge and elsewhere remained primitive until the development of the local canal system during the last 25 years of the 18th century. The arrival of the canals meant that Stourbridge was at last able to establish a line of communication with other large industrial towns in the region, as well as those markets along the River Severn. Equally, it also meant easy access to the abundant coal and mineral deposits around Dudley and Brierley Hill thereby ensuring a ready supply of good quality coal, fireclay and other minerals necessary to feed the insatiable appetites of local glass and ironworks. Unfortunately, shipping goods and materials by canal was costly in terms of time and local industrialists did not have time to spare. As a result, the eyes of industry turned towards the rapidly developing railway network.

Despite the fact that Stourbridge and its neighbouring 'Black Country' towns had been for many years recognised as an important manufacturing and mineral rich area, railways came to the area relatively late. If, though, the term 'railways' is considered in a wider sense, the town's association with this form of transport goes back much earlier, to the middle of the 17th century in fact. It would appear that the first known use of 'railways' in the locality was at Coalbournbrook, a hamlet just on the outskirts of Stourbridge. In 1665 this 'railway', one of two authorised by Parliament as part of an overall plan to make the Rivers Stour and Salwarpe navigable, entered service moving coal from a colliery in Pensnett to a wharf on the Stour. The coal was carried in horse-drawn waggons over wooden rails.

During the 1820s the Stourbridge firm of Foster, Rastrick & Company became involved in the manufacture of steam locomotives, in particular the *Stourbridge Lion* and the *Agenoria*. Both locomotives were built in 1829, however, their history is separated by the vast expanse of the Atlantic Ocean. The *Stourbridge Lion* left Stourbridge for Liverpool during February 1829 arriving in the United States on 13th May. After a static demonstration the 'Lion' made its working debut on the Delaware & Hudson Canal Company's railway on 8th August followed by a further trial on 9th September. Evidently, the Delaware & Hudson Canal Company was unimpressed and the locomotive was placed in store. By 1914 what was left

Agenoria c. 1860.

of the *Stourbridge Lion* had been reassembled and put on show at the Smithsonian Institution. Two other locomotives built by Foster, Rastrick & Company, the *Delaware* and the *Hudson*, both crossed the Atlantic although their final fate is not certain. Nearer to home *Agenoria* was to earn its corn on the Earl of Dudley's Shut(t) End Railway. The railway opened on 2nd June, 1829, *Agenoria* hauling two demonstration trains of 41 tons 18 cwt and 131 tons 10 cwt over the relatively level central section. The locomotive worked on the railway for about 35 years until a breakdown caused it to be abandoned and left to rot in a field. During 1884 *Agenoria* was rescued and after restoration was exhibited at the Wolverhampton & Staffordshire Fine Arts & Industrial Exhibition. Later, *Agenoria* visited several sites around the country until finally arriving at the National Railway Museum in 1974. The locomotive's designer, John Urpeth Rastrick was also a civil engineer who subsequently went on, especially during the 1830s and 1840s, to become associated with a number of railway schemes both locally and elsewhere. It was about this time that railway promoters began to take a serious interest in the construction of a railway to Stourbridge; it is also the starting point of the following narrative.

* * * * * *

Before proceeding to the main story a few lines regarding the general nature of the book itself. The inspiration behind it all came from the publication of a short article in the Railway Press relating to the 'Kingswinford Railway Walk' at Wombourne. In fact, a second article that was being prepared on the Railways of Stourbridge subsequently grew into what you see before you.

During the course of producing this work, it was pointed out that the subject area had already been well researched. To a certain extent this is true. This said, I felt that despite a number of excellent books that have been published which have included Stourbridge as part of a wider story, there was still much more to be written and consequently set out to provide the reader with a thorough and serious study which exclusively focused upon the development of the railway system in and around the town. However, whilst the basic aim remained unchanged, the discovery of more and more related information suggested that the initial geographical boundaries were going to be too restrictive and it was decided to extend these as far as Blower's Green on the former Oxford, Worcester & Wolverhampton Railway, and Old Hill on the Stourbridge Railway. Both railways were later absorbed by the Great Western.

The book itself is not directed at one particular section of the Railway readership. Hopefully, it will appeal to all those with an interest in railways in this part of the Black Country. It is a detailed history which recalls the sequence of events which ultimately led to today's railway operation in the area. The book places heavy emphasis on the 19th and early 20th centuries and fully utilises contemporary material, especially local newspaper reports to provide the reader with a flavour of the period and an understanding of the thinking at the time. This though, does not mean that the railway operation itself has been ignored: quite the contrary in fact. The freight and passenger services in the area, from the earliest days to the present, together with the associated motive power, have been covered at length. The reminiscences and experiences of local railwaymen bring to the text the personal touch of men who actually worked at Stourbridge depot and operated its services.

The book also covers two areas often neglected in works with wider geographical boundaries. Firstly, the private tramways and mineral railways which fed much lucrative business into the main line operation and secondly, the railway schemes proposed but never constructed, and very grand some of these schemes were. Both areas have been covered in some detail. One of the enduring mysteries of the latter is why the iron-making towns such as Kinver, Cookley and Wolverley that were located along the Stour Valley, were never connected to the rail network, despite the many schemes that were promoted to achieve this. Admittedly, Kinver did eventually become rail connected to Stourbridge in the form of the Kinver Light Railway, an electric tramway of most unusual construction. The story of this though forms part of a companion work which looks at the Tramways of Stourbridge.

Finally, I have laid claim to the view that this is an exhaustive study of all aspects of railway operation in the Stourbridge area. However, almost inevitably there will be omissions and I am sure there will be mistakes, all of which being solely attributable to the Author. Consequently, any additional material relating to the subject areas, or information leading to the rectification of errors, can be passed on via the publisher and would be very gratefully received.

OXFORD, WORCESTER, & WOLVERHAMPTON RAILWAY.

OPENING of the LINE between STOURBRIDGE, KIDDERMINSTER, DROITWICH, WORCESTER, PERSHORE, AND EVESHAM.

STOURBRIDGE TO KIDDERMINSTER, DROITWICH, WORCESTER, AND EVESHAM.

Miles	STATIONS.	WEEK DAYS.						SUNDAYS.			FARES FROM STOURBRIDGE.		
		1	2	3	4	5	6	1	2	3	1st Class	2nd Class	3rd Class
		1 2 3 Class Gov.	1 2 Class	1 2 3 Class	1 2 3 Class	1 2 3 Class	1 2 3 Class	1 2 3 Class	1 2 3 Class	1 2 3 Class			
		Morn.	Morn.	Aft.	Aft.	Aft.	Aft.	Morn.	Aft.	Aft.	s. d.	s. d.	s. d.
	STOURBRIDGE	8 5	11 5	2 5	3 30	6 20	9 0	7 0	1 0	5 10	..	..	..
7½	KIDDERMINSTER..	8 24	11 23	2 24	3 45	6 38	9 15	7 18	1 18	5 30	1 6	1 0	0 6
11	HARTLEBURY	8 35	11 33	2 35		6 48		7 28	1 28	5 41	2 3	1 7	0 11
18½	DROITWICH........	8 49	11 46	2 49	..	7 0	..	7 42	1 42	5 56	3 6	2 6	1 4½
19½	FEARNALL HEATH	8 56	11 53	2 56	..	7 7	..	7 48	1 48	6 3	4 0	2 10	1 7¼
22	WORCESTER.. { arr. { dep.	9 5 9 15	12 0 12 15	3 5 3 25	..	7 15 7 30	..	7 55 8 10	1 55	6 10 6 25	4 6	3 3	1 10
30	PERSHORE............	9 34	12 34	3 44	..	7 49	..	8 29	..	6 44	6 3	4 5	2 6
32½	FLADBURY	9 42	12 42	3 52	..	7 57	..	8 37	..	6 52	6 10	4 9	2 8½
36	EVESHAM	9 50	12 50	4 0	..	8 5	..	8 45	..	7 0	7 6	5 3	3 0

EVESHAM TO WORCESTER, DROITWICH, KIDDERMINSTER, AND STOURBRIDGE.

Miles	STATIONS.	WEEK DAYS.						SUNDAYS.			FARES FROM EVESHAM.		
		1	2	3	4	5	6	1	2	3	1st Class	2nd Class	3rd Class
		1 2 3 Class	1 2 3 Class	1 2 Class	1 2 3 Class	1 2 3 Class	1 2 3 Class Gov.	1 2 3 Class	1 2 3 Class	1 2 3 Class			
		Morn.	Morn.	Morn.	Aft.	Aft.	Aft.	Morn.		Aft.	s. d.	s. d.	s. d.
	EVESHAM	..	7 40	10 0	1 20	..	5 5	9 20	..	7 35	..	..	..
3½	FLADBURY	..	7 49	10 9	1 29	..	5 18	9 29	..	7 44	0 9	0 6	0 3
6	PERSHORE............	..	7 57	10 17	1 37	..	5 21	9 37	..	7 52	1 3	0 11	0 6
14	WORCESTER.. } arr. } dep.	..	8 11 8 20	10 33 10 45	1 50 2 0	..	5 35 6 0	9 55 10 5	2 15	8 8 8 20	3 0	2 1	1 2
16½	FEARNALL HEATH	..	8 26	10 52	2 7	..	6 7	10 12	2 22	8 27	3 6	2 6	1 4½
19½	DROITWICH........	..	8 34	11 0	2 15	..	6 15	10 20	2 30	8 36	4 1	2 10	1 7¼
25½	HARTLEBURY		8 45	11 11	2 26	..	6 26	10 31	2 41	8 47	5 3	3 9	2 1
29	KIDDERMINSTER ..	7 30	8 57	11 24	2 38	4 15	6 38	10 42	2 54	9 0	6 0	4 3	2 5
36	STOURBRIDGE	7 45	9 15	11 40	2 55	4 30	6 55	11 0	3 10	9 20	7 6	5 3	3 0

The OWWR timetable for May 1852. The first timetable to include Stourbridge.

Chapter One

The Early Days

The railway age dawned upon Stourbridge on 1st May, 1852. Shortly after 9 am, a train consisting of 21 carriages conveying Directors of the railway company, friends and relatives, departed from Stourbridge station (it was not known as Stourbridge Junction until much later) on a celebratory journey to Evesham calling at Kidderminster, Droitwich, Worcester and Pershore; a journey of 36 miles. The train, carrying upwards of 150 passengers, received a 29 gun salute as it steamed past Oldswinford church, near to White Hall, the residence of Mr Tredwells, the contractor involved in the building of the section between Stourbridge and Evesham. At Kidderminster, Droitwich and Worcester, the train was joined by the respective Mayor and Council members, each stop being accompanied by the sound of a brass band that had been accommodated in the leading carriage.

The Mayor of Evesham, together with members of the Council and prominent members of the community had assembled at the Old Town Hall, the procession moving off at 10.30 am toward the station in good time to meet the incoming 'special'. The train arrived at between 11.00 am and midday to a tumultuous welcome from a crowd estimated to be in the region of 10,000. The company Directors and accompanying dignitaries were then escorted to the Guildhall where a sumptuous lunch had been provided. Mr H. Workman, the Mayor of Evesham, presided over this excellent feast which was attended by 200 or so of the district's most noteworthy gentlemen. Among the guests were Lord Marcus Hill, Sir H. Willoughby, Mr J.H.H. Foley MP, Captain Rushout MP (Lord Ward's successor as company Chairman in 1851) and Mr Peto MP. Meanwhile, the remainder of the party numbering about 120 ladies and gentlemen, friends of Mr Tredwells, were being entertained at the 'Star Hotel' under the able presidency of Stourbridge's Captain Hickman. At 2.30 pm, well after the agreed time of return, the visitors made their way back to the station and boarded their train for the journey back to Stourbridge. Along the way the 'special' was again greeted with the discharge of cannon and the cheers of the large crowds that had gathered at the stations to witness this momentous occasion. On arrival at Stourbridge many of the guests departed for home undoubtedly well pleased with the day's events. However, for some the celebrations continued and for these it was back onto the train and a return to Kidderminster. Here they were met by the Mayor, Mr Grosvenor and the Town Council, the procession making its way to the 'Lion Hotel' where dinner was served. During the course of the evening it became abundantly clear that there was considerable support in favour of the proposed Oxford to Brentford Railway scheme which, if built, would have enabled company trains to run over the London & South Western Railway into Waterloo. At around 9.00 pm the party broke up and guests began to return to the station. Until now, the celebrations had gone according to plan: this situation though was about to change.

It would appear that the Mayor of Evesham had commandeered the train in order to return several of the company's Directors to Droitwich where they would catch their Midland Railway connection. However, the engine driver had apparently gone 'absent without leave' in Kidderminster, so it was David Joy, the company's locomotive superintendent, who had to take the engine and several carriages down to Droitwich. Having disposed of his passengers, Joy was in the process of preparing for the return to Kidderminster to pick-up the remaining Directors when disaster almost overtook the day's events. At Droitwich the locomotive had to run round its train. Unfortunately, the station master switched the wrong points at the north end of the station, causing the engine to come off the rails on the bridge carrying the line over the Birmingham-Worcester canal. Thankfully, the results of this incident, although extremely embarrassing, were not irredeemable as the locomotive did not at least disappear into the muddy waters below. However, it was not possible to re-rail it so Joy had to commandeer a spare engine from elsewhere, the train eventually arriving at Kidderminster at around 11.00 pm. Finally, with the rest of the party safely on board the train once again headed south and at nearly midnight it pulled into Worcester, the home of the company that had given its name to the line. That company: The Oxford, Worcester and Wolverhampton Railway (OWWR), or as it was to become known 'the Old Worse and Worse'.

The OWWR was not the first scheme to include Stourbridge. As early as 1824 there had been a proposal to build a railway between Gloucester and Birmingham, which would also serve as an outlet for the products of the fire-clay collieries and brickworks of Stourbridge. This scheme was abandoned in 1826. During 1833/34 two further projects were evaluated relating to a line between Gloucester and Birmingham. The first was a proposal known as the Cambrian, Gloucester, Birmingham & London Railway that would link the two cities via Worcester, Kidderminster, Stourbridge and Dudley. The second was virtually a direct link over the Lickey Incline. Despite widespread support little was done to further the interests of the Cambrian, Gloucester, Birmingham & London Railway and Gloucester was eventually linked to Birmingham via the Lickey Incline, the route having been slightly modified to include Cheltenham (the Birmingham and Gloucester Railway). The choice of the latter had been influenced by land prices, which being lower than those associated with the more westerly alternative due to the increasing prosperity of the Black Country and Worcestershire towns, had clearly outweighed the geographical disadvantages implied by a route over Lickey. This decision certainly displeased a number of interested parties, who subsequently met at Worcester to pass a resolution not to support any railway proposal for the area which did not identify a route through Worcester.

In 1835, the Grand Connection Railway promoted a further plan to link Gloucester and Birmingham via Worcester, Kidderminster and Stourbridge. However, after negotiations with the Birmingham and Gloucester Railway (B&G), the Grand Connection Railway decided to drop its Southern section between Worcester and Gloucester and concentrate instead on the Northern section from Worcester through Stourbridge to Wolverhampton where a connection with the Grand Junction Railway had been proposed. This scheme was thrown out by Parliament in May 1837 and although later in 1837 the Grand Connection Railway revived a much shortened version linking Stourbridge to Worcester, where it was to have joined the authorised Worcester branch of the B & G, this was not proceeded with.

During 1836/37 two schemes were proposed that would have joined Stourbridge and Birmingham. The first involved a line from Birmingham through Halesowen (where a branch to Dudley would have diverged), Cradley and Lye and was known as the Stourbridge, Dudley and Birmingham Railway. The Civil Engineer employed on this project was J.U. Rastrick, co-founder of the Stourbridge foundry and locomotive manufacturer 'Foster, Rastrick & Company', the firm responsible for building the famous *Agenoria*. The second was an intended branch to Stourbridge via Dudley that would have left the proposed main line between Birmingham and Wolverhampton at Burnt Tree. This was the Birmingham, Dudley, Stourbridge and Wolverhampton Railway.

In 1844, J.U. Rastrick was engaged as Civil Engineer on the Stourbridge & Birmingham Railway project. His proposal advocated a railway, including a branch to Spon Lane, which would have left a junction with the proposed Birmingham, Wolverhampton & Shrewsbury Railway to terminate at a Mr Collis's field in Stourbridge. In the same year, the promoters of the Shrewsbury & Birmingham Railway also laid plans for a branch to Stourbridge but this would have continued to Stourport having left the main line at Smethwick. On 3rd August, 1846, powers to construct a railway between Birmingham and Wolverhampton, over the route originally drawn up for the Shrewsbury & Birmingham Railway (S&B) were vested in the Birmingham, Wolverhampton and Stour Valley Railway Company (the latter was a joint venture including the S&B, London & North Western Railway (LNWR) & the Birmingham Canal Co.). The company had included the words 'Stour Valley' in the title in recognition of the absorption of the S&B's proposal to construct a branch to Stourbridge and Stourport through the valley of the River Stour. This branch, though, was never authorised and when the LNWR revived interest in its construction in 1852/3, Parliament's condition allowing the OWWR to have running powers over the main line into Birmingham (New Street) was considered too high a price to pay and the scheme was dropped.

By the end of 1844 railway 'mania' was sweeping the country and Worcestershire was no exception with a large number of schemes being promoted in the local press. However, like snow in the rays of the sun many of these just simply melted away to be forgotten. But there was one proposal which, despite the odds, survived to continue through Parliament during 1845 to finally receive the Royal Assent. This scheme was the Oxford, Worcester and Wolverhampton Railway, a broad gauge railway promoted with the assistance of the Great Western. However, two notable narrow gauge rivals of the OWWR, the Birmingham & Gloucester's 'Worcester and Wolverhampton Railway' and the London & Birmingham's Tring to Wolverhampton scheme were to be casualties of the Parliamentary process early in 1845. At the beginning of the year, the B&G's scheme was withdrawn in favour of the strongly supported London & Birmingham's (L&B) proposal. Subsequently, much to the surprise of its many advocates, the L&B's 'Tring Railway' then failed to win Parliamentary approval being thrown out in June 1845.

The B & G had proposed a line that would have left its own main line at Abbotswood along the authorised Worcester branch and then on to Kidderminster, Stourbridge, Dudley and finally Wolverhampton. However, the main threat to the OWWR appeared to be the L&B's scheme, known as the London, Worcester & South Staffordshire Railway (it is believed that this was originally called the London, Worcester, Rugby & Oxford Railway the name being changed with the introduction of an extension to Dudley and Wolverhampton). The L&B promoted a railway that would link Tring with Wolverhampton via a line through Banbury, Worcester, Stourport, the western edge of Stourbridge and Dudley, where a branch would be constructed to Sedgley and Brierley Hill. Remarkably, despite the support of the owners of 46 iron works, 57 furnaces and 98 collieries, including the trustees of Lord Ward whose estate produced upward of 1 million tons of coal and iron annually, as well as the Railway Department of the Board of Trade, Parliament rejected the scheme.

Although this book is about the railways of Stourbridge and the neighbouring towns, it might be useful to describe briefly the history of the OWWR as it was this company that first put Stourbridge onto the railway map. Plans for the new railway were first brought to the attention of local people on 22nd and 29th May, 1844, when the *Wolverhampton Chronicle* published the Prospectus of the Oxford, Worcester and Wolverhampton Railway. This document outlined the proposed construction of a line that would:

. . . branch out of the Grand Junction Railway at the station near the important manufacturing town of Wolverhampton . . . It will pass then through highly valuable mineral property, and in the immediate neighbourhood of the town of Dudley . . . passing several important ironworks, and through a densely populated manufacturing district to Stourbridge . . . From Stourbridge the line will proceed through Kidderminster . . . to Droitwich . . . to the city of Worcester . . . to Pershore, Evesham, Banbury and Oxford.

The Prospectus referred to the projected income that had been calculated by the promoters of the Grand Connection Railway. It was suggested that in view of the completion of certain main lines since the report of the Grand Connection Railway was published it was not unreasonable to suggest that the proposed line would achieve a similar, if not a better, result for its investors. The Prospectus went on to say, 'that there is not a line of country in the Kingdom now unoccupied by a railway which affords a greater prospect of remuneration, from the establishment of such a course of communication, than the present'.

However, supporters of the scheme, including manufacturers on both sides of the 'Ridge', but especially those to the west whose businesses were far removed from the existing railway network, were particularly keen to begin negotiations with a 'friendly' company that would back this venture. This 'friendly' company was the Great Western. Consequently, the inclusion of four Directors of the Great Western Railway Company on the scheme's management committee was seen by the *Chronicle* as guaranteeing the bona fides of the undertaking (the subsequent Act authorised six of the 16 Directors to be Great Western nominees). Unfortunately, the marriage between the OWWR and the GWR was to be quite a stormy affair and despite the fine words, the story of the line's construction was not to be quite so straightforward!

Stourbridge and its neighbouring towns and villages were located to the west of a ridge of ancient rock that had always proved to be a formidable obstacle to the development of transport communication in the Black Country. Although the western towns were served by an extensive system of canals that provided a cheap, if relatively slow, means for transporting the region's manufactured goods and raw materials, many industrialists considered that the area would benefit from the introduction of a railway system. Those who owned local industries had possibly cast an envious eye to the east of the region where on the other side of the 'Ridge' the Grand Junction Railway had built a line connecting Birmingham to the Lancashire town of Warrington, from which access to the major port of Liverpool and the city of Manchester had been made available, although, strangely, the line did actually bypass the important West Midland towns of Walsall and Wolverhampton. Traffic to London was carried by the London and Birmingham Railway but unfortunately, the development of a single trunk route from the capital to the industrial conurbations of Lancashire was hindered by company rivalry that was not resolved until the formation of the London & North Western Railway on 1st January, 1846.

To the supporters of the OWWR, the attractions of the scheme lay in the fact that it would provide access to both the developing markets in the North and those in and around London, in addition to providing competition with the unloved London & Birmingham which some felt had been guilty of exploiting its monopolistic position. On the other hand, the Great Western Railway saw the OWWR as an ideal opportunity to launch a two-pronged, broad gauge offensive aimed at extending Paddington's influence into the rapidly developing industrial centres in the northern counties of Victorian England. Already in 1844, the GWR had promoted the Oxford & Rugby Railway which was designed to provide a potential route into Yorkshire via Derby by connecting with the Midland Counties Railway at Rugby. It was therefore of considerable interest to the GWR that the route of the Oxford, Worcester & Wolverhampton Railway, having passed through the heavily industrialised Black Country, would subsequently join the Grand Junction Railway (GJR) just to the north of Wolverhampton. This link with the GJR would provide the GWR with the scope to pursue further its northern ambitions by securing a route to Crewe (assuming the co-operation of the GJR) and from there, the key Lancashire towns of Warrington, Liverpool and Manchester. Unfortunately, for the Great Western, there was considerable opposition to any broad gauge development and consequently all such proposals would be assured of a rough ride if and when they reached Parliament.

In 1845 the OWWR Bill was laid before Parliament and after extensive debate, both before a House of Commons Select Committee and in the Lords, the Bill received the Royal Assent on 4th August, 1845. The subsequent Act empowered the OWWR Company to build a broad gauge railway from a branch near Oxford, through Worcester, Stourbridge and Dudley to the GJR near its Wolverhampton station, which had been erected a mile to the north-east of the town at Wednesfield Heath. It also allowed mixed gauge track on that part of the line between the GJR and the B&G at Abbots Wood Junction.

The financial situation of the infant railway company was, from the outset, a critical factor to say the least and even before a rail was laid the company had incurred massive costs. Beset by continuing financial troubles and a simmering dispute with its sponsor the Great Western, the problems finally came to a head in 1850. During this year an Act of Parliament authorised the OWWR to raise additional capital and consequently the company attempted to sever its links with the Great Western. The break-up of this tentative alliance created a vacuum that both the LNWR and the Midland Railway were eager to fill and on 21st February, 1851 the OWWR entered into an agreement with both companies to work a 'standard gauge' line for 21 years. However, as the 1845 Act implicitly indicated that the line be broad gauge in construction in order that it may conform to Great Western Railway operation, an injunction was granted to the Great Western restraining the OWWR's action.

The bitterness between the OWWR and the GWR continued unabated for several years with the former paying scant attention to the latter's demand that the construction of broad gauge track should take priority. As a result the OWWR was built virtually as a standard gauge railway although stretches of mixed gauge line were constructed. However, apart from the stretch between Priestfield station and Cannock Road Junction which enabled the GWR's broad gauge trains to gain access to Wolverhampton (Low Level), much of it was only laid to give the impression of complying with the Act and very little could, or even did, carry broad gauge traffic. In November 1855, the OWWR announced in the *Wolverhampton Chronicle* its intention to present before Parliament a Bill that would seek powers to enable the company and the Great Western to enter into an agreement to allow the discontinuance of broad gauge rails on the OWWR. Eventually, on 1st March, 1858, the OWWR did succeed in obtaining release from its broad gauge obligations.

Despite the problems being experienced by the OWWR, construction of the line continued and Stourbridge was reached by the end of April 1852. Six months later, the six mile stretch of line between Stourbridge and Dudley was completed (initially, the line was single track between Brettell Lane and Dudley) and opened to freight traffic on 16th November, the *Wolverhampton Chronicle* reporting that a number of trains had been seen carrying coal from the various pits in the area. On Monday 20th December passenger services began between the two towns, the *Chronicle* reporting as follows:

> On Tuesday [14th December, 1852], Mr Galton, inspector of railways, paid a visit of inspection to that part of the Oxford, Worcester & Wolverhampton line which lies between Stourbridge and Dudley in order to see whether the works were in proper condition for passenger traffic. The last line of rails between Stourbridge and Kidderminster, hitherto not used for passenger traffic, also underwent his examination. The report being favourable, the line was fully opened between Dudley and Evesham on Monday [20th December 1852]; and the directors expect to be able to open the remainder of the line, from Evesham to Oxford, on the 15th of January next.

The route between Stourbridge and Dudley is noted for the 949 yds-long tunnel under the 'Ridge' and two viaducts located at Stambermill (190 yds-long) and at Parkhead (164 yards). Originally, there had been a third which had been built near Brettell Lane, but this was subsequently filled-in (more about this later). The construction of the tunnel represented a major engineering challenge requiring somewhere in the region of seven million bricks to complete, the internal linings being three feet thick. This stretch of line was to serve intermediate stations at Brettell Lane, Round Oak and Netherton. At first, 'Round Oak' was known as 'Brierley Hill & Round Oak'. However, as the station had been built primarily to serve the huge ironworks at Round Oak itself, and was approximately ½ mile from Brierley Hill town centre, the OWWR must have decided that the name was not quite appropriate. Consequently, during 1853, the station was renamed 'Round Oak & Brierley Hill'. Midway through 1857 'Brierley Hill' was dropped from the title and the station simply became known as 'Round Oak'. The good people of Brierley Hill did get their own station eventually, albeit one that was not that much closer to the town centre than the one at Round Oak! The new station opened on 1st December, 1858, the *Brierley Hill Advertiser* describing the occasion as follows:

> Opening of the new station on the Oxford, Worcester & Wolverhampton Railway. On Wednesday last a new station, situated between the Round Oak and Brettell Lane stations on the above railway, and to be called Brierley Hill station, was opened for traffic. The proceedings were entirely of an unceremonious character, the first train that stopped being simply welcomed by the strains of the Brierley Hill drum and fife band, under the direction of Mr Jackson. The horse road in Fenton-street, leading to the station, has been repaired, the footpath considerably improved by relaying and channelling, and gas lamps have been erected at intervals; so that the character of that once dark and murky place, heretofore known as Pinner's-lane has undergone a most beneficial modification. Apropos of the Oxford and Worcester Railway, it may be mentioned that arrangements have been made for lighting with gas the stations between Dudley and Wolverhampton that have hitherto only been lit by oil lamps.

Netherton station was also to undergo a number of name changes as well as one relocation. Initially, 'Netherton' appears to have been located within the area later to be occupied by Blower's Green sidings, probably very close to where the goods shed was to be built. However, on 1st March, 1878, the station was closed and 'Dudley (South Side) & Netherton' was opened to replace it. This station was located about 300 yards closer to Dudley tunnel, thereby allowing it to accommodate passenger traffic off the Dudley to Old Hill branch which had also been opened on 1st March. On 21st August, 1921, the station was renamed 'Blower's Green'. During 1895 a fifth station was built on the line just to the north of Round Oak. Opened on 1st April, Harts Hill & Woodside had a relatively short working life being closed on 1st January, 1917 after having been in operation for less than 22 years.

Returning to the line in general, the standard (narrow) gauge track between Stourbridge and Evesham had been constructed in such a way as to allow the installation of an outer third rail which would enable the OWWR to comply with its broad gauge obligations. The sections between Droitwich and Stourbridge, and Norton Junction and Evesham opened on 1st May, 1852 (those between Worcester and Norton Junction, and Worcester and Droitwich had opened on 5th October, 1850 and 18th February, 1852 respectively), with regular passenger services between Evesham and Stourbridge commencing almost immediately. However, according to the enabling Act, the mixed gauge track would be laid in a northerly direction from the connection with the Midland at Abbots Wood Junction, implying that in the opposite direction, from Norton Junction (where the Abbots Wood branch joined the main OWWR) to Wolvercot Junction, track would be on the broad gauge. By February 1852 the GWR had become aware that the company was laying narrow gauge track southwards from Norton Junction and subsequently sought an injunction in March 1852. However, the injunction was refused by the Vice-Chancellor, Sir J. Parker, on the grounds that the Act did not specifically forbid the laying of narrow gauge track south of Norton Junction and that the OWWR possessed sufficient funds to complete the whole line on the mixed gauge thereby permitting the GWR to work it throughout. By the Spring of 1853, a mixed gauge line from Evesham to Wolvercot Junction had been constructed which seemed to force the GWR to consent to traffic off the OWWR, irrespective of gauge, running into its Oxford station over the mixed gauge track of the Oxford and Rugby line. The battle over, the OWWR arranged for an opening ceremony to be held on 21st April but a series of misfortunes resulted in its postponement until 7th May. Unfortunately, the Board of Trade Inspector then refused to pass the line for public working as the broad gauge rails had not been laid at certain locations and the junction at Wolvercot remained unfinished. The company, not to be put off by such trivial matters, carried out the 'opening' as arranged and at virtually first light a 26-carriage train, hauled by two locomotives, left Dudley for Wolvercot, where it was met by a second 'special' train that had been generously provided by the GWR to convey the party down to Oxford. The celebrations did prove to be a little premature for it was not until 2nd June that the Board of Trade Inspector, Captain Galton, to the great relief of the company's Directors, finally decided that the line met the required standards. The railway between Evesham and Wolvercot Junction opened for public use on Saturday 4th June, 1853.

North of Stourbridge, the railway reached Wolverhampton in December 1853 when a standard gauge connection was made with the LNWR at Tipton, thereby allowing trains off the OWWR to reach the town's Queen Street station via the LNWR's main line. With the OWWR now able to reach Wolverhampton there was a proposal to abandon the remaining five miles of its own authorised route from Tipton through Priestfield to a new station at Wolverhampton. However, the GWR needed the projected 'Low Level' station and actually approached Parliament for authorisation to complete the line from Priestfield to Wolverhampton. Parliament, though, was of a mind to insist upon the OWWR completing the route itself. Consequently, a reluctant company, spurred on by the threat of penalties hanging heavy over it, continued its route from Tipton to Priestfield where it made a junction with the GWR. From there the line continued to Wolverhampton where it joined the Shrewsbury & Birmingham Railway at Cannock Road Junction. This section was completed during April 1854. All that was now left was the stretch from Cannock Road Junction to the LNWR at Bushbury Junction and by July 1854 this too had been brought into use. This final stretch of track was initially for freight only, the line not being passed for passenger traffic until three months later, although passenger services from Wolverhampton (OWWR) to Tipton via intermediate stations at Bilston and Daisy Bank commenced on 1st July, 1854 (Priestfield station actually opened a few days later). And so the OWWR was finally finished, 10 years after the scheme was first proposed. It had been a very hard struggle, but the alternative route from London to Wolverhampton via Worcester, Stourbridge and Dudley had now been completed.

This part of the story ends on a sad note. It was reported in the *Brierley Hill Advertiser* on 20th August, 1859 that Stourbridge's former Chairman of the OWWR, Francis Rufford, had recently been committed to a lunatic asylum in Sutton Coldfield. Perhaps the problems that he had faced during the construction of the line, added to his own bankruptcy shortly after he left the company, had at last taken their toll?

Chapter Two

Expansion of the Network

The Main Line From Stourbridge to Birmingham

By 1860, plans were afoot to expand the railway network around Stourbridge. The formation of the West Midland Railway on 14th June, 1860, brought about by the merging of the OWWR with the Newport, Abergavenny & Hereford Railway and the Worcester & Hereford Railway, created the conditions for the construction of a further six lines in the new company's area, one of which was to become known as the Stourbridge Railway. The Stourbridge Railway Company was incorporated on 14th June, 1860, thereby obtaining authority to build a line from the OWWR at Stourbridge to Old Hill, a distance of 3½ miles which was to include two branches; the first was to Cradley Park and The Hayes, whilst the second was to bring a line into the Corngreaves Iron Works. Earlier, at a public meeting held at Cradley to obtain support for the line, it had been explained by the Chairman of the soon-to-be-formed Stourbridge Railway Company, Mr Akroyd, that the proposal would require financing to the sum of £80,000 to be raised through the issue of 4,000, £20 shares. In the light of current revenue per mile, the meeting required little persuading that the scheme would be viable and the proposal was adopted unanimously. It was subsequently reported that the first sod was lifted in a field adjoining Stourbridge station on Monday 11th February, 1861. This auspicious occasion, however, did not seem to generate very much by way of interest, the event passing without ceremony.

During the following year, on 1st August, 1861, the company, despite stiff opposition, especially from the LNWR and the Birmingham Canal Company, was authorised to build an extension to this line, thereby taking the route from Old Hill to a junction with the LNWR at Smethwick. Trains off the West Midland line would then be able to gain access to Birmingham (New Street) station via the LNWR main line. This Act was the Stourbridge Railway (Extension) Act, 1861. In effect, to carry out the powers authorised by the Stourbridge Railway Acts, it was necessary to create, at least nominally, two separate companies, i.e. The Stourbridge Railway Co. and The Stourbridge Railway (Extension) Co. Contemporary reports suggest that this was done in order to improve the chances of obtaining Parliamentary approval more easily than if a single scheme had been proposed for the line as a whole.

The first 2¼ miles to Cradley was constructed reasonably easily, although this section of line did have one formidable obstacle that would require some ingenuity to overcome. At Cradley Forge it was necessary to construct a bridge across the Stour at a point just to the south-west of Cradley station. The line was planned to cross the river at a height of 35 feet and great difficulty was encountered in finding a suitable location to lay the sort of foundation necessary to bear the weight of both the embankment and the brickwork. Eventually, having dug down to a depth of some 20 feet, a suitable stratum was found which enabled a foundation to be laid and the bridge built. The bridge was of quite substantial construction being approximately 13 feet thick at the base and 7 feet at the top, requiring upwards of three million bricks to be used. The nature of the ground at the site required the bridge to be constructed at a skew of 50 degrees to the line of the river.

On Saturday 14th February, 1863, with this first section of line almost finished, an inspection was carried out on behalf of the Board of Trade by Captain Rich (Royal Engineers). The inspection was carried out in the presence of Mr Akroyd (Chairman, Stourbridge Railway Company), Mr Harwood (Solicitor), Mr Wilson (Consulting Engineer, West Midland Railway), Mr Green (Resident Engineer, Stourbridge Railway), Mr Tinckham (Sir Morton Peto's agent - Sir Morton was a major railway contractor who also became Deputy Chairman of the OWWR from 1856) and Messrs Cleasby, Roberts and Heppingstall (West Midland Railway). The inspection was reported in the *Brierley Hill Advertiser* as follows :

He [Captain Rich] arrived at Stourbridge Station about eleven o'clock and at once proceeded to inspect the new signals, which the junction of the line with the West Midland have rendered necessary. The points at the junction were next looked at and then the bridge was tested in the usual manner, by running locomotives over it at different degrees of speed, while the deflection was taken underneath by an instrument used for that purpose. All the bridges on the line are girder bridges, with arched brickwork in the space between the girders. The inspection of the one junction having been completed, the Inspector proceeded along the line on two locomotives told off for the purpose. As the bridges were reached, the engines were stopped, and the same tests were applied as those used on the first. At the Lye station the signals were inspected and tested. This station is scarcely finished yet, but when a permanent station-house has taken the place of the temporary box which at present supplies the place of a house, it will certainly be a credit to the Lye as well as to the line. The approach from the road is easy, the platforms are roomy and commodious, and, so far as it has been finished, it has been so both tastefully and substantially. At Cradley Forge there is the greatest and most important engineering work of this portion of the line, in the shape of a bridge which spans the Stour . . . From this bridge to Cradley Heath Station is but a short distance, and after a few minutes spent there the engines whisked the party in a few minutes back to Stourbridge Station . . . But though the face of matters show that the scenic glory of the district is gone, the evidence on every hand of industry and enterprise show, on the other hand, that 'every yard of it is traffic'. . .

This section of line, together with a ½ mile-long branch to Corngreaves works and collieries, was subsequently opened on 1st April, 1863. In June of the same year, the ¾ mile-long branch from Lye to The Hayes goods station was completed. This branch also provided access to a number of local collieries (*see Chapter Five*).

In accordance with the agreements made with the Stourbridge Company on 20th May, 1861 and 25th July, 1863, the West Midland Railway was to work the Stourbridge to Old Hill and then the Old Hill to Galton Junction sections immediately on opening. However, the latter agreement was in reality made with the Great Western Railway Company as the West Midland Railway had been absorbed by that company following the passing of the Great Western Railway (West Midland Railway) Amalgamation Act of 13th July, 1863, effective as from 1st August, 1863.

Twelve months after the line to Cradley had opened, in April 1864, at the eighth half-yearly meeting of the Stourbridge Railway Company, it was reported that traffic on the section had far exceeded the expectations of the Directors with freight being consigned from the goods stations at Lye and Cradley to 271 different stations throughout the United Kingdom. However, the good news was speedily followed by the bad with the announcement that the proportion of the line's traffic receipts to be awarded to the company as determined by the Great Western was £1,532 18s. 0d. gross, £732 16s. 11d. net after subtraction of interest awarded on the debenture stock: these figures were not easily accepted by the company's Directors. It was also made known that as well as providing a passenger link to Birmingham, the Great Western was very keen to utilise the line to bring coal from South Wales into the West Midland industrial centres. At present this traffic was taken into the area by the Midland Railway, therefore with the opening of the Stourbridge Railway the Great Western would be able to compete with the Midland for this very lucrative traffic.

By September 1865, the Board of Trade had inspected the section between Cradley and Old Hill and issued the appropriate certificate. A new company had set up adjacent to Cradley station (the Staffordshire Public Chain and Anchor Testing Company Limited), thereby generating further traffic for the line to carry. However, the Great Western seemed a little slow in commencing services on the section much to the displeasure of freight customers located on the line and according to Mr Swindell, a major shareholder in the Stourbridge Company, getting the GWR to move was like trying to 'move a mountain'. The mountain was eventually moved and the section was opened on 1st January, 1866 thereby completing the first phase of the line which would eventually link Stourbridge and Birmingham. However, progress seems to have been hindered in the construction of the second phase of the line, that between Old Hill and the LNWR at Smethwick, by the need to bore a 896 yds-long tunnel located some 600 yds to the east of Old Hill station. This tunnel was to pass through the formidable West Midlands ridge, an undertaking made more difficult by the constant need to rid the workings of water. In fact between April and August, 1864 the tunnel had only been extended by 253 yards, i.e. from 457 yards to 710 yards in five months.

The construction of the tunnel was the source of an interesting dispute during 1865. Apparently, Sir Morton Peto's contractor was producing bricks for the tunnel lining out of excavated clay, a process that was perfectly legitimate and recognised as so in the contract for the work. However, Mr Swindell objected to this at the tenth half-yearly meeting of the company held in April 1865. It was argued that this practice was detrimental to local business, a fact that had not been contemplated in the Act. Another shareholder, Mr W.B. Collis had been supplying the bricks for the tunnel and was obviously a little peeved at losing the order. Sir Morton Peto, a wily old campaigner, had clearly seen an opportunity to decrease his costs and had seized the chance immediately. The meeting had also been informed that the Directors had applied to Parliament for powers to raise additional capital to meet the requirements of providing additional sidings and works.

One cost that was difficult to foresee in the estimates for the railway was that incurred through legal action taken against the company. In March 1865 an action was taken against the Stourbridge Railway Company and the Great Western Company by Messrs Barrs and Company, Rowley, the latter claiming compensation in the sum of £32,000 for land, severance and increased difficulty in working their mines due to railway lines crossing their property. The court did find in favour of the plaintiff, although the award of £11,830 10s. 0d. plus costs of £5,082 15s. 0d., to be apportioned between the Stourbridge Railway Company, the Stourbridge Railway (Extension) Company and the Great Western Railway Company, was substantially lower than the company had hoped to obtain.

The second phase of the line from Old Hill to Smethwick (the Stourbridge Extension), was eventually opened on 1st April, 1867, the line connecting into the LNWR at Galton Junction and giving access to Birmingham (New Street). The completion of the line between Stourbridge Junction and Smethwick was not, however, the end of the story for the Great Western, which, having a major interest in the line being constructed by the Stourbridge Railway Company, clearly did not wish to see all the benefit accrue to its main rival. Consequently, some years earlier, the Great Western and West Midland Railway Companies had proposed to extend the line from a junction at Smethwick to the Great Western main line at a junction between West Bromwich and Handsworth, north of Birmingham. The result of the efforts of the companies to secure authority for this proposal was reported at a shareholders' meeting in September 1862:

The Great Western Railway Company, now in alliance with the West Midland Railway Company, after a most protracted and obstinate opposition by the London North Western Company, in Committees of both Houses of Parliament in the last session, obtained authority to construct a line of railway from the Stourbridge extension railway at Smethwick to the Wolverhampton and Dudley line at West Bromwich, by which means the traffic off the Stourbridge line will have direct and independent communication with Birmingham and the entire Great Western lines.

It was also mentioned at this same meeting that Parliament had authorised the company to build a branch line from Halesowen via Old Hill to the OWWR at Netherton Junction near Dudley, the line being seen as a valuable feeder route into the Stourbridge to Birmingham main line.

The section from Smethwick Junction to the Great Western main line at Handsworth Junction, made under the Great Western Railway Additional Powers Act, 1862, was also opened on 1st April, 1867, thereby enabling passengers access to Birmingham (Snow Hill) as well as Birmingham (New Street). The works on the whole line had cost £379,242 1s. 3d. with £138,564 8s. 9d. being costed to the Stourbridge Railway and £240,677 12s. 6d. to the Stourbridge Extension, although it was estimated that a further £15,000 would be needed to complete the outstanding work on the line satisfactorily.

Prior to the opening of the Stourbridge Extension Railway, Birmingham-bound passengers travelling from Stourbridge, Kidderminster etc., had quite a journey in front of them. One option was to continue to Wolverhampton where trains to Birmingham ran from the LNWR's Queen Street station over the Stour Valley line and from 14th November, 1854, from Wolverhampton (Low Level) via the former Birmingham, Wolverhampton & Dudley Railway into Birmingham Great Western (later Snow Hill). Alternatively, some would alight at Dudley and travel over the South Staffordshire Railway through Wednesbury and into Birmingham via Bescot Junction and Perry Barr. The journey time over this route was, on average, 55 minutes which persuaded others to leave the train at Dudley Port (Low Level) and either walk to the High Level platforms where a Birmingham bound train could be caught, or take to the canal, boarding a swift packet boat which sailed to Birmingham on three days per week. However, this tiresome trip via Bescot was soon to be considerably shortened when the South Staffordshire Railway (SSR) opened Sedgeley Junction on 2nd January, 1854. The junction was built to gain access to the LNWR's Stour Valley line at Dudley Port (High Level) from the SSR's Dudley/Walsall line by way of the Sedgeley Loop. With the cooperation of all three companies concerned, the OWWR, SSR and the LNWR, a through service between Kidderminster, Stourbridge Junction, Dudley and Birmingham (New Street) was subsequently inaugurated on Saturday 1st March, 1856. This new service had an immediate impact on journey times to and from Birmingham and Stourbridge passengers were now able to get to the city in five minutes under the hour, or to put it another way, in about the same time that the original journey had taken from Dudley to Birmingham over the South Staffs route! For those with local knowledge, the spelling of 'Sedg(e)ley' with an additional 'e' must be quite puzzling. The junction was constructed by Sedgley Road East in Tipton and was shown on early OS maps as 'Sedgley Junction'. Why the railway company chose to spell it differently remains a mystery. Through trains via Sedgeley Junction ceased within a few months of the opening of the Stourbridge Extension on 1st April, 1867, the LNWR introducing through services to Stourbridge Junction, Kidderminster, Worcester and Hereford via Galton and Smethwick Junctions on the same day.

On 1st February, 1870, the GWR absorbed the Stourbridge Railway Company, the agreement being confirmed on 31st July, 1871 by the Great Western (Additional Powers) Act, 1871, thereby completing a process which had begun under the provisions of the Great Western (Further Powers) Act, 1866. However, an episode involving the disappearance of the Company Secretary, W.T. Adcock, ensured that the takeover did not pass without incident. It would seem that Mr Adcock had issued £52,000 of false stock which being almost identical to the genuine stock, meant that it was almost impossible to distinguish between the issues. The situation had of course been made more difficult by the fact that at the time of the fraud's discovery, the powers of the Stourbridge Railway Company were being vested in the Great Western. Consequently, company stock was in the process of being transferred to the Great Western Railway and it had become an argument as to who would have been responsible for relieving the bond holders of their loss. However, the problem was resolved when it was decided to acknowledge both types of bond and treat the holders equally. The fate of Mr Adcock is not clear although it would seem he was not brought to justice. He did apparently write to the Chief Constable at Worcester, but this was all that was heard from him. It was reported that he had been seen at Worcester (Shrub Hill), probably on his way to Gloucester where he may have had relatives, but this was not confirmed and Mr Adcock subsequently disappeared. This was the second major fraud in recent railway history, the first being perpetrated by a Leopold Redpath at the Great Northern Railway during 1856.

Stourbridge to Wolverhampton via the Wombourn Branch

In 1925, a through route was opened between Oxley sidings, on the main line between Wolverhampton and Shrewsbury, and Kingswinford Junction on the former OWWR main line just south of Brierley Hill station. The route was originally conceived as a means to link Wolverhampton with Bridgnorth via the village of Wombourn(e). However, the plan to swing the line west was 'postponed' and instead it continued south to eventually link up with the former OWWR's 'Kingswinford branch'. The Kingswinford branch itself had opened to traffic on 14th November, 1858 and had reached its termini at Oak Farm Colliery and Himley Colliery by 1860, some 3½ miles from the main OWWR route from which it had diverged at Kingswinford Junction. The termini on the branch were located just to the north of Shut End and it was also near Shut End that one of Stourbridge's steam locomotive celebrities had some years earlier made the headlines.

On 2nd June, 1829 the steam locomotive *Agenoria* made its debut on the Ashwood branch of the Shut End Railway which ran from Dawley Brook to the Ashwood basin on the Staffs & Worcester canal. Designed by the engineer on the Shut End Railway, John Rastrick, *Agenoria* was built by Foster, Rastrick & Co. at its works in Amblecote. The locomotive was employed on the central, and reasonably level section of the railway situated between two very steep inclines that comprised the rest of the line. Coal was transported over these steep inclines through the use of a self-acting system which enabled empty wagons to be drawn up the slope by the movement of full wagons in the opposite direction. The Shut End Railway was for many years physically isolated from the rest of the Earl of Dudley's Pensnett Railway, which itself had come into existence in the 1840s. However, the situation changed in 1865 when the two railways were linked. Over the years the Pensnett Railway developed into a system which linked numerous collieries, ironworks and canals in Cradley Heath, Dudley, Gornal, Kingswinford, and, of course, Round Oak steelworks in Brierley Hill. This extensive network represented approximately 35 miles of track, with junctions with the GWR at Baggeridge, Round Oak and Cradley Heath.

Returning to what has become known as the Great Western Railway's Wombourn branch, the 12½ mile branch opened as a through route for freight traffic on 11th January, 1925 and for passenger and parcels services on 11th May, 1925. The completion of this branch enabled traffic from the North West to reach destinations in the South, and vice versa, without having to negotiate the congested lines around Wolverhampton and Dudley. The passenger service between Stourbridge Junction and Wolverhampton (Low Level) via Wombourne was comprised of seven services each way daily utilising single class steam railmotors. In addition to the direct services between the two towns, the first railmotor from Wolverhampton (the 6.55 am) terminated at Wombourn, whilst the 4.45 pm from Wolverhampton terminated at Brettell Lane. In the opposite direction, the 6.15 pm from Stourbridge connected with the 6.25 pm railmotor from Brettell Lane to Wolverhampton. Unfortunately, poor receipts from passenger traffic led to services being withdrawn on 31st October, 1932. However, the line did possess a healthy freight traffic with inter-regional goods, coal from South Wales and coal from the local collieries very much in evidence. Although this type of traffic prolonged the life of the branch, its existence as a through line eventually came to an end on 1st March, 1965 when the line north of Baggeridge Junction was closed to all traffic. In effect, what remained was virtually the original 'Kingswinford branch' as constructed by the OWWR. Later, on 1st April, 1968, the branch was reduced still further, terminating at the Pensnett Trading Estate although, in 1994, even this stretch of line gave the impression of being abandoned and was in a state of semi-dereliction. At the time of writing the future of this branch is unknown, although it is believed that there may be plans to develop the site with the rail link providing the central feature. Railtrack (Midlands) had indicated that freight trains could begin using the branch again as early as Spring 1995, however, by the end of that Summer, it still appeared that the branch was out of use.

WOLVERHAMPTON, TETTENHALL AND STOURBRIDGE JUNCTION.
(Rail Motor Car, One Class only. Week-days only.)

	a.m	a.m.	a.m.	p.m	p.m.	p.m.	p.m.	p.m.	p.m
Wolverhampton (LL) dep	8 0	9 15	11 45	12F45	12J50	2G50	2S37	6 10	9 0
Dunstall Park „	8 3	9 18	11 48	12F48	12J53	2G53	2S40	6 13	9 3
Tettenhall „	8 10	9 25	11 55	12F55	1J 0	2G40	2S47	6 20	9 10
Compton Halt „	8 13	9 28	11 58	12F58	1J 3	2G43	2S50	6 23	9 13
Penn Halt „	8 18	9 33	12 3	1F 1	1J 8	2G48	2S55	6 28	9 18
Wombourn „	8 22	9 38	12 7	1F 6	1J12	2G53	3 1	6 35	9 25
Himley „		9 43		1J13		3G59	3S 6	6 40	9 30
Gornal Halt „		9 49		1J19		3G 5	3S12	6 46	9 36
Pensnett Halt „		9 52		1J22		3G 8	3S15	6 49	9 39
Bromley Halt „		9 55		1J25		3G11	3S18	6 52	9 42
Brockmoor Halt „		9 58		1J28		3G14	3S21	6 55	9 45
Brettell Lane „		10 0		1J30		3G16	3S23	6 57	9 47
Stourbridge Junct'n arr.		10 6		1J35		3G22	3S30	7K24	9 53

	a.m	a.m.	a.m.	p.m.	p.m	p.m.	p.m.	p.m
Stourbridge Junct'n dep.	6 50	.	10 22	.	18K33	4 38	7 40	
Brettell Lane „	6 56	...	10 28	...	18J2	4 44	7 46	
Brockmoor Halt „	6 58	.	10 30	.	18J4	4 46	7 48	
Bromley Halt „	7 1	...	10 33	...	18J7	4 49	7 51	
Pensnett Halt „	7 4	.	10 36	.	18J0	4 52	7 54	
Gornal Halt „	7 7	...	10 39	...	18J3	4 55	7 57	
Himley „	7 12	.	10 44	.	18J8	5 0	8 2	
Wombourn „	7 20	8 25	10 50	12 10	1 55	2S 5	5 6	8 9
Penn Halt „	7 25	8 30	10 55	12 15	2 0	2S10	5 11	8 14
Compton Halt „	7 30	8 35	11 0	12 20	2 5	2S15	5 16	8 19
Tettenhall „	7 33	8 38	11 3	12 23	2 8	2S18	5 19	8 22
Dunstall Park „	7 41	8 47	11 11	12 31	2 16	2S26	5 27	8 30
Wolverhampton (LL) arr.	7 46	8 50	11 16	12 34	2 19	2S31	5 31	8 33

(Saturdays excepted)

F—Saturdays only, also runs on Thursday, July 21st and Fridays, July 22nd and 29th. G—Saturdays excepted. J—Saturdays excepted; will not run Thursday, July 21st and Fridays July 22nd and 29th. K—Passengers change at Brettell Lane. S.—Saturdays only.

Timetable showing the steam railmotor service from Wolverhampton to Stourbridge for 18th July to 11th September, 1932.

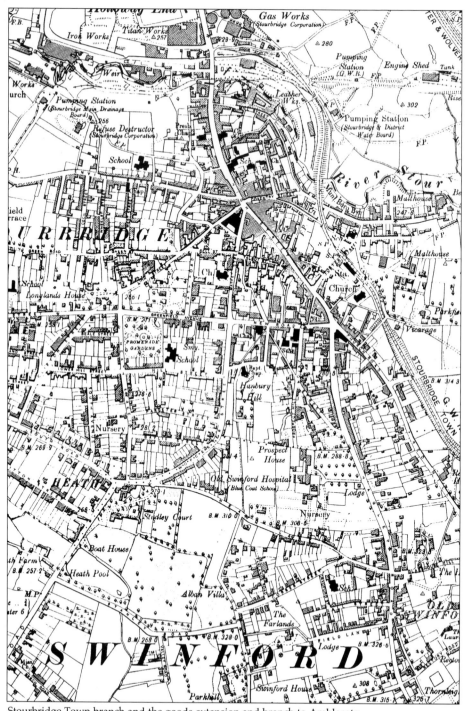

Stourbridge Town branch and the goods extension and branch to Amblecote.
Reproduced from the 6", 1921 Ordnance Survey Map

Chapter Three

Local Facilities:
Stations, Yards and Locomotive Depot

Before the Age of the Train

Predating the coming of the railway to Stourbridge were the canals. The Act authorising the construction of the Stourbridge canal was passed as early as 2nd April, 1776. The line of the canal was to be from a junction with the Staffordshire and Worcestershire canal (opened 1772) at Stourton/Stewponey, where it was raised via four locks and then continued at the same level to the Stourbridge basin in Amblecote. The canal crossed the River Stour on a two-arched aqueduct constructed of blue brick facing bricks supported on sandstone piers. This aqueduct is still in use today. At Wordsley Junction a branch was constructed as a navigable feeder which supplied water to the canal from the three Fens Pool reservoirs, Grove, Middle and Fens Pool itself. Due to the ever steepening incline, this feeder branch required a flight of 16 locks within the space of just over one mile to raise the canal the 145 feet to enable it to reach the Leys before continuing on the level to the Fens Pools. At the top of this flight of locks a second branch was constructed at what became known as Leys Junction which took the 'Stourbridge' to the 'Ninelocks' at Black Delph and the beginning of the Dudley canal. The original nine locks were built in 1779, just to the south of the present flight, but due to subsidence caused by coal extraction from the nearby 'Thick Coal' seam, the locks had to be replaced in 1856. The original bottom and top locks were, however, retained and supplemented by the construction of a further six locks. Although the site is still known to locals as 'Nine Locks', the existence of only eight must be a constant source of mystery to the unsuspecting visitor. The main line today is the line from Stourton through to Black Delph with the Stourbridge arm now classified as a branch.

The Stourbridge town branch of the canal originally terminated to the west of Lower High Street in the form of a basin that later served the ironworks of John Bradley. In the 1830s the canal was extended by 230 yards under the roadway via a very low tunnel, so low as to prevent access for cabin boats. This extension was built to serve Foster and Orme's ironworks, although following the construction of the gasworks, liquid cargoes would also have been shipped out. There was also a plan to extend the canal along the Stour Valley towards Halesowen, but the coming of the railway effectively put a stop to this.

The Stourbridge Town Branch and the Goods Extension and Branch to Amblecote

On 5th July, 1965 the large goods yard located on the eastern side of Lower High Street was finally closed down by British Rail so ending more than 100 years of freight handling in the Amblecote area (Amblecote lies immediately adjacent to Stourbridge). Today, there is no trace of the railway, the site now largely occupied by the Mill Race Trading Estate. However, in the middle of the 19th century a railway to Stourbridge was the principal item on the town's agenda.

The years between 1844 and 1874 saw a number of schemes prepared in connection with railways to the area. Some of these proposals involved the construction of branches into the town, while others were much grander, arriving at Stourbridge from as far away as West Bromwich, Smethwick and Dudley. The majority, of course, were not constructed, although, these too helped to place Stourbridge on the railway map and therefore played an important part in the history of the town's railway development.

The Oxford, Worcester and Wolverhampton Railway was to promote a number of branches to the town as well as larger schemes aimed at bringing other Black Country areas into its railway network. The company's original Act of 1845 authorised the construction of four branches, one of which would have left the main line north of Stambermill viaduct to terminate on the south side of the Stourbridge canal in Amblecote on the site of James Foster's ironworks. However, problems relating to the construction of the main line itself put these plans 'on hold' and it was subsequently not constructed. From then on, the OWWR, its successor the West Midland Railway, the Great Western Railway and even the London & North Western were all to become involved in the railways to Stourbridge.

During 1852/53, the LNWR promoted a 'Branches to Stourbridge' Bill. This railway was to leave the Stour Valley line between Birmingham and Wolverhampton just to the north of Smethwick, and would continue to Stourbridge via Blackheath, Cradley Heath and Lye. Near Lye a branch would leave the main line at or near Hungary Hill brickworks, terminating in the vicinity of the OWWR station at Chawn Hill on the outskirts of Stourbridge. The main line itself would continue towards Stourbridge and on reaching Portobello would diverge, with one line terminating at a station in Foster Street, whilst the other would continue to Amblecote where it would end on land belonging to James Foster at or near the canal basin. This scheme was very similar in direction to one proposed by the Birmingham, Wolverhampton and Stour Valley Railway, one of three plans promoted in 1846. The others were proposals put forward by both the Birmingham, Wolverhampton and Dudley Railway (BW&D) and the OWWR. The former promoted a line which would leave the BW&D near West Bromwich, joining the OWWR via an east to south connection before dropping down to pass under the OWWR and continuing to Amblecote where it would terminate at the canal basin. The OWWR proposal corresponded very much with the BW&D, although the latter's line would have swung north at Old Hill towards Netherton rather than continue eastwards towards Birmingham. All three schemes received strong support from groups outside of Parliament, however, Parliament itself remained unconvinced and rejected each on the grounds that their preambles had not been proven. Incidentally, the LNWR route laid out in 1853 was quite closely followed by the later Stourbridge and Stourbridge Extension railways, the latter, though following a route that probably carried the line further south of Blackheath and Cradley Heath, but north of Lye.

The passing of the Oxford, Worcester and Wolverhampton Railway (Branches and Extensions) Act, 1853 authorised 'a branch or extension railway, commencing by a junction with the main line of the Oxford, Worcester and Wolverhampton Railway in the Hamlet of Amblecote . . . and terminating at or near the Turnpike Road from Stourbridge to Dudley', this Act giving a clear indication that a line into the district was once again high on the company's agenda. However, not all were in favour of such a development with the result that a petition against the line was sent to the Stourbridge Improvement Commissioners on 12th July, 1853. The branch, which would have left the up line via a north facing junction at Amblecote before dropping down on the east side of the line then to pass under it, would have terminated on the south side of the Stourbridge canal basin.

Also in 1853 the OWWR promoted the 'Cradley loop'. This was to have left the main line at Blower's Green, passing through Netherton before swinging south-west near Cradley Heath and through Lomey Town to Lye before dropping below the main line just north of Chawn Hill, where it was to connect with branch lines that were subsequently authorised by the Oxford, Worcester and Wolverhampton (Stratford and Stourbridge Branches) Act, 1854. The first of these branches was to diverge from the main line just to the north of the station at Chawn Hill and terminate at a station in Foster Street, whilst the second would leave the main line south of the station to terminate at the canal basin in Amblecote. The 'Cradley Loop' also included a branch which would leave the main line just beyond Lye to form an east to south connection with the main line at Stourbridge station. The 1853 Bill did not proceed, but instead a modified plan appears to have been produced in 1854. Also known as the 'Cradley loop' this proposal followed a very similar line to the original. However, the line terminated at a junction with the main line station and the branch to Corngreaves, as shown in the 1853 version, was extended to form the 'Outer loop' which took the railway through Reddall Hill, near to Old Hill, before rejoining the 'Inner loop' (i.e. the original 'Cradley loop') to the north of Netherton, near to the Buffery Ironworks. The line then continued to the main line which it joined via a junction at Blower's Green. However, this too was not proceeded with.

In September 1856, a public meeting of Stourbridge ratepayers met to discuss the way the rates were being spent. The Town Commissioners had spent approximately £200 on opposing the proposal put forward by the OWWR to construct a road crossing which apparently was located just outside the Commissioners' jurisdiction in Amblecote. What seemed to annoy the ratepayers most, however, was the fact that the Commissioners had supported the LNWR's Stour Valley line proposal into Foster Street, reference being made to the fact that the Chairman (Mr Akroyd) owned property in the street, implying perhaps that vested interests were playing an unacceptable part in the decisions being taken.

The first tangible evidence of railway development did not come until 1858 when the OWWR agreed to construct a siding alongside the canal basin. A year later, on 30th July, 1859 a branch was completed from the OWWR main line to the north of the viaduct, probably very close to where the junction to the engine shed was to be located, to the ironworks that had been built on the western side of Lower High Street (the opposition to the road crossing presumably had been overcome). The *Brierley Hill Advertiser* reported the event as follows:

On Saturday, a work which had been actively carried on for the last three months was to such an extent completed as to allow some show of an opening ceremony. This work is the new branch railway connecting the lower part of the town with the main branch of the OWWR. This branch has been designed for goods traffic, Messrs Bradley & Co's & Messrs Keep and Watkins' works being traversed by the branch, in the former of which is the terminus; but we hope that it will ultimately be adopted for passenger traffic also and as such it would be a great public boon. A double line of rails will be laid down when the line is finally completed. It leaves the main line at the Stourbridge side of the Amblecote cutting, and hence there is a descent to Parkmoor Hill, where a great deal of time and labour has been expended in cutting deeply through the declivity. Messrs Bradley & Co's works are reached by crossing the High Street on the level and by a couple of bridges thrown across the Stour.

Shortly before five o'clock on Saturday evening, an engine and three trucks, two of them containing five tons of pig iron each, the other Mr Wilson, of the OWWR Co., Mr Stokes, from Messrs Bradley's and other gentlemen, started from the main line, and went as far as the upper end of the Parkmoor Hill colliery. There the engine was detached, and the trucks were drawn the remaining distance by four powerful horses, ridden by navvies in white slops, and with gay colours streaming from their caps. A union jack was also hoisted, and a band of music enlivened the proceedings. A great number of workpeople assembled, who having giving vent to some cheers, the ceremony concluded by the trucks being driven back in the same manner as they were brought down. In the evening a dinner was held at the Talbot Hotel, to which the contractors and managers of the above works sat down; and the employees on the line also sat down to an excellent dinner provided by Mr Abraham Brown, of the Star and Anchor Inn, Coventry Street.

The above extract makes it clear that there was a hope that the branch would be available for passenger traffic. However, due to the steepness of the incline (1 in 14), which necessitated traffic having to be winched up and down using a cable attached to a stationary engine, it was doubtful that such traffic could be handled safely. On 3rd November, 1877 there was an accident on the incline which vindicated the concern in very dramatic fashion. The following report appeared in the *Brierley Hill Advertiser*:

On Saturday morning a number of railway trucks laden with coal, iron etc were being lowered down the short branch line at Amblecote when the wire rope gave way beneath the strain upon it. The signalman at the bottom of the incline discovered the trucks were loose before he reached his box and he fortunately had time to turn them off the main line (which crosses the turnpike road) into a short siding, which ends or did end, in a good stout sand embankment. There were 18 or 19 trucks on the move and the force with which they came carried away the embankment and wrecked the first half dozen wagons, while others were damaged. We understand it is only usual to lower about four trucks at once and that the large number which started down on Saturday morning were sent along through some mistake in a signal. The branch line now being made into Stourbridge will do away with the necessity of working trucks up and down the Amblecote branch by a stationary engine.

The existing main line station was located approximately ½ mile from the town centre, in Halfpenny Hall Lane (later to be renamed Junction Road). It had always been considered that this location was too far from the town centre businesses to actively encourage people from outside the district to shop there. Consequently, there were a number of plans drawn up during the 1860s and 1870s to replace the original goods branch line with one that was constructed for the conveyance of passenger as well as freight traffic and which would connect to the main line station. However, only the railway authorised under the 1874 Act was, ultimately, to be constructed.

An Act authorising the Stourbridge Railway Company to construct a new branch that would terminate in Foster Street received the Royal Assent on 5th July, 1865 (The Stourbridge Railway Act, 1865). This branch was to leave the Stourbridge Railway just beyond Lye passing under this and the OWWR main line before terminating at Foster Street. Just 12 months after becoming law, the Act was overtaken by a second plan which virtually made the 1865 Act redundant. On 16th July, 1866, the Stourbridge Railway (Further Powers) Act, 1866 authorised the construction of a 'Deviation Railway or Branch' that would leave the main line just south of the station to curve round in the direction of the town centre. It would then have continued to a station in Foster Street via a short stretch of the branch authorised by the Act of 1854. Unlike the 1865 proposal, this scheme enabled trains to reach the town from off both the Stourbridge Railway and the OWWR.

On 13th July, 1868 The Stourbridge Railway Amendment Act, 1868 extended the powers of the Stourbridge Railway Company with respect to the branch, increasing the statutory time period governing the line's completion to 31st December, 1869 (thereby repealing Section 24 of the 1865 Act and Section 22 of the 1866 Act which had allowed 3 and 2 years, respectively, for the line's completion). However, the company then applied to the Board of Trade for an Abandonment Order on 4th March, 1869. The reason for the application was due to the Great Western Railway having obtained powers under 'The Great Western Railway Act, 1868' to construct 'another' Branch Railway to Stourbridge commencing by a junction with its own railway to the south of Stambermill viaduct and terminating at a station to be built at the bottom of High Street near the canal. Apparently, it had been fully explained to Parliament that it was never contemplated actually building the two branches, the Stourbridge Railway's powers being extended to safeguard against any eventuality that might have hindered the passing of the Great Western Bill, thereby keeping the project alive. Under the circumstances the Board of Trade authorised the abandonment on 23rd July, 1869. Unfortunately, authorisation for the construction of the Great Western branch was allowed to lapse leaving the town without its passenger branch and the original goods line into Amblecote still *in situ*.

However, on 30th June, 1874, a further Act was passed authorising the Great Western Railway Company to build a new branch line from the south end of Stourbridge station terminating at the goods station at the eastern end of the canal basin at a junction with the existing goods branch. The Act also authorised the abandonment of the Great Western Railway Act, 1868 and the remaining railway line and incline of the existing goods branch. Although the line would still be steep (a 1 in 67 incline between the Junction and the Town and 1 in 27 beyond), it was deemed to be suitable for locomotive-hauled passenger and goods traffic. The company though, was seemingly reluctant to press ahead and it was to be a further four years before work commenced on the line. Finally, after many acrimonious exchanges between the company and Stourbridge's Improvement Commissioners, the branch was completed and by August 1879 the line was ready to accept traffic. The 6th August saw the line inspected by Major-General Hutchinson of the Board of Trade, the event being reported in the *Brierley Hill Advertiser* as follows:

Stourbridge-Inspection of the New Branch Line

The Stourbridge Branch Railway was opened for traffic on Wednesday last, and the occasion was made use of to present Mr Henry Hughes, Chairman of the Commissioners, with an address and to entertain him to dinner in acknowledgement of his long service to the town, and especially in connection with the obtaining of a central station.

The new branch line into the town was inspected on Wednesday by Major-General Hutchinson, Board of Trade Inspector. The railway, which is a double line, leaves the main line by a sharp curve at Churchill, a few hundred yards on the Worcester side of the present Stourbridge station; and after passing over a high embankment near Oldswinford church it is conducted through a deep cutting along Red Hill to Foster-street, running under the Station-road a yard or two below the brow of the hill, and thence along the bottom of Rev. T. William's garden. At Foster-street, which is crossed by a bridge, is placed the town station, which will be the terminus of the line as far as the present passenger traffic is concerned. Beyond, the railway is continued over Birmingham-street and another embankment, to the field called 'Mill Meadow', where a goods station is in course of erection, and extensive works are being carried out to accommodate the goods traffic from the bottom of the town and the vicinity. This part of the line crosses Birmingham-street by a bridge a short distance from the Cliff corner, the street being made to slope on both sides to preserve a sufficient passage below the bridge for wheel traffic. The embankment spans the bed of the Stour and carries the line with a steep decline to Mill Meadows.

Whether the company will think well to continue the railway for passengers past this point, and so provide the much wanted accommodation for the district beyond, is not at present known; but there seems to be a very prevalent opinion that it would be possible to connect the branch with the main line again, somewhere towards Brettell-lane, so that the present objectionable viaduct at Stamber Mill might be superseded.We cannot say whether such a project might be feasible. The passenger station in Foster-street, where Major-General Hutchinson's inspection ended, is a commodious and convenient one, upon the right-hand side of Foster-street, looking away from the town. The building is one block with a long platform, sheltered by a light and handsome glass roof; and opening upon the platform are the suite of waiting rooms, booking office and rooms for officials, with between them and the street a spacious standing ground for vehicles. Of the roads and paths which have had to be either stopped, diverted or otherwise interfered with in the construction of the line, there are several of considerable importance.

Foster-street and Birmingham-street are by some thought to be much damaged by the alterations to the levels and the bridges, while others fail to see that these alterations have materially affected the value of the streets as arteries of the town. Angel-street, which is totally stopped, is perhaps one of the most-felt losses. Station-road is not materially affected as the line runs under it. Mr Grierson, the Manager of the Great Western Railway, has promised to arrange for the opening of the line on Monday the 18 inst. if it is passed by the Board of Trade; and we understand that the train service will be laid out to give every accommodation as regards the traffic between Stourbridge and Birmingham.

Travelling away from the town, the trains from Stourbridge to the junction are timed at the latter to catch all the trains to Birmingham with the exception of the 10.25 am; all those to Kidderminster and Worcester except the 6.10, 9.43 and 11.30 am and 10.41 pm; and all in the direction of Dudley excepting the 8.15 am, and 1.35, 4.35, 9.50, 10.46 and 11.50pm. Entering Stourbridge, trains from the junction to the town run in connection with all the trains from Birmingham except the 9.45 and 11.43 pm; all from Dudley except the 10.38 and 11.35 pm; and all from Kidderminster except those at 10.42 am; 9.45 and 10.44 pm. The public will see therefore, that the facilities for getting into and out of Stourbridge are very considerable.

As it happened, the line did not open for passenger traffic until Wednesday 1st October. The *Brierley Hill Advertiser* once again reported the event:

The line was opened without ceremony and no doubt the heavy rain which fell about the time prevented many from attending to witness the starting of the first train. If anything can be concluded from the number of passengers on the opening day, we should judge that the line will be considered a great public convenience. At 4 o'clock in the afternoon, a number of the Improvement Commissioners of the town with their Chairman (Mr Henry Hughes) and the Town Clerk (Mr Taylor) as well as several of the leading tradesmen, made a trial of the line by taking a trip to the junction station and back, a saloon carriage being placed at their disposal by the Railway Company. All considered in this at any rate - that the travelling was easy and comfortable. The timetable issued for the new line shows 19 trains running each way between 'Stourbridge Junction' as the old station is now called by the Directors, and 'Stourbridge', which name is henceforth to be borne by the new station in Foster-street. These trains are for week days only, the Directors not thinking it worthwhile to run Sunday trains at present.

Following the opening ceremony, the guests repaired to the Talbot Hotel where dinner was laid for 50 people. Among the guests at the meal which was presided over by Mr W.J. Turney with Messrs E. Stringer and J. Taylor as vice-chairmen, were the other Mr H. Hughes (GWR divisional superintendent, Birmingham), Mr T. Bantock, the Wolverhampton division cartage agent, Mr T. Kinsey (agent) and Messrs Pritchard and Noble, station masters for the Town and Junction stations respectively, as well as notable residents including the Reverend Sherrard who spoke of a hope that the line would be extended towards Kinver and the surrounding districts. As will be seen later, similar views were to be expressed by many people in many areas. Finally, the church's other notable present, the Reverend Maginnis, made the point regarding the Town station becoming the main station in Stourbridge with the Junction its subordinate. This was a view which was to stimulate much discussion during the last few years of the century.

On 1st January, 1880 the branch was declared open for the conveyance of freight to the goods depot in Amblecote. The fate of the original goods (incline) line is not clear; it probably just fell into disuse and eventually 'disappeared'.

Some time after the opening of the goods branch, an additional siding was added which continued north to the local authority gas works. This was probably opened quite late in the 19th century, or even during the early 20th century (it was not there in 1884, but had been constructed by 1903) to bring coal into the plant. It may also have been used to ship out coke and other by-products from the coal gas-making process. The siding became redundant at about the time of the closure of the works in 1963 as part of the Gas Board's policy of centralising gas production at a few major plants.

Although the Town branch seems to have been planned to run as a double track for the whole of its length, the Ordnance Survey map of 1885 shows that the line was only double to just beyond Angel Street. So, even though space did seem to have been provided to accommodate the second line, this may never have been utilised. The GWR branch terminated in the goods yard at the level crossing in High Street, Amblecote, the line which actually continued across the High Street being a private siding which ended on the far side of Bradley's ironworks near the elbow in the Stourbridge canal.

During June 1895, the Great Western carried out major alterations to the goods station in Amblecote. The company had purchased the old Mersey Wheel and Axle Works that was located close to the Stourbridge canal and was to convert this into a freight handling facility. Unlike its predecessor the building was to be of two storeys, the first floor being used to store grain. The facility would be served by two tracks, a loading platform, seven cranes and a gas-engined hoist to lift bags of grain into the storage area. The facility would also provide improved grain handling from canal boats to road transport. The existing iron loading shed would remain, but the canal was to be widened to improve access. Office accommodation would be provided at the front of the site adjacent to Lower High Street. In 1901 the disused goods station located just to the south-west of the original Junction station (closed in 1901) was dismantled and re-erected on the south side of Amblecote goods yard, replacing a much larger shed which had been demolished. It has been recorded that one of the clerks who started his railway career at the goods yard progressed to become the goods manager of the whole Great Western system. By the 1920s the handling capacity of the goods depot was in excess of 230, four-wheeled wagons.

The decision to build a new main line (Junction) station at Chawn Hill had the immediate effect of making the existing connection from the branch to the main line redundant. The Great Western Railway (Additional Powers)Act, 1897 had, however, made provision for the construction of a new loop that would join the existing branch near Parkfield. During work on making the new line it was necessary to blast a path through sandstone rock in order to create a suitable cutting. Unfortunately, this operation had a permanent effect on some of the town's oldest residents. A group of rooks who for many years had made their homes in the elms near Job's Lane decided to 'move on', presumably to some quieter corner of Victorian England.

World War I placed considerable demands on railway resources in the district, with the result that the Town branch was temporarily closed to passenger traffic on 1st April, 1915. As a result of this measure, the Great Western introduced an omnibus service between the Town and Junction stations. During the war buses were converted to run on coal gas held in a large balloon located on top of the vehicle. If Great Western practice followed that adopted by Midland Red, there would have been two types of gas balloon employed: one being fitted behind the advertisement boards which, when empty, tended to fall over the vehicle; the second was a rigid-sided balloon. On 28th February, 1919 this service was withdrawn the moment passenger services on the branch were reintroduced. An interesting bus service, also operated by the Great Western, was that between Stourbridge and Bromsgrove via Clent which commenced on 13th February, 1905. The two omnibuses to be used on the route (one would be in use whilst the other was spare) were delivered to Stourbridge on 11th February. The buses were built by the Milnes-Daimler Company of Tottenham Court Road, London at a cost of £1,200 each. These petrol-engined, 24 hp, double deckers were designed to carry 36 passengers, 20 on the upper deck and 16 below. The journey time between the termini was expected to be 35 minutes. However, the service was withdrawn on 5th August, 1916 and was not reintroduced at the end of the war. During the General Strike, the bus service between the Town and Junction stations was resumed on 7th May, 1926 to cover for withdrawn train services. The use of buses remained until 10th July, 1926.

The Town passenger station was just one 298 ft platform with brick buildings covered by a full length awning. The branch itself was in most part double track (the goods line on the embankment which carried the line across the Stour and into the yard was single track), workings being controlled by a signal box situated near the south-east end of the station platform. However, in order to make economies, on 27th August, 1935 the Great Western introduced modified working arrangements which dispensed with the conventional up/down system, replacing it with what was, in effect, the introduction of two independent single lines; one for passenger trains, which terminated just beyond the station, and one for freight which continued through the station into the goods depot in Amblecote. As a result of this, the company was able to close the branch signal box on 25th August, 1935.

British Rail announced early in 1964 that both Amblecote Goods Depot and Stourbridge Town station were to be closed as part of an economy measure to be carried out under the Beeching Plan. However, by September 1965 the Mayor of Stourbridge, Councillor E.J. Broughton, a former railwayman himself, was able to announce that the threat of closure to the Town station had been removed. Unfortunately, the goods depot was not so lucky.

The running down of the goods yard probably began as early as 1960 when the siding to Turney & Co. was taken out of use. This was followed by the closure of the gas works siding on 31st May, 1963. Meanwhile, the private siding agreement between BR and Bradley & Co. was terminated during July 1962 and in March 1965 all trackwork to the west of the level crossing which served the company's works was withdrawn from use. Shortly afterwards, in May 1965, the siding to D.F. Fellows was also closed. The last freight train to leave the yard did so on 30th April, 1965 and by 5th July all work at the yard ceased. The goods line itself remained open until 20th September, 1965, but after this date the track was lifted, its removal being completed by October 1967. Foster Street bridge, which had been rebuilt in November 1957, was demolished on the last Sunday of September 1967 thereby severing completely the link between Amblecote goods yard and Stourbridge Junction.

By November 1970 the passenger service to the Town station was again jeopardised when British Rail proposed closure of the line in the face of an operating loss of £30,000 per year. Thankfully, the threat was again staved off. The old Town station, which had been unstaffed

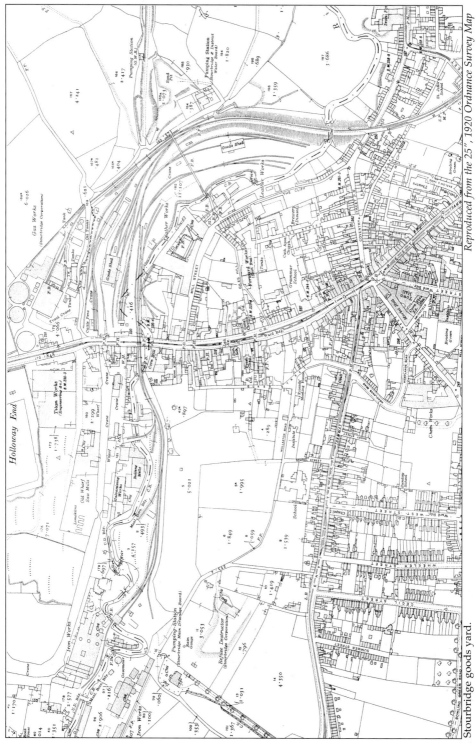

Reproduced from the 25″, 1920 Ordnance Survey Map

Stourbridge goods yard.

GWR buses outside Stourbridge Town station in 1910.

Dudley Public Library

'57XX' class 0-6-0PT No. 3729 leaves Stourbridge (Amblecote) goods yard for Stourbridge Junction on 2nd November, 1957.

E.J. Dew

'57XX' class 0-6-0PT No. 9613 comes off the Stourbridge goods branch at the head of a class 'K' freight on 24th March, 1951.   *B.W.L. Brooksbank*

An overall view of Amblecote goods yard, not long before closure, with a 350 hp diesel shunter in the distance.   *E.J. Dew*

'14XX' class 0-4-2T No. 1458 stands at Platform 1 at Stourbridge Junction with the auto-trailer service for Stourbridge Town *c.* 1950. *D.K. Jones*

Stourbridge Town station on the 18th June, 1966. In the paltform stands a train consisting of a single car unit coupled to a trailer car. This view clearly shows the goods branch continuing on to Amblecote goods yard. *G.D.A. Hingley*

The unstaffed Town station is seen at the end of 1978. In February 1979 the station was demolished.   *D. Allen*

A view looking towards the new station at Stourbridge Town on 12th August, 1995. Class '153' No. 153 356 is handling the branch service.   *Author*

from July 1967, lasted for another 12 years until in February 1979 the buildings were demolished and the platform cut back almost 70 yards to make way for a combined bus and railway terminus. Originally, material salvaged from the station was to be used in the reconstruction of a GWR station at Tyseley Railway Museum although it appears that these materials were eventually used throughout the site.

At the beginning of February 1994 all traces of the old station were swept away in a £380,000 rebuilding which saw a new 170 ft platform, together with booking office and passenger waiting area, built adjacent to Vauxhall Road. The new station was also provided with a lengthy safety zone created by the moving of the buffer stops some 30 yards further up the line. The branch was actually closed to traffic during the rebuilding, passengers being provided with a free bus service. The station reopened on Monday 25th April, 1994, although the official opening by Councillor Fred Hunt was not until several days later on 3rd May.

Stourbridge Main Line Station and Marshalling Yard

Opened on 1st May, 1852 by the Oxford, Worcester and Wolverhampton Railway, Stourbridge station was from the earliest days an important location on the OWWR's main line and by 1857 as many as 25 passenger trains were calling there each weekday. These services included four through trains running in each direction between the LNWR stations at Wolverhampton (Queen Street) and London (Euston Square). Stourbridge's position was further strengthened in 1867 when the Stourbridge Extension reached the GWR main line between Birmingham and Wolverhampton. This provided the GWR with a direct route to South Wales via Worcester and Hereford. Unfortunately, as the level of traffic increased, so did the public's awareness of the station's inadequacies. This led to an ever growing demand for improved facilities.

The Directors of the Great Western Railway decided in 1871 that Stourbridge station was in need of a 'face-lift' and consequently the existing platforms and buildings were rebuilt and/or renewed. The so-called 'new' accommodation was in fact comprised of a building formerly located at Slough which had been dismantled and re-erected at Stourbridge. The 'new' buildings were located on the down side of the main line between the old waiting room and the goods station. This arrangement provided for better booking facilities, an improved general waiting room and two ladies' waiting rooms. At the opposite end of the platform two gentlemen's toilets had been provided (first and second class!) together with office accommodation for Mr Phillips the station master and Mr Warner the company's goods agent. Both platforms had been raised and extended. Although the Directors were not totally satisfied with the result, it was the best that could be done with the money available. The modifications had cost approximately £1,200 and had been carried out by Mr H. Lovatt of Wolverhampton. The original buildings on the up platform were modified and raised to platform level, although the old buildings on the down side were still to be so treated. The former were used as a general waiting area, as well as providing a room for both guards and porters, whilst the latter would eventually be converted for use as a parcels office, telegraph office and toilet. Oddly, a footbridge across the lines was not provided although it was the Directors' intention to erect one as soon as possible. By September of the same year the station buildings had been appropriately furnished by Mr E. Stringer's 'Furnishing Establishment'. The passenger footbridge had also been completed thereby enabling passengers to cross safely what were by now very busy lines. By 1883 passenger figures were reported to be in the region of 80,000 per half year, a fact that encouraged the belief that obtaining a refreshment license would not be an unprofitable venture. At the Worcester County Licensing Committee held on 6th October such a license was granted to Mr W.T. Davies.

Throughout the 1890s, the townspeople of Stourbridge became increasingly alarmed at the level of traffic being handled at the main line station with the result that the GWR came under mounting pressure to provide better facilities. A look at the GWR timetable of 1900 shows

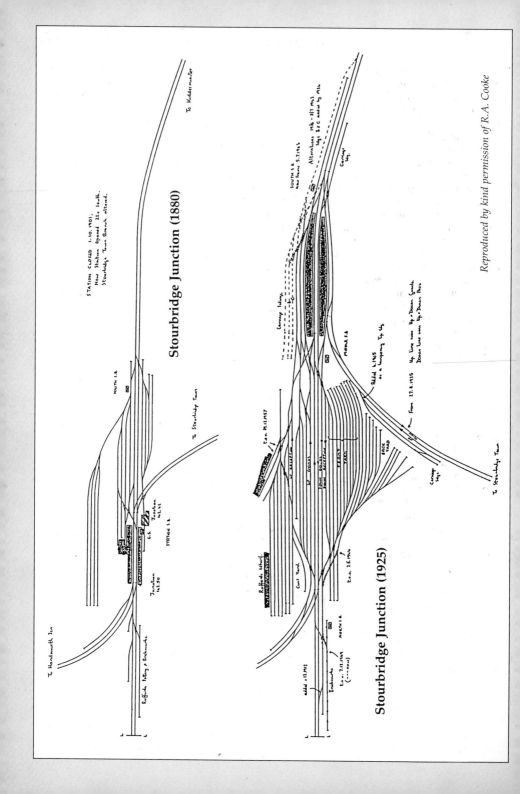

Stourbridge Junction (1880)

Stourbridge Junction (1925)

Reproduced by kind permission of R.A. Cooke

why there was such concern. Compared to 1852 when the station was first opened, the number of weekday passenger services that were now using Stourbridge Junction had increased enormously. On the Stourbridge Extension Railway (this term commonly refers to the full length of the Stourbridge Railway & Stourbridge Extension) there were 23 up trains, i.e. to Birmingham (Snow Hill), whilst in the opposite direction, 22 trains headed out of Snow Hill towards the Black Country. As a matter of interest, seven of the former and six of the latter connected with LNWR trains at Smethwick Junction. On the ex-OWWR route, traffic was even greater with local stopping services and longer distance passenger trains between Wolverhampton and Worcester accounting for 29 up and 32 down services each weekday. Additionally, there was the last service from Snow Hill which departed at 11.25 pm and ran via Dudley to Stourbridge Junction where it arrived at 12.24 am. It should be remembered that the Junction station only possessed two through lines and therefore with 107 passenger trains per day, plus the frequent Town 'shuttle' services and around 50 daily freight trains to accommodate, the lines around the station did become quite congested. In view of this, it is perhaps understandable that fears regarding the ability of the railway company to handle this amount of traffic safely had been growing steadily for some time.

As early as October 1891, Stourbridge Improvement Commissioners had approached the GWR requesting that passenger accommodation and safety at the station be improved. On 16th October, a relatively minor collision had occurred between the 8.36 departure to the Town and an empty passenger train standing on the up line brought about by the incorrect operation of the points. Although the damage sustained was slight, the 'Town' engine did have to be replaced thereby delaying the train's arrival at Foster Street by some 30 minutes. This mishap was sufficient to raise fresh doubts in the minds of local people, especially in view of the amount of traffic the station was now having to deal with on a day-to-day basis. The local press saw the incident as a timely reminder that traffic handling facilities at the station were now inadequate and that a town the size of Stourbridge deserved better railway accommodation.

The news in 1893 that negotiations were taking place between Droitwich Council and the Great Western to build a new station for the town acted as a further incentive for Stourbridge's representatives to press the company to review its policy. However, it was not until the end of 1895 that the GWR decided that the time was right to improve arrangements at Stourbridge. It was subsequently announced that a new, much larger station would be constructed approximately ½ mile to the south of the existing structure on a site to the rear of Oldswinford Castle. The station approach would be via Brook Road or as it was more usually known, the 'Labour in Vain' Road, after the nearby public house of the same name. The 1896 Railway Bill would authorise the company to construct a new loop that would leave the main line 16 chains north of the bridge over the road leading to Hagley, terminating by a junction with the existing Town branch near Red Hill House, at a point 14½ chains south-east of the bridge carrying Junction Road over the branch. This would mean that Town branch trains would have to join the main line before gaining access to the station.

During February 1896 it had been suggested that a completely new bridge be built at Chawn Hill, and it is presumed that this proposal relates to the one which was subsequently built to carry the Town branch directly into platform No. 1 of the Junction station. Stourbridge Council's Highways and Improvement Committee had recommended that £200 be contributed to the costs of the bridge which would have a span of not less than 35 feet, total width not to exceed 70 feet and the height to remain the same as the existing bridge. The committee was of the opinion that if the company did not accept this offer then the clerk would be instructed to petition against the Bill in Parliament and to use all 'means necessary e.g. counsel, Parliamentary agents, witnesses and incur such other expenses as he may see fit in support of such petition'.

If the company accepted the offer an application to the Local Government Board for sanction to obtain a loan would be made. However, the reply from the company's solicitor was not too encouraging as it stated that the Directors expected the Council to find at least

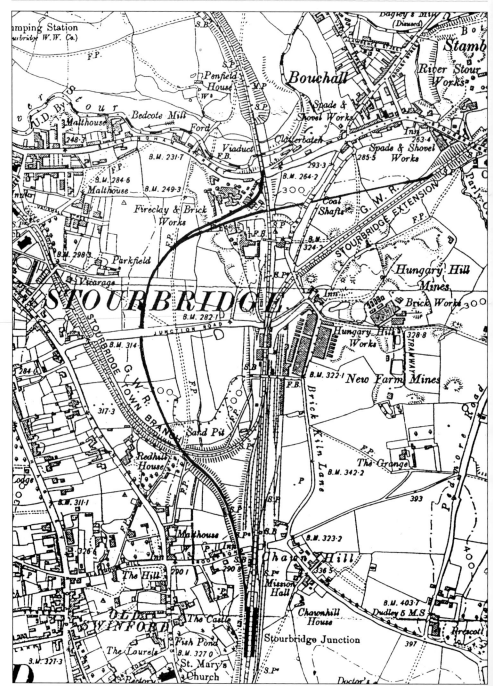

Proposed alternative routes of 1896 and 1897 at Stourbridge Junction based on local reports.
Reproduced from the 6", 1903 Ordnance Survey Map

half the cost. In view of this demand the Council decided to petition against the Bill in Parliament, although only insofar as it related to the Chawnhill bridge.

During 1896, but more especially in 1897, a demand arose that had laid dormant for a number of years. There had been a view that the principal station for the town should be considerably closer to the centre than the one located at the Junction. In December 1896 it had been suggested in Council that the proposed Town branch should be upgraded and extended so as to enable the Foster Street station to replace the Junction as the main line station for the town. The suggested line would continue into Amblecote where it would rejoin the main line to Dudley, north of the engine shed in the vicinity of the Amblecote Road. Although this implied overcoming steep gradients both into and out of the town, the latter was compared to that encountered on the line to Cradley. Beyond the station a branch off the main line could then be built to Whittington and along the Stour Valley to Cookley, Wolverley and Kidderminster and on to Stourport. No provision was made, though, to accommodate passenger traffic to or from the Stourbridge Extension Railway.

A more serious recommendation, however, was made in 1897 when plans were drawn up on behalf of the Council to construct a completely new station built at a different location which would handle all passenger traffic off the former Oxford, Worcester & Wolverhampton Railway and the Stourbridge Extension Railway. The proposal advocated that a new station be built at Red Hill replacing both the Junction and the Town stations. This station would be served by a line leaving the existing main line at Chawnhill bridge, and follow the line of the proposed branch to the town until reaching the new station at Red Hill. Trains for Dudley and Wolverhampton would then rejoin the main line via a curve taking the line past Parkfield, where it would rejoin the main line at a junction just to the south of Stambermill viaduct at Portobello. Trains for Cradley and Birmingham would leave the curve, probably between Parkfield and Portobello, and after passing under the Dudley line, would rejoin the main line in the vicinity of Hungary Hill. The existing main line between Chawnhill bridge and Rufford Works would then be freed to handle freight traffic.

On 19th January, 1897, a deputation from Stourbridge Council met Mr Wilkinson, General Manager of the Great Western, at Paddington regarding the company's proposed new station and the Council's alternatives. The company recognised that a large section of the public did want a station nearer the town, but if this was not possible, then this would be offset by a 'first class station' that would have a train service to and from the town which would meet all passenger trains to arrive at the Junction. Furthermore, the station had been designed with the company's traffic arrangements in mind, hinting that any alternative would be quite unsuitable. Predictably, in the following April, the company advised the Council that the Directors had rejected the alternatives and confirmed that the new station would be built at Chawnhill in accordance with the original plans. It was, however, promised to provide a Town service which would meet all trains at the Junction.

The new line from the existing Town branch into platform 1 of the Junction station was built under the Great Western (Additional Powers) Act, 1897 which authorised the construction of a railway '(No. 5) 3 furlongs and 8.12 chains in length . . . commencing by a junction with the OWWR and terminating by a junction with the Stourbridge Town branch railway'. Clause 45 of the Act had been inserted, 'For the protection of Urban District Council of Stourbridge and in respect of the bridge over the road leading from Old Swinford to Chawn Hill which was to have a clear span of not less than 33 feet between abutments and a headway of not less than 14 feet'. The company also undertook to divert the footpath leading from Job's Lane to the station.

An amusing incident accompanied the final days of the old Junction station. The last train to the Town having got the 'right away' pulled out in a cloud of steam and whistle blowing only for it to be discovered, to quote the local paper, that 'like one of Bo-peep's sheep, it left its tail behind it'. The locomotive had moved out leaving part of its train at the platform. However, after much shouting, gesticulating and waving of lamps, the train halted and reversed to pick-up the remaining carriage, the engine driver's face probably being similar in hue to that of a matador's cape.

A staff group pose for the photographer in this view of the original station at Stourbridge Junction.

Lens of Sutton

The original station at Stourbridge Junction *c.* 1900. This station was closed when the new station opened on 1st October.

Stourbridge Library Collection

A few days before the official opening of the new station, the local press were allowed to carry out an inspection of the site. The *County Express* was of the opinion that the Great Western Railway Company had fulfiled its promise to give Stourbridge really first-class accommodation. The newspaper described the station and surrounds as follows:

A strict eye upon the question of dividends sometimes delays and blocks necessary improvements but one cannot pass the 700 ft length of platform at the new Junction without feeling the station buildings have been erected upon happy lines, and have a refreshing appearance. There is a delightful feeling of cleanliness and roominess, so very different from the dark cramped state we all know so well under the old conditions.

One cannot fail to be struck by the enormous engineering work which has had to be accomplished in connection with the new scheme. The main roadway has been increased from a two-rail width to a seven-rail width, while a long embankment has been made forming a line which runs from the new station to the old Junction. In the last named work, and a tenth only of the total, between 80,000 and 100,000 cubic yards of ballast have been absorbed, and a cubic yard of ballast will roughly weigh a ton. Much of this ballast has come from the Hayes Lane, whence a large cinder mound has been transplanted, but a considerable quantity has come from Langley Green. The widening of the line has necessitated the widening to a considerable extent of the old Chawnhill bridge, and the building of a second to carry the town line.

The approach to the new station from the Chawnhill Road, is quite ornamental. There is a fine sweep of well-made, gravel-red drive, which leads to the booking hall, which is on a much lower level than the platforms. Upon entering one finds to the left the booking office, smaller than the old one, but quite large enough for all requirements, as the telegraph instruments, instead of being in the office, will be accommodated in a special room on the down platform. To the right of the entrance lie the parcels and ticket collectors' offices while in front is the broad, handsome, and well lighted subway, lined with glazed bricks, and from which lead just as broad and just as handsome flights of stone steps to the two platforms overhead. For passengers' luggage two lifts are provided, one to each platform, while exceedingly plain directions are exhibited, showing from which platforms trains depart Birmingham, Wolverhampton or Worcester-wards.

The station itself comprises of two 'island' platforms, upon each of which are waiting rooms, refreshment rooms and supplementary places. Overhead glazed covering protects passengers and officials from the inclemency of the weather, and we noted that the covering projects quite a foot over the edge of the platform, so that passengers alighting in wet weather are protected. Facing towards the old station, the west or down platform will afford accommodation on its west side for the town service, and on the right of the same the main down line trains, i.e., to Wolverhampton and Birmingham. On the second platform (that on the up-side) the main up line trains to Worcester, Hereford, London etc, will come in on the west side, while local traffic will be accommodated on the east. Mention should be made of the small etceteras which, small in themselves though they be, go to make up a sum total of comfort not to be despised. The stained glass in the refreshment room windows, for instance, is unique, and has been used, so we are informed, in but few stations. The fittings in the waiting rooms and bars, and, in fact, everywhere, seem to be of the latest type, and the company are to be congratulated upon the thoroughness with which all the details have been looked after. Not the least improvement will be the use of incandescent gas lights, which have been installed throughout. We might add that on the down platform are situated the station master's office and the telegraph office.

The safety of the public ever demands perfect signalling and telegraphic systems, and these have all to be in readiness to come into use the moment the old station is vacated. As a matter of fact, the two new large signal cabins have been in use for some time, and all is now in readiness to connect up the telegraphic system at a moment's notice. The important matter of water supply has received attention by the erection of a great tank, capable of holding 24,000 gallons of water.

The contractor for the building was Mr Herbert of Wolverhampton, who has been occupied with the work from June of last year till the beginning of the present month. The construction was carried out under Mr Monckton (from the Engineers Office Wolverhampton) and Inspectors Simpson and Hancox.

At last, the great day arrived: the new Stourbridge Junction station was set to be opened

Opening day of the new Stourbridge Junction station on 1st October, 1901.

Stourbridge Library Collection

Stourbridge Junction station *c.* 1905.   *Dudley Library Services*

with all the pomp and ceremony the occasion deserved. The time was 6.07 am on 1st October, 1901 when the first train, with inspector Lodge in charge, rolled into the station to be greeted by flowing champagne and some hearty cheers. Six hours earlier, at midnight, the permanent way gang led by Mr Simpson, had broken the connection to the old station from the Town and by 5 am work had been completed in respect of connecting the line to the new loop. The formal opening took place at 12.30 pm against a setting prepared on the Town platform by Mr W.C. Simpson of Paddington and Mr A.C. Allnatt and his assistants who had decked out the platform and awning with flags and bunting. Shortly before 12.30 pm the unmistakable sound of the special train could be heard climbing the gradient of the Town branch and then round the bend it came, a formation of first class carriages and saloons hauled by a locomotive bedecked in flowers and flags. The train pulled up at the platform and disgorged its specially invited passengers comprising council members and prominent residents of the town. The Deputy Chairman, Mr J.E. Jones, accompanied by his wife, opened the proceedings with a short commentary on the history of the railway and how improved trade had underlined the need for better railway accommodation at the town. However, he was of the opinion, and speaking as a Stourbridge man and representing the views of a great many in the town, that the arrangements were not yet totally satisfactory. They would have liked the station to be nearer the town, but as this was not now possible, matters would be improved by arranging the town service to connect with every main line arrival (the service had been improved, see below). At the end of his address the station was opened with the words: 'It is now my pleasing duty to declare this new Junction station open and I hope that it will tend to the mutual advantage of the company and the Stourbridge people'. The station was then opened in 'the name of the Great Western Railway and of the Stourbridge Urban Council'.

At 1.15 pm the guests again boarded the special and departed for the Town where they were entertained to lunch at the Talbot Hotel. It had originally been hoped that amongst the guests would have been at least one Director of the company. However, had the Council expected this on the day, they were to be disappointed as no one from Paddington attended. The company, though, was well represented by local management in the form of Mr E. Murphy (superintendent of the Birmingham District), Mr E.A. Scaife (district goods manager, Worcester) and Mr J.A. Robinson (divisional locomotive superintendent). The absence of a Director did not, however, seem to diminish the occasion, local people seemingly well pleased with the station now provided (approximately £100,000 had been spent on the works as a whole). A notable absentee from the opening was the Chairman of the Council, Mr Isaac Nash, who must have been very indisposed to miss such an important event.

The train service to and from Stourbridge Town prior to the opening of the new Junction station had been:

18 services from the Town to the Junction, between 7.42 am and 8.27 pm.
18 services to the Town from the Junction, between 8.10 am and 8.58 pm.
No Sunday Service.

However, as from 1st January, 1902 there was a significant improvement in the number of services between the two stations. According to the timetable for the period, trains ran as follows:

28 services from the Town to the Junction, between 6.07 am and 10.32 pm.
28 services to the Town from the Junction, between 7.57 am and 10.15 pm.
Sunday services introduced, 9 from the Town and 8 from the Junction running between 8.50 am and 9.12 pm and 9.08 am and 9.02 pm respectively.

It was reported in the local press that the improved level of service to the Town had been achieved, at least in part, by the Council making strong representations to the GWR's General Manager, Mr J. Wilkinson. It was probably on the strength of one of these communications

The south end of the new station at Stourbridge Junction in the early 1900s with a passenger
train in the platform.   *Lens of Sutton*

Stourbridge Junction station looking north *c*. 1960.   *Lens of Sutton*

that the existing 9.00 pm weekday departure from the Town was discontinued at the end of December 1901, to be replaced in the January timetable by the 10.05 pm departure timed to connect with the 10.16 pm to Kidderminster.

As stated above, the new station comprised two 700 ft-long island platforms served by four through passenger lines. The location of the station now facilitated the construction of large marshalling yards just to the north on land left vacant by the move. In 1909, additional sidings were provided and the horse landing stage extended. Workings through the station were controlled by two signal boxes, Middle being located just beyond the north end of platform 1, and South box which was situated to the south of platform 4. A third, known as North signal box, was located near the junction of the two main lines just beyond the site of the old station. Stourbridge South signal box was closed on 30th December, 1973, and the North box followed on 29th July, 1978. The remaining signal box (Middle) was modernised to enable it to control the new colour light signalling that had been installed in the area. Semaphore signalling remained in use at Kingswinford Junction into the early 1990s; these too have been replaced by colour light signalling, although at least two semaphores are in place just beyond the junction alongside Transrail's Moor Street Steel Terminal sidings.

If the men who built the new Junction station were to return today what would they see? Probably just a shadow of the glorious days of 1901. The most obvious is the reduction in track-work around the station. The contraction began in the 1960s with the closure of the marshalling facilities and although a number of sidings remain in use on the down side of the main line these are largely overgrown and only hold the occasional track maintenance train. The station retains but three of its original four platforms. No. 4 no longer exists and a car park now occupies the site of the up relief line and the two up goods lines which once ran through. Platform 1 is still the platform for the Town branch, however, this was made into a 'dead-end' during January 1971 when the connection to the down main line at the south end of the platform was severed and the down goods loop removed.

On Monday 29th January, 1996, Centro continued to underline its commitment to improving public transport facilities in the West Midlands when a half-million pounds refurbishment programme was begun at Stourbridge Junction. Along with improvements to the toilet block and passenger waiting areas, new lifts are to be provided and the dark and uninviting subway between the booking office and the platforms is to be renovated. By July 1996 work had almost been completed on the subway and the improved lighting and colourful decor has certainly made this area more 'customer friendly'. In addition to the work currently being undertaken, there are plans to install in the centre of the car park a 'feature time piece' the design of which, according to a Centro representative, may well be considered 'provocative'!

Stourbridge Locomotive Depot

The GWR engine shed at Stourbridge was a brick-built structure with gable ends. Constructed in 1870, it appears to have been built to replace the original single-road, wooden building that had been erected by the OWWR at Dudley in 1854. The shed was located on the west side of the former OWWR main line to Dudley approximately ½ mile to the north of Stourbridge Junction station. Engine movements to and from the shed, and the two nearby through sidings, were controlled by Engine House signal box (later Engine Shed signal box). By the beginning of the 20th century the number of through sidings had been increased to five with access from the northern end to the down main line being controlled by Engine Shed ground frame. Although the sidings and ground frame were taken out of use during February 1968, Engine Shed signal box survived for a further 15 months before finally closing on 11th May, 1969.

The 156 ft by 20 ft four-road shed (one of which ran through the shed to the fitting shop to the rear) could hold up to 20 locomotives and was equipped with both coaling stage and a 45

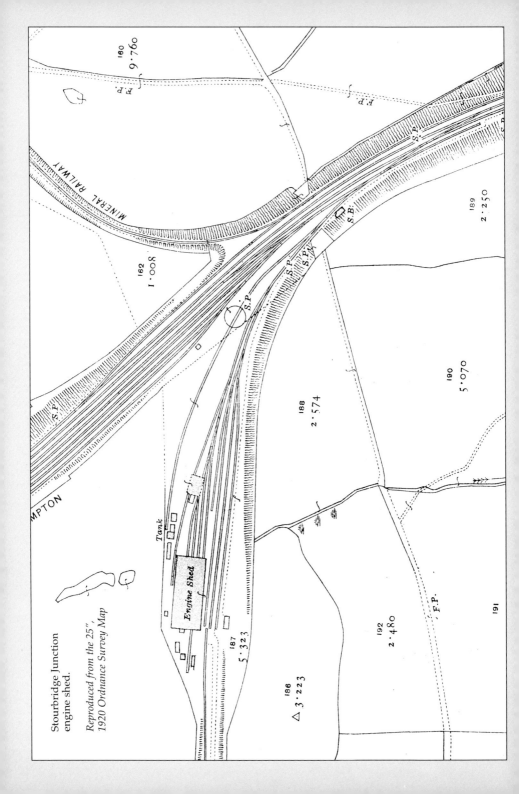

Stourbridge Junction
engine shed.

*Reproduced from the 25″,
1920 Ordnance Survey Map*

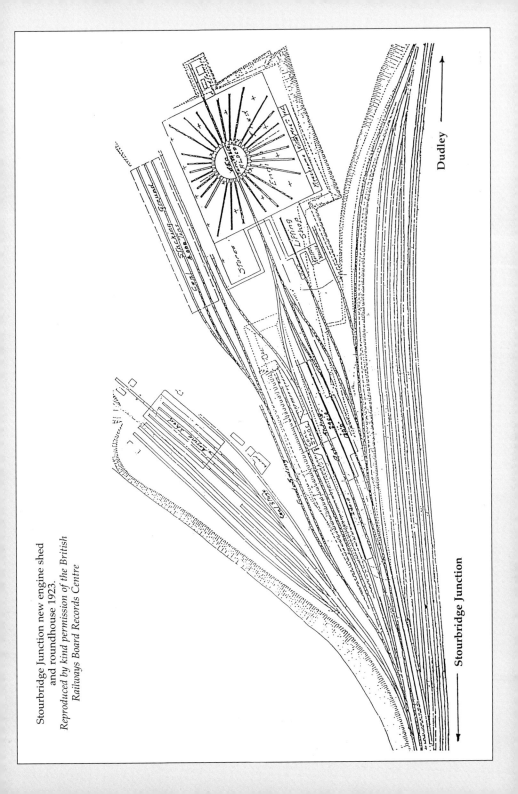

Stourbridge Junction new engine shed
and roundhouse 1923.
*Reproduced by kind permission of the British
Railways Board Records Centre*

Dudley →

Stourbridge Junction

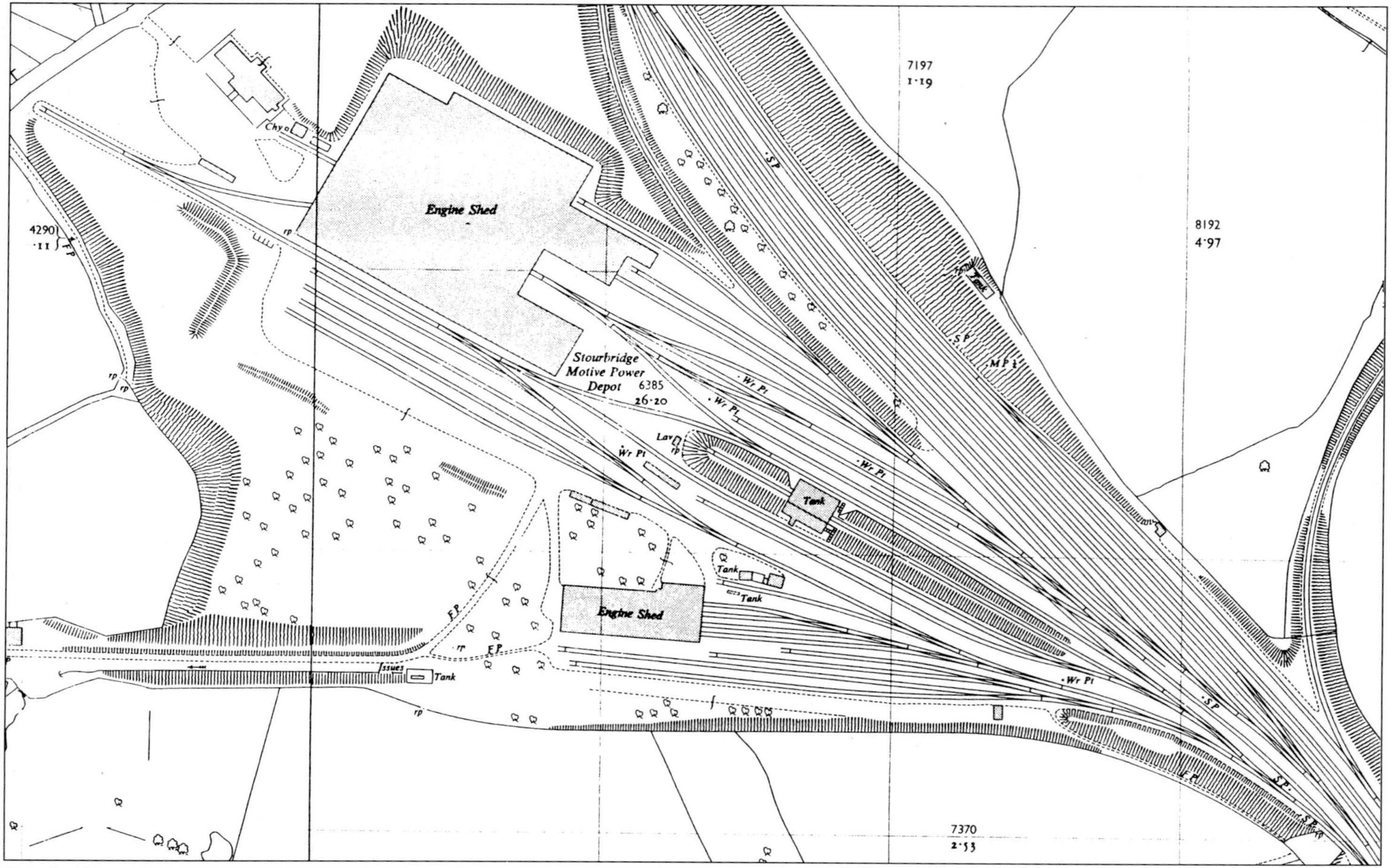
Engine Shed
Stourbridge
Motive Power
Depot
6385
26·20
Engine Shed
Tank
Tank
Tank
Tank
Tank
Issues
Chy
Lav
Wr Pl
Wr Pl
Wr Pl
Wr Pl
Wr Pl
S.P
S.P
S.P
S.P.
M.P.
F.P.
F.P.
7197
1·19
8192
4·97
7370
2·53
4290
·11

Stourbridge motive power depot.

Reproduced from the 25", 1956 Ordnance Survey Map

Stourbridge depot yard on 22nd April, 1962 with an assortment of ex-GWR and ex-LMS types on view. *R.S. Carpenter Collection*

An interior view of the roundhouse at Stourbridge depot on 22nd April, 1962. Amongst the pannier tanks is 'Austerity' 2-8-0 No. 90148. *R.S. Carpenter Collection*

Stourbridge shed yard from the coaling plant *c.* 1963.   *R. Williams*

ft diameter turntable, as well as office and mess-room facilities. Near to the turntable stood the engine house which once held the machinery for working the original incline to the goods yard. However, by the turn of the century this building had been demolished. On 8th February, 1926 the shed was closed to steam when the new depot was opened next to Engine Shed sidings, although it subsequently came in useful as a store for steam railmotors and later for GWR diesel railcars and diesel multiple units. During World War II, facilities at the new shed became over-stretched by the demands of wartime traffic and so in 1944 the old building was once again utilised to service steam locomotives. During 1956 the shed was partly rebuilt to accomodate the new dmus and a refuelling point was located just outside. The original slated timber-framed roof and wooden doors were replaced although the side walls and offices remained intact.

Plans for the construction of a new depot were drawn up as early as 1916, but wartime demands resulted in the temporary postponement of the project. Revised plans were drafted in 1923 and the facility was constructed in 1926. The contract for building the shed went to Messrs A.H. Guest Ltd at a cost of £119,230. The new structure was built around a 65 ft turntable that directed locomotives onto any one of 28 storage and maintenance roads, one of which left the rear of the shed to the sand drying room just beyond. In the 1940s, a doorway was constructed in the rear wall and the track extended outside. Track was then laid from this extension, along the south-west wall and back to the lines at the front of the shed, thereby providing an emergency exit from the shed if the main entrance road became blocked. A new brick-built coaling stage was provided, as were ash disposal facilities. During World War II, the coal stage was extended to enable locomotive tenders or bunkers to be filled from both right- and left-hand sides of the building. The coal stage supported a 75,000 gallon water tank located on top. The shed's 219 ft by 255 ft locomotive holding area was supplemented by the provision of a repair shop that was equipped to carry out light or running repairs to its own or visiting locomotives. There were also offices, a boiler house which accommodated two old locomotive boilers that provided steam for power, heating and boiler washouts, and a mess-room. The new shed had the distinction of being the last roundhouse to be built by the GWR. Both old and new sheds closed completely to steam on 11th July, 1966 although the 'Railmotor' (old) shed was used to stable dmus until 6th May, 1968. The roundhouse was also used to stable diesel locomotives and also played host, during 1967, to Ivatt Mogul No. 46443 and Collett 0-6-0 No. 3205 on their way to preservation on the Severn Valley Railway. Although both sheds had been demolished by June 1969, Stourbridge Junction continued as a signing-on point until the end of the 1980s. Initially, it had been the intention of the London Midland Region to close Stourbridge Train Crew Depot (TCD) to footplate staff on 11th April, 1988. However, ASLEF succeeded in negotiating a postponement until Saturday 9th July, 1988 when around 50 train crew were made redundant or redeployed. Will Stourbridge Junction have a TCD again? Well, by June 1998 conductors were once again reporting to the station although whether this facility will be extended to include drivers remains to be seen.

The depot ran a locomen's 'Mutual Improvement Class' on a voluntary basis from an old carriage body to the rear of the depot and it was here that both passed firemen and drivers would pass on the finer points of enginemanship to would-be drivers at the shed. Some drivers would even continue this tuition on the footplate if they felt their mate was keen and eager to learn.

Originally, Stourbridge's GWR shed code was STB, however, from 1948 under BR, this changed to 84F. Subsequently, as a by-product of the takeover of Western Region territory in the West Midlands by the LMR on 1st January, 1963, this became 2C on 9th September of the same year. Today, the site of the engine sheds has been completely covered by a new housing estate whose roads have been thoughtfully named after Great Western locomotive superintendents and chief mechanical engineers.

Stourbridge Loco Mutual Improvement Class of 1927.   *D. Harris Collection*

Collett '2251' class 0-6-0 No 3205 stands on the turntable in Stourbridge Junction on 25th March, 1967 before leaving for the Severn Valley Railway.   *E.J. Dew*

Stourbridge Engine Shed signal box on 15th September, 1963. *Joe Moss Collection*

Stourbridge diesel depot on 22nd April, 1962. This building was the former railmotor shed and was rebuilt during 1956 to house dmus. *R.S. Carpenter Collection*

Table One

Typical Working Arrangements for Stourbridge Drivers and Firemen *c.* 1955

Link	*Range of Work*
No 1 or Top Passenger Link	Passenger work only. Operate services over the Worcester to Wolverhampton line and the Stourbridge Extension to Birmingham (Snow Hill). Also services between Birmingham-Lapworth/Leamington Spa/Stratford-on-Avon.
No. 2 or Bottom Passenger Link	Mainly local passenger work over the Wolverhampton-Worcester line and the Stourbridge Extension to Birmingham (Snow Hill). Also Dudley-Birmingham via Swan Village and workmen's specials, Old Hill-Halesowen-Longbridge. Where no return passenger work was available, crews employed on freight turns e.g. deliver E.C.S. to Tyseley, go light engine to Bordesley Jn to take trip working to Stourbridge Jn.
Auto-train or Diesel Car Link	Stourbridge Jn-Stourbridge Town. Dudley-Old Hill.
Freight Link (a.k.a. Double Home Link)	Long distance/express freight services to or from the Stourbridge Jn Crews normally relieved at Oxley Branch Jn on northbound freights and at Hereford on South Wales services.
Top Bank Link	Trip workings to Oxley Sidings and Bordesley Jn.

	No. 1	Blower's Green and Bromley Basin early service.
	No. 6A	Blower's Green and Windmill End branch.
	No. 7	Hartlebury service/Elmley Lovett sidings.
	No. 8	Halesowen evening service (to Queen's Head).
	No. 9	Cannock Road, Wolverhampton.
	No. 10	Halesowen to Rowley Regis-Oldbury and Langley Green.
	No. 12	Brettell Lane and Dudley.
	No. 15	Cradley-Rowley Regis-Oldbury and Langley Green night service.
	No. 16	Halesowen assistant engine and Oldbury, Langley Green and Dudley late service.
	No. 17	Halesowen to Longbridge service. Kingswinford branch service.
Bottom Bank Link	No. 2	Halesowen morning service.
	No. 3	Stourbridge goods branch.
	No. 4	Lye and Cradley Heath.
	No. 5	Rowley Regis service.
	No. 6	Corngreaves service.
	No. 11	Old Hill goods service.
	No. 13	Lye, Hayes Lane and Timmis' sidings.
	No. 14	Halesowen and Canal Basin afternoon engine.
	No. 18-20	Train banking engines.
Shunt Link		Stourbridge Shed and Engine Shed sidings. Stourbridge Jn yards and carriage sidings. Sidings at Brettell Lane, Kingswinford, Pensnett, Bromley Basin, Round Oak, Blower's Green and Dudley; Lye, Cradley, Langley Green and the Oldbury branch.

Chapter Four

Train Services Through Stourbridge

The Route to London

Following the opening of the Oxford, Worcester and Wolverhampton Railway, the company entered into an agreement with the London & North Western Railway in September 1853, which would eventually allow all passenger traffic to leave the OWWR south of Handborough and run, via the 'Yarnton Loop' (opened on 1st April, 1854) and Bletchley into the LNWR's terminus at London (Euston). Access to the LNW Stour Valley Line (just to the north of Tipton (OWWR) station via the 'Tipton Curve') had already been gained on 1st December, 1853 thereby enabling the company to run trains directly into Wolverhampton (Queen Street) station. Consequently, with the opening of the Yarnton Loop a through route from Wolverhampton, Dudley, Stourbridge and Worcester into the nation's capital city was assured. Services between Wolverhampton and London (Euston) over this route commenced on 1st April, 1854.

The weekday timetable for July 1857 (*Table Two*) shows four workings daily each way between Wolverhampton and Euston. The first up and the last down trains were designated 'Expresses' and probably worked straight through to each terminus. The remaining services would, however, be comprised of both OWW and LNW carriage stock, the latter being attached/uncoupled at Handborough. LNW locomotives apparently worked through from Bletchley to and from Handborough with these through carriages. Passengers could, of course, continue their journey to Oxford where they might catch a broad gauge connection into London (Paddington). This was the original service with trains from Worcester and the Black Country terminating at Oxford. The introduction of the Euston service meant that passengers wishing to continue to Oxford would have to wait at Handborough until the Euston portion had entered the Yarnton Loop. The remaining carriages, usually about two or three, would then continue to Oxford hauled by an OWWR locomotive.

From 1st July, 1861 the OWWR (now part of the West Midland Railway) was managed by a Joint Committee of 18 Great Western Directors plus six from the West Midland Railway, until the formal absorption of the company by the Great Western Railway on 1st August, 1863. The principal effect of this arrangement was the termination of the through services to/from Euston on 1st October, 1861 and the establishment of Paddington as the London terminus for trains using the OWWR (*Table Three*). The takeover by the GWR led to a substantial increase in the number of services to and from the capital running over the OWWR as far as Stourbridge Junction and beyond. For example, in October 1886, there were six trains to the Black Country from Paddington and five in the opposite direction, including one express service each way. By July 1900 the number of down services had been increased to eight, whilst the number of London-bound trains had been strengthened to seven. The July timetable indicated that the two expresses over the route (1.40 pm departure from Paddington arriving Stourbridge Junction at 4.55 pm and the 12.30 pm departure from Stourbridge Junction arriving Paddington at 4.10 pm) ran non-stop over the section between Worcester and London.

An interesting point was made by a correspondent writing under the pseudonym 'Tempus' in the 8th August, 1896 edition of the *County Express*. The writer suggested that in the 1860s, the early morning service between Stourbridge Junction and London (Paddington) was considerably quicker than the service currently in operation. As shown on page 58, this seems to be a valid point:

Table Two

The Oxford, Worcester and Wolverhampton Railway July 1857

Down Trains - Weekdays

	am	am	am	am	am	pm	pm	am	pm	pm	pm	pm
LONDON, Euston Square d.					6.15			9.30			12.30	5.00
Watford								10.00			1.00	
Tring											1.30	
Bletchley					7.30			10.50			2.05	6.10
LONDON, Paddington d.								9.15			11.00	4.50
Reading								10.00			12.00	5.37
Didcot											12.27	6.10
OXFORD a.								10.35			12.50	6.30

	123	1&3 K	123	123	1&2 K	1&2 K	123	1&2 K	123	123 K	12&P	Ex12
OXFORD d.					8.15			11.30			2.50	6.45
Handborough for Blenheim					8.30			11.45			3.10	7.00
Shipton					9.10			12.20			3.50	7.35
Adlestrop & Stow Road					9.25			12.30			4.06	7.45
Moreton					9.35			12.40			4.20	7.55
Blockley					9.42			(pm)			4.30	
Campden					9.50			12.50			4.35	
Honeybourne					10.00						4.45	
Evesham		7.15			10.10			1.10			5.00	8.25
Fladbury		7.22			10.15			1.17			5.07	
Pershore		7.30			10.20			1.25			5.15	8.35
WORCESTER a.		7.45			10.35			1.45			5.33	8.50
WORCESTER d.		7.55	8.45		10.50	12.00		2.00		3.45	5.45	9.00
Fernhill Heath			8.52			12.07				3.52	5.52	
Droitwich			9.00		11.02	12.15		2.10		4.00	6.00	9.15
Hartlebury			9.15			12.30		2.25		4.15	6.15	
KIDDERMINSTER	7.35	8.25	9.25		11.25	12.40		2.35		4.25	6.25	9.30
Churchill			9.32			12.50				4.35	6.35	
Hagley		8.32	9.37								6.40	
STOURBRIDGE	8.00	8.40	9.45	10.30	11.40	1.00	1.45	2.50	3.50	4.45	6.45	9.45
Brettell Lane	8.06		9.50	10.35	11.45	1.06	1.50	2.53	3.56	4.50	6.51	9.50
Round Oak	8.12	8.47	9.55	10.42	11.50	1.12	1.57	3.00		4.55	6.57	9.55
Netherton	8.18		10.00	10.48	(pm)	1.20	2.03		4.08	5.00	7.02	
DUDLEY a.	8.23	8.55	10.10	10.53	12.00	1.25	2.08	3.10	4.13	5.05	7.10	10.05
DUDLEY d.	8.25		10.20	10.55		1.35	2.10	3.15	4.15	5.15	7.20	
Tipton	8.30		10.25	10.59		1.40	2.15	3.20	4.20	5.20	7.25	
Prince's End	8.34		10.28	11.03		1.43	2.19	3.23	4.24	5.24	7.28	
Daisy Bank	8.38		10.32	11.07		1.47	2.23	3.28	4.28	5.28	7.32	
Bilston	8.42		10.36	11.11		1.50	2.27	3.31	4.32	5.32	7.36	
Priestfield	8.45		10.40	11.15		1.55	2.30	3.35	4.35	5.35	7.40	
WOLVERHAMPTON (OWW)	8.55		10.45	11.20		2.00	2.40	3.45	4.40	5.40	7.50	

	123	1&3 K	123	123	1&2 K	1&2 K	123	1&2 K	123	123 K	12&P	Ex12
DUDLEY d.		9.00	10.30		12.05			3.20			7.15	10.10
Tipton		9.05	10.35					3.25				10.15
Deepfields			10.40					3.30			7.25	10.20
Ettingshall & Bilston			10.45									
WOLVERHAMPTON (LNW)		9.20	10.50		12.15			3.40			7.35	10.30

Passengers by trains marked K will go between Kidderminster and Birmingham without change of carriage.

Table Two

The Oxford, Worcester and Wolverhampton Railway July 1857

Up Trains - Weekdays

		am Ex12	am 12&P	am 123	am 1&2 K	am 1&2 K	am 123	pm 1&2 K	pm 123	pm 1&2	pm 123 K	pm 123	pm 123	pm 1&2 K
WOLVERHAMPTON (LNW)	d.	6.00			9.45	11.05		12.40			5.00			7.35
Ettingshall & Bilston					9.50	11.10								
Deepfields		6.05			9.55	11.15		12.45			5.05			
Tipton		6.10			10.00	11.20		12.50			5.10			
DUDLEY	a.	6.15			10.10	11.25		12.55			5.15			7.45
WOLVERHAMPTON (OWW)			8.15	9.10		11.00	11.45		2.45	3.30	4.40	5.30	6.30	
Priestfield			8.20	9.15		11.05	11.50		2.50	3.35	4.45	5.35	6.35	
Bilston			8.23	9.18		11.10	11.53		2.53	3.38	4.50	5.38	6.38	
Daisy Bank			8.27	9.22		11.15	11.56		2.57	3.40	4.55	5.41	6.40	
Prince's End			8.31	9.27		11.20	12.01		3.01	3.42	5.00	5.46	6.43	
Tipton			8.36	9.30		11.25	12.04		3.04	3.45	5.05	5.50	6.48	
DUDLEY	a.		8.40	9.34		11.30	12.10		3.10	3.55	5.10	5.56	6.50	
DUDLEY	d.	6.25	8.45	9.36	10.20	11.35	12.12	1.10	3.12	4.00	5.20	5.58	7.00	7.48
Netherton			8.50	9.41	10.25	11.40	12.17		3.17	4.05	5.25	6.03	7.05	
Round Oak		6.30	8.55	9.46	10.30	11.45	12.22	1.15	3.22	4.10	5.30	6.07	7.10	
Brettell Lane		6.35	9.00	9.51	10.35	11.50	12.27	1.20	3.27	4.15	5.35	6.13	7.13	7.58
STOURBRIDGE		6.40	9.05	10.00	10.40	11.55	12.35	1.25	3.35	4.20	5.40	6.20	7.20	8.03
Hagley			9.10			(pm)				4.25	5.45			
Churchill			9.15				12.02				5.50		7.30	
KIDDERMINSTER		6.52	9.25		10.55		12.10	1.40		4.35	6.00		7.40	8.15
Hartlebury			9.35				12.18	1.48		4.45	6.08			
Droitwich		7.10	9.50		11.10		12.30	2.00		4.55	6.20			8.35
Fernhill Heath			9.58								6.28			
WORCESTER	a.	7.25	10.10		11.25		12.45	2.15		5.10	6.40			8.50
WORCESTER	d.	7.30	10.15				12.50			5.15	6.50			
Pershore		7.45	10.30				1.05			5.30	7.10			
Fladbury			10.37				1.12			5.37	7.17			
Evesham		7.55	10.48				1.20			5.45	7.25			
Honeybourne			11.00				1.30			5.55				
Campden			11.13				1.45			6.05				
Blockley			11.20				1.50			6.10				
Moreton		8.25	11.30				2.00			6.20				
Adlestrop & Stow Rd		8.35	11.40				2.10			6.30				
Shipton		8.45	11.55				2.25			6.40				
Handborough for Blenheim		9.05	12.25				2.50			7.05				
OXFORD	a.	9.30	12.45				3.15			7.30				
OXFORD	d.	11.38	2.00				4.08			8.00				
Didcot		12.15	2.18				4.40			8.23				
Reading		12.50	2.52				5.08			9.13				
LONDON, Paddington	a.	2.25	3.30				5.40			10.15				
Bletchley		10.05	1.59				3.30			8.00				
Tring		10.35	2.32				4.27							
Watford							4.53							
LONDON, Euston Square a.		11.25	3.30				5.35			9.30				

Passengers by trains marked K will go between Birmingham and Kidderminster without change of carriage.

Table Three

The West Midland Railway January 1862

Down Trains - Weekdays only

Stations	am 123	am 123	am 1&2	am Parl K	pm 1&2	am 1&2	pm 1&2 K	pm 1&2	pm 1&2	pm 1&2
LONDON Paddington				6.00		9.35		1.30	3.30	6.30
OXFORD d.				8.35		11.20		3.25	5.30	7.55
Handborough for Blenheim				8.50		11.35			5.45	
Shipton				9.20		12.05		4.00	6.15	
Adlestrop & Stow Road				9.35		12.20		4.10	6.30	
Moreton				9.45		12.30		4.20	6.40	8.40
Blockley				9.54		12.40			6.50	
Campden				10.00		12.45		4.35	6.55	
Honeybourne			9.08	10.10		12.55		4.45	7.05	
Evesham			9.20	10.25		1.10		5.00	7.20	8.55
Fladbury			9.27	10.32		1.18			7.28	9.03
Pershore			9.35	10.40		1.25		5.15	7.35	9.10
WORCESTER a.			9.55	11.00		1.45		5.30	7.55	9.25
WORCESTER d.		8.45	10.10	11.10		2.02	4.45	5.45	8.05	9.28
Fernhill Heath		8.52		11.17		2.08	Sat		8.12	
Droitwich		9.00	10.25	11.25		2.15	only	6.00	8.20	9.40
Hartlebury		9.15		11.40		2.30		6.15		
KIDDERMINSTER	7.55	9.25	10.45	11.50	12.45	2.40	5.30	6.25	8.40	9.55
Churchill		9.35		11.57	12.52	2.50	5.37			
Hagley	8.05	9.40		12.05	1.00		5.45		8.50	
STOURBRIDGE	8.12	9.50	11.00	12.15	1.07	3.00	5.52	6.40	9.00	10.10
Brettell Lane	8.17	9.55		12.20	1.12	3.05	5.57	6.45		
BRIERLEY HILL	8.20	9.59		12.24	1.16		6.01		9.10	
Round Oak	8.23	10.05		12.28	1.19	3.10	6.04	6.50		
Netherton		10.12		12.35	1.26	3.15	6.10			
DUDLEY a.	8.35	10.17	11.15	12.40	1.33	3.25	6.20	7.00	9.20	10.27
DUDLEY d.	8.45	10.22	11.18	12.45	1.40	3.30	6.25	7.05	9.25	
Tipton	8.49	10.27		12.50	1.45		6.30			
Prince's End	8.52	10.30		12.53	1.48	3.35	6.33	7.10		
Daisy Bank	8.55	10.34		12.56	1.51	3.38	6.36			
Bilston	8.58	10.38		1.00	1.55	3.41	6.40	7.15	9.35	
Priestfield	9.01	10.42		1.05	2.00	3.45	6.45	7.20		
WOLVERHAMPTON (LL)	9.10	10.50	11.30	1.15	2.10	3.55	6.50	7.25	9.45	
BIRMINGHAM New St	9.10	11.05	12.30	1.30	2.15	6.20	7.05	8.25	10.15	

Passengers by trains marked K will go between Kidderminster and Birmingham without change of carriage.

Table Three

The West Midland Railway January 1862 (continued)

Up Trains - Weekdays only

Stations	am 1&2	am Parl	am 1&2 K	am 1&2	am 1&2	pm 1&2	pm 1&2 K	pm 1&2	pm 123	pm 123	pm 1&2 K
BIRMINGHAM New St		6.00	8.00	10.20	11.30	1.00	2.30	4.15		6.30	8.00
WOLVERHAMPTON (LL)		7.30	8.45	10.20	11.55	1.25	2.35	4.20	5.40	7.10	8.15
Priestfield		7.35		10.25			2.40	4.25	5.45		
Bilston		7.38	8.50	10.28	12.02	1.30	2.43	4.28	5.48	7.15	8.20
Daisy Bank		7.42	8.53	10.31		1.33	2.47	4.32	5.51	7.19	8.25
Prince's End		7.45		10.35	12.07	1.36	2.51	4.36	5.55	7.23	8.30
Tipton		7.50		10.40	12.10		2.55	4.40	6.00	7.26	
DUDLEY a.		7.55	9.02	10.45	12.15	1.40	3.00	4.45	6.05	7.30	8.35
DUDLEY d.	6.15	8.00	9.05	10.55	12.20	1.50	3.10	4.55		7.35	8.40
Netherton		8.05		11.00			3.15	5.00			8.45
Round Oak		8.10		11.05	12.28	2.00	3.20	5.04		7.45	8.50
BRIERLEY HILL		8.14	9.12	11.09			3.23	5.07		7.48	
Brettell Lane	6.25	8.18		11.12	12.33	2.05	3.25	5.10		7.51	8.55
STOURBRIDGE	6.30	8.25	9.20	11.18	12.40	2.10	3.30	5.15		7.56	9.00
Hagley		8.32		11.25			3.37	5.22			9.05
Churchill		8.40		11.32			3.45	5.30			9.10
KIDDERMINSTER	6.45	8.48	9.35	11.40	12.55	2.25	3.53	5.37		8.10	9.20
Hartlebury		8.55			1.05			5.45		8.18	
Droitwich	6.55	9.10	9.50		1.20	2.45		6.00		8.30	
Fernhill Heath		9.20								8.38	
WORCESTER a.	7.10	9.30	10.05		1.35	3.00		6.10		8.48	
WORCESTER d.	7.15	9.40	10.15		1.45			6.25		9.00	
Pershore		9.55	10.30		2.00			6.40		9.15	
Fladbury		10.02			2.07			6.47		9.22	
Evesham	7.40	10.10	10.45		2.15			6.55		9.30	
Honeybourne		10.20	10.55					7.08			
Campden		10.25	11.10					7.20			
Blockley		10.40						7.28			
Moreton	8.05	10.50	11.25		2.45			7.35			
Adlestrop & Stow Rd		11.00			2.55			7.45			
Shipton		11.20			3.10			8.00			
Handborough for Blenheim	8.40	11.50			3.35			8.30			
OXFORD a.	8.55	12.05	12.15		3.50			8.45			
LONDON, Paddington	10.30	2.30	2.30		5.40			10.30			

Passengers by trains marked K will go between Birmingham and Kidderminster without change of carriage.

Year	Departure	No. of Stops	Arrival	Journey Time
1862	6.30 am	6	10.30 am	4 hours
1875	6.10 am	10	10.25 am	4 hours 15 mins
1896	6.00 am	6*	10.25 am	4 hours 25 mins

* It is thought that this train may have stopped at more stations than stated, the source timetable that appeared locally being a summarised version of the 'official' copy.

The GWR Timetable for January to April 1902 showed the following weekday services between Wolverhampton Low Level, Stourbridge Junction & London:

Table Four

Down	arr. Stourbridge Jn	Notes
9.45 am to Wolverhampton	3.28 pm	(6)
9.50 am to Wolverhampton	1.53 pm	(1/4)
1.40 pm to Stourbridge Junction	4.55 pm	(2)
1.45 pm to Stourbridge Junction	5.36 pm	(6)
1.50 pm to Wolverhampton	7.10 pm	(4)
4.45 pm to Wolverhampton	8.34 pm	(1/4)
6.50 pm to Wolverhampton	11.40 pm	(4)

Up	arr. Paddington	
5.55 am from Stourbridge Junction	10.25 am	(4)
7.20 am from Wolverhampton (dep. Stourbridge Jn 8.14 am)	12.00 nn	(1/4)
8.30 am from Wolverhampton (dep. Stourbridge Jn 9.03 am)	2.10 pm	(5)
10.18 am from Stourbridge Junction	2.33 pm	(6)
12.37 pm from Stourbridge Junction	4.10 pm	(3)
1.12 pm from Wolverhampton (dep. Stourbridge Jn 1.45 pm)	5.50 pm	(4)
3.45 pm from Wolverhampton or 4.33 pm from Stourbridge Jn	8.45 pm	(4/7)
4.50pm from Wolverhampton (dep. Stourbridge Jn 5.43 pm)	10.50 pm	(6)

Notes
(All Through Carriages (TC) attached/detached at Worcester Shrub Hill)
(1)   TC to/from Hereford and/or Malvern.
(2)   TC off 'Worcester, Malvern & Hereford Corridor Express'
(3)   TC onto 'Hereford, Malvern, Worcester & London Corridor Express'.
(4)   TC to/from Wolverhampton and/or Stourbridge Junction.
(5)   May have combined with 7.45 am departure from Shrewsbury via S.V. line.
(6)   Passengers probably required to change trains at Worcester
(7)   The 3.45 pm ran via Worcester Foregate Street so TC may have been detached at Stourbridge for the 4.33 pm departure?

During February 1905 news broke that a new express was to be introduced to the line. Departing from Wolverhampton at 7.50 am, the train would call at Dudley (8.02 am), Stourbridge Junction (8.14 am), Kidderminster (8.26 am), Droitwich Spa (8.39 am) and would then run non-stop from Worcester (dep. 8.55 am) to London (Paddington) arriving there at 11.10 am. The return would leave Paddington at 4.45 pm, arriving Wolverhampton at 8.04 pm. On 1st March, 1905 the express began its inaugural journey to be met at Dudley by Mr C. Aldington, the assistant superintendent of the District, accompanied by a group of newspapermen who had been specially invited by the GWR to sample the delights of travel by the new train. The journey from the Junction to London took 2 hours 56 minutes, 8 minutes ahead of schedule. Apparently, the quickest journey previously had been 3 hours 35 minutes, probably the 12.35 pm departure comprising through carriages attached at Worcester to 'The Hereford, Malvern and Worcester Corridor Express', arriving Paddington at 4.10 pm. The new express had a Breakfast Car attached for the up journey and a Dining Car for the return.

As the years passed by, the former OWWR north of Worcester gradually lessened in importance, the Great Western seeming to lose interest in the running of fast trains over the section. Probably this had something to do with the opening of the more direct route between Paddington and Banbury via Bicester in April 1910, which substantially reduced the route mileage between Wolverhampton and Paddington in comparison to that of the OWWR. However, whatever the reason, the fact remains that by the early 1920s, express services as such were no longer running over the Stourbridge, Dudley and Wolverhampton line, instead, through trains were either 'semi-fast' (additional stops at principal intermediate stations) or 'slow' (calling at all intermediate stations); this was certainly a far cry from the heady days of 1905! To illustrate these arrangements relevant details have been extracted from the Working Time Tables for 11th July, 1921:

Table Five

Up Services	Notes
7.15 am Wolverhampton-Paddington (7.54 am dep. Stourbridge Jn) arr. 11.15 am	(1)
8.20 am Wolverhampton-Paddington (9.12 am dep. Stourbridge Jn) arr. 2.15 pm	(2)
4.05 pm Wolverhampton-Paddington (4.47 pm dep. Stourbridge Jn) arr. 9.20 pm	(3)
Down Services	
9.45 am Paddington-Wolverhampton (2.03 pm arr. Stourbridge Jn) arr. 3.00 pm	(4)
1.30 pm Paddington-Wolverhampton (4.48pm arr. Stourbridge Jn) arr. 5.45 pm	(5)
1.35 pm Paddington-Stourbridge Junction arrive 5.44 pm	(6)
4.45 pm Paddington-Stourbridge Junction arrive 8.01 pm	(7)

Notes

(1)   An ordinary passenger train as far as Kidderminster, the first stop from Wolverhampton was at Dudley. From Kidderminster the train ran under 'A' headlamps combining at Worcester with the Hereford-Paddington express. This made one intermediate stop at Oxford.

(2)   Ran as an ordinary passenger train throughout, calling at all stations.

(3)   Worked under 'A' headlamps throughout calling only at principal stations.

(4)   'A' headlamps from Paddington to Worcester stopping only at principal intermediate stations. Headlamps changed to 'B' at Kidderminster, called at all stations to Wolverhampton Low Level.

(5)   Non-stop Paddington to Worcester express. Although the timetable is not specific, it is thought that in addition to the Hereford portion through carriages also worked to Wolverhampton under 'A' headlamps. This was certainly the case in 1922.

(6)   Running under express headlamps to Worcester, this train called at principal stations. From Worcester the train continued under 'B' headlamps stopping at all stations to Stourbridge.

(7)   Working under 'A' headlamps throughout, this service only called at Oxford before Worcester. From Worcester the through portion called at all stations to Stourbridge Junction except Churchill and Hagley (where stops were made only on notice being given to the guard at Worcester).

Moving forward to the winter of 1922, through trains to and from the capital remained very similar to the above, apart from some service re-timings. However, one notable addition to the timetable was the 1.19 pm departure from Kidderminster which conveyed through carriages to Paddington. By this time Kidderminster seems to have been given a much higher profile by the GWR, a view that the Public Timetable for 2nd October, 1922 seems to support.

Stourbridge Junction looking south *c.* 1960.   *Lens of Sutton*

Station approach at Hagley.   *Lens of Sutton*

Hagley station looking south *c.* 1960. *Lens of Sutton*

Hagley station looking north in 1962. *Joe Moss Collection*

Churchill & Blakedown station in the early 1960s.   *Joe Moss Collection*

The station frontage at Kidderminster in the early 1900s is seen in this commercial postcard.
Lens of Sutton

Dean 'Single' 4-2-2 No. 3050 *Royal Sovereign* is seen at Stourbridge Junction *c.* 1910.

D.K. Jones Collection

Class '455' 'Metro' 2-4-0T No. 976 departs platform 3 at Stourbridge Junction with an up local service bound for Kidderminster *c.* 1925. *Real Photographs*

'Bulldog' class 4-4-0 (possibly No. 3308 *Falmouth*) leaves Stourbridge Junction on a
Wolverhampton to Paddington express.   *Stourbridge Library*

'Bulldog' class 4-4-0 No. 3300 (*Pendennis Castle*) passes through Pedmore, just to the south of
Stourbridge, with a Worcester to Birmingham service. The locomotive is by this time un-named,
the plate being removed during May 1923 to avoid duplication with the new 4-6-0 'Castle' class
locomotive of the same name.   *Real Photographs*

'Star' class 4-6-0 No. 4031 *Queen Mary* leaves Stourbridge Junction with the 'all stations' Wolverhampton (Low Level) to Oxford service on 16th October, 1949. *W.F. Deebank*

'Castle' class No. 5010 *Restormel Castle* waits with the 9.10 am departure from Stourbridge Junction to Oxford (ex-Wolverhampton (Low Level) at 8.14 am) on 4th April, 1954. *W.F. Deebank*

Table Six

Through Passenger Trains - Wolverhampton, Stourbridge Junction, Oxford & Paddington

3rd July to 24th September, 1939

Headcode			arr. Stourbridge Jn	Notes
A	10.15 am	Paddington-Wolverhampton	1.32 pm	(1)
B	11.32 am	Oxford-Wolverhampton	2.55 pm	
A	12.45 pm	Paddington-Stourbridge Jn	3.49 pm	(6)
A	1.45 pm	Paddington-Stourbridge Jn	5.35 pm	(1)
B	3.42 pm	Oxford-Wolverhampton	7.17 pm	
A	4.45 pm	Paddington-Wolverhampton	8.04 pm	(1)

Headcode			arr. Paddington	Notes
B	6.50 am	From Wolverhampton (dep. S. Jn 7.45 am)	11.10 am	(2)
B	8.23 am	From Wolverhampton (dep. S. Jn 9.15 am)	2.10 pm	
B	11.55 am	From Wolverhampton (dep. S. Jn 12.45 pm)	4.20 pm	(7)
B	4.10 pm	From Wolverhampton (dep. S. Jn 4.48 pm)	9.20 pm	(2)

Sundays			arr. Stourbridge Jn	Notes
B	5.52 pm	Oxford-Wolverhampton	arr. S. Jn 9.10 pm	
B	9.30 am	Stourbridge Jn-Oxford	arr. Oxford 12.40 pm	

7th October, 1946 to 4th May, 1947

Headcode				Notes
A	1.45 pm	Paddington-Wolverhampton	arr. S. Jn 5.52 pm	(1)
A	4.45 pm	Paddington-Wolverhampton	arr. S. Jn 8.29 pm	(1/6)
B	6.50 am	From Wolverhampton (dep. S. Jn 7.42 am)	arr. London 11.30 am	(3)
B	8.18 am	From Wolverhampton (dep. S. Jn 9.15 am)	arr. Oxford 12.46 pm	
B	12.05 pm	From Wolverhampton (dep. S. Jn 1.00 pm)	arr. London 5.05 pm	(3)
B	1.55 pm	From Wolverhampton (dep. S. Jn 2.45 pm)	arr. Oxford 5.25 pm	(3)
Sundays				
B	4.05 pm	Paddington-Wolverhampton	arr. S. Jn 9.13 pm	
B	8.00 am	From Wolverhampton (dep. S. Jn 9.17 am)	arr. London 1.55 pm	(5)

13th June to 18th September, 1955

Headcode				Notes
A	1.45 pm	Paddington-Wolverhampton	arr. S. Jn 5.48 pm	(1/6)
A	4.45 pm	Paddington-Stourbridge Jn	arr. 8.22 pm	(1/6)
B	8.14 am	From Wolverhampton (dep. S. Jn 9.10 am)	arr. Oxford 12.37 pm	
A	8.19 am	From Kidderminster	arr. London 11.27 am	
A	2.25 pm	From Wolverhampton (dep. S. Jn 3.00 pm)	arr. London 6.35 pm	(4)
Sundays				
B	4.45 pm	Paddington-Wolverhampton	arr. S. Jn 9.19 pm	
B	7.55 am	From Wolverhampton (dep. S. Jn 9.15 am)	arr. London 2.00 pm	

17th June to 15th September, 1957

Headcode				Notes
A	1.45 pm	Paddington-Stourbridge Junction	arr. 5.48 pm	(1/6)
A	4.45 pm	Paddington-Kidderminster	arr. 8.03 pm	(6)
B	8.14 am	From Wolverhampton (dep. S. Jn 9.10 am)	arr. Oxford 12.37 pm	
A	8.19 am	From Kidderminster	arr. London 11.30 pm	(8)
A	2.15 pm	From Wolverhampton (dep. S. Jn 3.00 pm)	arr. London 6.35 pm	
Sundays				
B	4.45 pm	Paddington-Wolverhampton (arr. 10.05 pm)	arr. S. Jn 9.17 pm	

Notes

1. 'B' headlamps from Worcester (Shrub Hill).
2. 'A' headlamps from Worcester (Shrub Hill).
3. 'A' headlamps from Stourbridge Jn.
4. Terminates at Oxford SO.
5. 'A' headlamps from Oxford.
6. Conveys TC for Hereford.
7. 'A' headlamps from Kidderminster.
8. Combined with 7.45 am ex-Hereford.

Express services over the ex-OWWR to and from Paddington were being advertised by principal station and Kidderminster was now featuring alongside Worcester, Malvern and Hereford. The town's increased railway status had of course been strengthened by the introduction of its own through service to London which combined with the 12.50 pm ex-Hereford express at Worcester and arrived at Paddington at 4.15 pm. With the exception of this service, all others continued to convey through portions to or from stations in the Black Country. Sometime between 6th July,1936 and 1939 this through service from Kidderminster was extended to depart from Wolverhampton (Low Level).

The Great Western's prime interest lay with the London(Paddington)-Worcester expresses and several of these ran non-stop between the two cities, such as the 'Worcester, Malvern & Hereford Corridor Express' of 1902 and the 'Worcester, Malvern, Hereford & Kidderminster Express' of 1922 which conveyed slip carriages released at Kingham. However, apart from these early examples, express (or possibly semi-fast) services would call at the more important stations such as Oxford, Kingham (for trains to Chipping Norton or Cheltenham Spa), Moreton-in-Marsh, Campden and Evesham. The company had always recognised that the route to Worcester alone could not generate sufficient passenger business to ensure the viability of fast services over the line, and had therefore widened the catchment area for these trains by introducing intermediate stops in the Cotswolds and extending services to the Malverns and Hereford in one direction, and the Black Country in the other. Consequently, the 'slow' and 'semi-fast' services to the latter did play an important role in relation to these expresses acting as feeder services to/from the many intermediate stations along the route.

The Paddington-Worcester-Hereford element evolved into a major service whilst the through trains to/from Stourbridge, Dudley and Wolverhampton gradually went into decline and eventually faded away completely.

The prestigious 'London, Worcester, Malvern and Hereford Corridor Express' of 1902 completed the journey to Hereford in 3 hours 15 minutes. At this time there were three up and two down services between Hereford, Worcester and Paddington (the 4.45 pm ex-Paddington terminated at Great Malvern at 8.07 pm) in addition to three services running to and from Paddington and Hereford via Gloucester. By 1922 the fastest service between Paddington and Hereford was the 'London, Malvern and Hereford Express' which left London at 1.30 pm arriving at Hereford at 4.40 pm. By the summer of 1935, there were five fast trains operating each way over the Malvern/Hereford section, three to/from Hereford, including the 'Worcester, Malvern & Hereford Express', and two from and to Malvern.

The GWR's policy of naming trains after the principal towns and cities on the route continued into the late 1930s. The Public Timetable for 30th September, 1935 to 5th July, 1936 gave the 10.15 am and 4.45 pm Paddington departures as the 'Worcester, Malvern, Hereford, Droitwich Spa & Kidderminster Expresses', whilst the 12.45 pm included 'Cheltenham Spa' in its list of destinations. The up services, the 8.09 am and 1.20 pm trains from Kidderminster, were described in similar fashion but in reverse order. Stourbridge Junction was the principal destination for the through portions off the 12. 45pm; the untitled 1.45 pm and the 4.45 pm, although the 10.15am ex-Paddington terminated at Wolverhampton (Low Level). In the opposite direction, the 8.09 am departure from Kidderminster conveyed through carriages from Wolverhampton.

After World War II, the significance of the Malvern/Hereford route measurably increased and Hereford became firmly established as the principal destination beyond Worcester relegating Malvern to an intermediate stop on the route. Unfortunately, accompanying this move was an equally noticeable downturn in the fortunes of the Worcester-Stourbridge-Wolverhampton through services as *Table Six* attempts to illustrate. As mentioned above, the line from Worcester (Shrub Hill) to Stourbridge and Wolverhampton had been for many years very much a subsidiary route with virtually all of its London trains operating as locals stopping at intermediate stations along the way. At least Stourbridge did have a through service to the nation's capital but this position was soon to change.

By 1951 down through services were confined to two trains, the 1.45 pm and the 4.45 pm departures from Paddington. These conveyed through carriages which went forward to

'Hall' class 4-6-0 No. 5909 *Newton Hall* on a southbound service on 15th September, 1956.

H.C. Casserley

No. 5046 *Earl Cawdor* at the north end of Stourbridge Junction, possibly with the fast service from Worcester (Shrub Hill) to Wolverhampton (Low Level) on 9th February, 1957.   *J.W. Gibbs*

Brush Type '4' No. D1628 heads a passenger train through Hagley on 28th June, 1966. By this time the station canopy had been removed on the northbound platform.   *G.D.A. Hingley*

Wolverhampton (Low Level) at 4.53 pm and 7.36 pm respectively. In the opposite direction the two through trains to Paddington (ex-Wolverhampton at 6.50 am and 12.08 pm) were supplemented by two connecting services, the 11.10 am departure from Stourbridge Junction and the 3.45 pm ex-Wolverhampton. These services enabled passengers to continue their journey to London on the 12.15 pm and 6.05 pm services from Worcester (the 11.00 am and 4.48 pm departures from Hereford).

As far as Sunday services were concerned, from *circa* 1947 the GWR, and later BR(WR), operated a late afternoon through service from Paddington via Stourbridge Junction which arrived at Wolverhampton (Low Level) at about 10.00 pm. During 1946/7 the up train, the 8.00 am departure from Wolverhampton (9.17 am from Stourbridge), ran from Oxford under 'A' headlamps reaching Paddington at 1.55 pm. By 1951 this service had been altered to terminate at Oxford at 12.22 pm.

By the mid-1950s there were still a handful of through services working over the OWWR north of Worcester as can be seen from *Table Six*. By this time five down through trains left Paddington for Hereford, the city having taken over as the final destination for all expresses over the route.

By the summer of 1963 the Hereford expresses had increased to six down and seven up, whilst through weekday workings between London and Stourbridge had ceased. Its main line status almost gone, Stourbridge Junction was becoming little more than a remote outpost for suburban traffic, a victim of the dmu revolution. There was, though, one remaining through working from London, the 5.00 pm (Sundays) departure from Paddington to Stourbridge Junction arriving at 9.15 pm. However, if passengers did wish to travel over the ex-OWWR route to Stourbridge Junction on Mondays to Saturdays, through carriages were conveyed by the 5.50 pm (6.05 pm SO) from Evesham arriving at the Junction at 7.10 pm (7.23 pm SO). Passengers could join this train after arriving at Evesham on the 3.15 pm express from Paddington to Worcester and Hereford.

This was not quite the end of main line passenger traffic to and from London over the ex-OWWR north of Worcester. By 1955 the Western Region had introduced the 8.19 am through service from Kidderminster. This combined at Worcester (Shrub Hill) with the 7.45 am ex-Hereford to form the 9.00 am departure to Paddington arriving there at 11.27 am. The Hereford-Worcester-Paddington line did not at this time possess a titled train, however, this omission was rectified in the Winter Timetable of 1957 when the 'Cathedrals Express' was born, the title being bestowed upon the 7.45 am Hereford/8.19 am Kidderminster through train and the 4.45 pm return. By the Summer of 1963 the up train departed Kidderminster at 8.30 am for Worcester (Shrub Hill) where it joined up with the main Hereford portion. The return working left London at 5.15 pm arriving Kidderminster at 8.37 pm (8.54 pm SO). This service continued to fly the main line flag until withdrawn during 1965; the last reminder of the line's former glory was no more.

The demise of the London connection did not pass without protest, although it took almost 30 years before a service of sorts was reinstated. In 1993 it was decided to upgrade the Stourbridge line between Birmingham (New Street) and Worcester to 'Express' status and to introduce a new through service from the West Midland's principal city to London (Paddington). This service commenced during October 1993 with one 'Turbo Express' to Paddington leaving Birmingham (New Street) at 9 am, calling at Stourbridge Junction at 9.20 am and arriving in the capital at 12.15 pm. As the return working was the 12.48 pm from Paddington arriving at Stourbridge Junction at 3.36 pm, it can come as no surprise that the train was not a complete success. The up departure continued to run until May 1995 although the down service was withdrawn after just 12 months.

'43XX' class 2-6-0 No. 4360 heads a South Wales express from Birmingham (Snow Hill) to Cardiff passing Stourbridge up sidings in the early 1920s.   *Real Photographs*

'Saint' class 4-6-0 No. 2920 *Saint David* working the 1.00 pm Birmingham to Cardiff express at Stourbridge Junction on 12th September, 1947.   *P.J. Garland*

The South Wales Expresses

In addition to the Wolverhampton to London services, Stourbridge Junction also played host to cross-country through services between the West Midlands, Newport and Cardiff. The process of connecting the West Midlands with South Wales probably began with the construction of the Shrewsbury & Hereford Railway (S&HR) and the Monmouthshire Railway's Newport & Pontypool line during 1852/53. This continued with the building of the Newport, Abergavenny & Hereford Railway (opened in 1854) and the Worcester & Hereford Railway (which joined the S&HR at Shelwick Junction: opened September 1861) and was completed with the opening of the Stourbridge Extension on 1st April, 1867. What was missing though, was a direct link with the Great Western Railway station at Newport which was situated on the GWR main line to Cardiff. This omission was eventually rectified with the opening of the Pontypool, Caerleon & Newport Railway in September 1874 which joined the South Wales main line at Maindee West Junction.

The opening of the route between the West Midlands and South Wales led to the inauguration of services between Birmingham (Snow Hill) and the Principality, although through trains were possibly not introduced until the 1880s. By August 1887, one through service was in operation each way between Cardiff and Birmingham via Hereford, Worcester and Stourbridge. This was the 10.00 am departure from Snow Hill arriving Cardiff at 3.00 pm, and the 1.00 pm ex-Cardiff which reached Birmingham at 6.15 pm. Services were subsequently improved and certainly by 1895 these had become known as the 'South Wales Expresses'. From the beginning of 1902 there were eight such workings operating. Of the four Birmingham to Cardiff services, the 11.38 am, the 3.55 pm and the 5.50 pm departures stopped at Smethwick Junction, whilst the 10.15 am ran non-stop to Stourbridge Junction. In the opposite direction, two of the four expresses called at Smethwick Junction, the others continuing non-stop from Stourbridge Junction to Birmingham (Snow Hill). However, the last express from Cardiff, the 4.12 pm departure arriving Stourbridge Junction at 7.42 pm, would stop at Smethwick Junction on notice being given to the Guard at Stourbridge. The 'South Wales Expresses' were usually very well patronised and therefore often required additional motive power to be attached at Stourbridge Junction to climb over the steeply graded Old Hill Bank on the Stourbridge Extension.

Services running over the South Wales route to and from the North West and West Midlands were sometimes quite complex affairs. Many of the services from Shrewsbury had dual destinations, Cardiff and Bristol, and were therefore required to divide into two separate trains, usually at Pontypool Road. However, the Cardiff portion of these services would now include those carriages forming the Birmingham-Cardiff expresses which had been attached at Hereford. Return workings were treated in similar fashion, trains combining at Pontypool Road and West Midland through carriages being detached at Hereford. However, as will be seen later, there were two exceptions to this general rule.

An example of one of these very interesting workings can be found in the 9.30 am departure from Cardiff to Birmingham in 1902. This train left the Welsh capital at the same time as an express from Bristol (Temple Meads), the latter arriving at Pontypool Road 10 minutes after the express from Cardiff. The two were then combined and departed at 10.29 arriving at Hereford at 11.17 am. Here, the Birmingham portion was detached and would leave for the Black Country at 11.30 am, six minutes after the departure of the Shrewsbury-bound train. Trains for the North West would continue over the Shrewsbury & Hereford Railway to Crewe. Trains for the West Midlands would also take the Shrewsbury & Hereford Railway before diverging eastwards at Shelwick Junction over the Hereford and Worcester line to Worcester (Foregate Street), Stourbridge Junction and ultimately Birmingham. Altogether three departures from Cardiff and Bristol combined at Pontypool Road before dividing again at Hereford for Shrewsbury and Birmingham. However, the 12.45 pm departure from Cardiff to Birmingham did not combine with a South West to North West service and therefore had a relatively straightforward journey back to the West Midlands, although it did convey through carriages for the Shrewsbury line which had to be detached at Hereford. The 12.45 pm express reached Stourbridge Junction at 3.51 pm (4.20 pm at Snow Hill) which at 3 hours and 6 minutes represented the fastest of the four services from the Principality. This time compared very favourably to the swiftest express from Stourbridge to Cardiff which was the 10.43 am departure (the 10.15am from Snow Hill) which took just 3 hours and 5 minutes to reach the Welsh capital. For reasons as yet unexplained, the 12.45 pm departure was required to stop at Ledbury on Tuesdays only.

A similar pattern of working applied in the opposite direction, a good example of this being the 3.55 pm departure from Snow Hill. At Hereford this train combined with the 5.00 pm departure from Shrewsbury before dividing at Pontypool Road to form the 7.09 pm to Bristol (Temple Meads) and the 7.16 pm to Cardiff (General). There was though an exception, this being the 10.15 am from Birmingham. At Hereford, through carriages off the 10.38 am from Shrewsbury to Bristol (Temple Meads) were attached to the Birmingham-Cardiff express. Then, as two independent trains, they left Hereford for their respective destinations in South Wales and the South West of England. Incidentally, all services between Birmingham and Cardiff conveyed through carriages for Ross-on-Wye, although there were only two services back to Birmingham. Through carriages for the Ross service were handled at Hereford.

By October 1922, these complex services remained unchanged. At this time the Public Timetable showed three services in each direction operating as through trains, Birmingham-Cardiff. However, to complicate matters, a summary table had also been included headed 'Through Services Birmingham, Malvern, Hereford and Cardiff' which shows seven services to Cardiff and six in the opposite direction. Basically, through services to and from Birmingham (Snow Hill), Stourbridge Junction and Hereford would therefore have been of two types: i) the principal services between Birmingham and Cardiff operating in fixed carriage formations; and ii) through carriages which were conveyed on other principal services to be attached/detached at Hereford.

By 1935, services between Birmingham and South Wales using the West Midland section had been reduced to three trains in each direction. With one exception journey times over the route were not particularly inspiring, being anything between 3 hours 21 and 3 hours 55 minutes; the exception though was considerably quicker. The 8.00 am departure from Snow Hill raced to Cardiff in 3 hours 1 minute stopping only at Smethwick Junction, Stourbridge Junction, Kidderminster, Worcester (Foregate Street), Great Malvern, Hereford, Pontypool Road and Newport. This departure was possibly the fastest-timed service over the route and certainly in later years no other known trains, either steam hauled or diesel, ran to such a tight schedule. In addition to the South Wales services there were four trains from Snow Hill to Hereford and three back to Birmingham.

In contrast to 1902 and 1922, the train services of 1935 were quite straightforward affairs, formations, by and large, remaining unchanged throughout the journey, although the 9.30 am departure from Cardiff did convey through carriages for Manchester (London Road) 'Saturdays Only' which went forward on the 11.40 from Hereford. There was, of course, one exception, this being the 12.35 pm 'Cardiff to Birmingham Express' which conveyed through carriages for Manchester (London Road) and Birkenhead as far as Pontypool Road (arriving at 1.11 pm). At Pontypool Road they were detached and made ready for re-coupling to the following 'West to North Express', the 8.52 am from Plymouth due at Pontypool Road at 1.21 pm. Shunters at Pontypool Road, though, must not have looked forward to its arrival as they were allowed less than four minutes to couple up the carriages, the train being due to depart for Shrewsbury at 1.25 pm to be followed 10 minutes later by the 'Cardiff to Birmingham Express'.

The last timetable issued by the GWR, dated 6th October, 1947, showed little change to the cross-country operation with three services each way being operated Monday to Friday, plus a 'Saturdays Only' departure from Birmingham (Snow Hill) at 9.45 am. However, by the Summer of 1951, weekday services to South Wales via Stourbridge Junction had been increased to four, although there were still only three return workings. The fastest service at this time was the 8.00 am from Snow Hill which arrived in Cardiff at 11.32 am. Holidaymakers to Wales were catered for by a 'Saturdays Only' working from Kidderminster to Barry Island which ran between 21st July and 25th August inclusive. The return service, from 28th July to 1st September, continued to Stourbridge and terminated at Birmingham (Snow Hill).

On 9th June, 1958 services between Birmingham (Snow Hill) and Cardiff via Stourbridge Junction were increased and accelerated by the introduction of new Swindon-built 'Cross Country' diesel multiple units. The transition from steam to diesel traction was to provide passengers with six trains in each direction, a much more even spread of departure times and an overall running time for most of the services of between 3 hours 10 and 3 hours 15 minutes, leading to a reduction of something in the order of 15 to 40 minutes on previous journey times. The 1963 Summer Timetable shows that weekday westbound trains left Birmingham at two-hourly intervals between 8.05 am and 2.05 pm and then at 6.05 pm and 8.05 pm, whilst the first in the opposite direction left Cardiff (General) at 7.35 am and then every two hours from 9.40 am to 3.40 pm with the last departure at 6.45 pm. These included one through train from Carmarthen. Intermingled with these services were two afternoon trains from Birmingham to Hereford and two evening and two morning trains in the opposite direction. At this time the quickest service over the route was the 10.05 am from Birmingham which completed the 118 mile journey to Cardiff in 3 hours 12 minutes. With the withdrawal of main line services from Snow Hill during March 1967, trains using the Stourbridge loop were transferred to New Street. As a result things changed dramatically and by the end of the decade trains to and from Cardiff via Stourbridge Junction had been withdrawn. However, a series of major improvements during the 1980s led to the introduction, on 11th May, 1987, of a through service between Birmingham (New Street) and Cardiff via Stourbridge Junction, Worcester (Shrub Hill), Gloucester and the Chepstow line to Newport. The weekday service consisted of six trains each way running at two-hourly intervals with an overall journey time of about 2½ hours. On 14th May, 1990 the service was rerouted to run to Worcester via Bromsgrove.

The 1997 Summer Timetable identified three new services working over the Stourbridge loop between Birmingham New Street and Cardiff via Worcester (Shrub Hill) and Gloucester. Running on Sundays these services are the 11.45 and 11.55 departures from Birmingham and Nottingham respectively, whilst in the opposite direction there is a 11.05 departure from Cardiff. None of these trains stop at Stourbridge Junction or any of the intermediate stations to Birmingham, passengers can however alight or join at Kidderminster.

Finally, special mention should be made of the important role the Worcester-Stourbridge Junction-Wolverhampton line played as an emergency route to accommodate diverted traffic off the West to North main line. It is known that on at least five occasions during the 1950s/60s, the route was used by such trains due to incidents which occurred north of Hereford. These diversions occurred on 1st April, 1953 after a derailment at Broomfield; 23rd February, 1954 when both tracks at Condover near Shrewsbury were blocked following a derailment; on 6th September, 1956 after a collision between a parcels and passenger train at Ludlow and then two other derailments, also at Ludlow, on 15th March, 1957 and 24th March, 1960. Most diversions arrived at Shrewsbury by way of Wellington, Wolverhampton (Low Level), Stourbridge Junction and Worcester (Foregate Street) although non-passenger carrying traffic not needing to call at Shrewsbury would take the Market Drayton line to or from Crewe. However, whilst the 1956 mishap led to South Wales traffic being diverted over this route, some trains from the West of England followed the Midland Railway route from Bristol to Abbots Wood Junction. From there they continued via Worcester (Shrub Hill), joining the route of other 'North & West' trains at Worcester Tunnel Junction.

An unidentified outside-framed 0-6-0 is seen heading south from Stourbridge Junction with what may be a special working.   *Stourbridge Library*

A '3600' class 2-4-2T approaches Stourbridge Junction with a local service.   *Stourbridge Library*

Local and Through Services

Stourbridge Junction is located on the busy commuter route between Worcester and Birmingham. It also possesses one of the most intensively worked branch lines in the country. As a result, platforms there rarely remain empty for long. Today, all passenger traffic north of Stourbridge runs via Lye, Cradley and Old Hill and over the Stourbridge Extension Railway to Birmingham, although for many years the Junction was the terminus for local stopping services which operated over the OWWR to and from Wolverhampton (Low Level) via Dudley. A glance at some of the old timetables relating to this line shows that whilst originally the workings were perhaps a little haphazard, by 1855 a pattern of local services had begun to emerge with Kidderminster very much to the fore. However, two years later Stourbridge had gained the lion's share of the Wolverhampton stopping trains with three down and four up services, the remainder being shared between Kidderminster (one each way), Worcester and Evesham.

The opening of the Stourbridge Extension on 1st April, 1867 meant that the GWR's direct route between Birmingham, Worcester and Hereford was finally complete. As mentioned previously, there already existed a service to Birmingham from Kidderminster which had been introduced on 1st March, 1856 when the OWW, LNW and South Staffordshire railways co-operated in the running of through carriages to Birmingham (New Street) via Stourbridge Junction, Dudley, the Sedgeley Loop and Dudley Port (High Level). The *Wolverhampton Chronicle* dated 19th March, 1856 advised its readers that through trains would run direct from Kidderminster at 8.00 am, 9.30 am, 12.45 pm, 4.20 pm and 5.40 pm, return services leaving Birmingham at 9.30 am, 12.30 pm, 4.20 pm, 6.00 pm and 8.05 pm. Later, a number of trains operating between Wolverhampton (LNWR Queen Street and the OWW stations) and such places as Worcester, Evesham and Oxford, including Sunday services which had been introduced by July 1857, took over the Kidderminster through portions to and from Dudley, a note in the local timetables indicating that passengers would be carried 'between Birmingham and Kidderminster without Change of Carriage'. The opening of the more direct route over the Extension led to these services being withdrawn, although it is thought that this did not occur immediately, local timetables indicating that through carriages continued to operate until August 1867. Passengers to/from Birmingham now had the choice of travelling with the LNWR via Galton Junction or the GWR via Handsworth Junction. Initially, the LNWR operated seven weekday through trains to/from the Worcester-Hereford line together with four in each direction on Sundays, the company's carriages being conveyed by GWR trains to or from Smethwick Junction where the trains divided or combined. At this time the GWR was running the same number of 'locals' between Stourbridge Junction and Snow Hill. By 1900 the LNWR Sunday services appear to have ceased whilst one weekday train terminated/originated at Smethwick Junction. On 1st January, 1917 the LNWR withdrew its through carriages. Up to the opening of the Extension, the GWR had operated nine services each way between Stourbridge Junction and Cradley.

Local services were often contentious issues between Stourbridge's elected representatives and the GWR. In November 1883, for example, Stourbridge Commissioners had asked for an additional evening train from Stourbridge Junction to Dudley. The company's reply, declining the request, was that on average the loading on the last two trains from the Junction was often no more than one passenger per train yielding receipts of between 1s. 0½d. and 1s. 4d. Almost five years later, a similar appeal was made for an extra train over the Extension to Birmingham calling at Lye, Cradley and Old Hill. The existing last service left the Junction at 7.47 pm, which was seen by many as being far too early. Consequently, in May 1888, a deputation from the Stourbridge Improvement Commissioners met the Directors to promote their cause. One of the principal arguments used to justify the introduction of the later train was the splendour of the new Town Hall, which would be certain to attract many more visitors to the town. It is hard to imagine today that such an argument would be used to help increase rail services to the town, but evidently the company thought that there was a case to

'455' class 'Metro' 2-4-0T No. 1445 heads a train of 6-wheeled stock past Stourbridge Middle
signal box towards Wolverhampton *c*. 1925. During the 1920s this locomotive was allocated to
Stourbridge.   *Real Photographs*

'2021' class 0-6-0PT No. 2102 brings a two-coach (including auto-trailer No. 111) local service
from Old Hill into Stourbridge Junction *c*. 1925. No. 2102 was probably allocated to Stourbridge
at the time this view was taken.   *Real Photographs*

'3600' class 2-4-2T No. 3605 coasts into Stourbridge Junction with a train from Birmingham (Snow Hill) comprising 4-wheeled stock, probably *c.* 1920s.   *Real Photographs*

'3901' class No. 3920 inside-cylindered prairie tank makes a smoky departure from Platform 2 at Stourbridge Junction with a fast service to Birmingham (Snow Hill) probably sometime in the mid-1920s. This locomotive was rebuilt in 1910 from Dean Goods No. 2502.   *Real Photographs*

'43XX' class 2-6-0 No. 5368 passes Stourbridge Junction up sidings with a fast service from Birmingham (Snow Hill) to Malvern in the 1920s.   *Real Photographs*

'5101' class 2-6-2T No. 5110 on a Birmingham (Snow Hill) to Stourbridge/Kidderminster local on 10th September, 1949. The carriages are steel-panelled bow-ended 4-coach sets.

H.C. Casserley

justify a later train and by 1889 one had been introduced, a 10.53 pm departure. During 1890 this service was replaced by one even later; an 11.12 pm departure which called at all stations to Birmingham (Snow Hill), with the exception of Rowley and Soho, arriving at 11.56 pm. As it happens, even this action received criticism as the gap between the penultimate and the last departure from the Junction was, by 1893, 3 hours 22 minutes.

Straying slightly from the main theme, an interesting service was run in February 1896. Stourbridge Football Club was playing an away match at Derby County and the GWR arranged a 'football special' to take local followers to the match. Also during 1896 the Great Western came under strong criticism from Stourbridge Council regarding services to and from Stourbridge Junction and Wolverhampton. The journey from the Junction, even when stopping at all 11 intermediate stations, could be achieved in 43 minutes: this was the schedule for the 8.00 am departure from Stourbridge Junction. However, several services were taking in excess of an hour with the stop at Dudley for one train being as long as 23 minutes. A letter of complaint was sent by Stourbridge Council to the General Manager of the GWR. Letters were also sent to the Town Clerks of other Authorities served by the line aimed at drumming up support for the Council's stand. In April 1898, the company announced the introduction of a new local service between Stourbridge Junction and Wolverhampton (Low Level). A workmen's train was to be run, departing from the Junction at 6.00 am, calling at all stations to Wolverhampton. A similar service would be operated from the latter leaving at 5.55 am. Both services were timed to connect with the 6.27 am departure from Dudley to Birmingham.

The continuing expansion of industrial and commercial activities in Birmingham and the Black Country in the first part of the 20th century implied a major requirement for a quick and efficient transport system to cater for the needs of an increasingly large and mobile labour force. This development had been anticipated by the British Electric Traction Company Limited (BET) which, as the 19th century drew to a close, had taken over the steam tramway between Stourbridge and Dudley. The BET subsequently introduced electric traction and within a few years a modern tramway network had evolved which linked Stourbridge, Dudley, Old Hill, Cradley, Lye, Brierley Hill, Kingswinford and Kinver. The railways too responded to the challenge with the result that by 1902 there were between 10 and 12 stopping trains in each direction operating over the route serving the rapidly developing commuter corridor between Birmingham, Cradley, Stourbridge and Kidderminster with the majority either starting or terminating at Kidderminster itself. In addition to these were several longer distance 'slow' or 'semi-fast' workings which catered for passenger traffic from off the Worcester-Hereford line. One of these was the 8.00 am departure from Hereford which was described in the timetable as the 'Hereford Express'. This train called at Ledbury, Colwall, Great Malvern, Malvern Link, Worcester (Foregate Street), Kidderminster, Stourbridge Junction arriving at Birmingham (Snow Hill) at 10.05. There did not seem to be a similar down working, although there was a 'semi-fast' which departed Birmingham at 4.25 pm, arriving Hereford at 7.35 pm.

The years between the two World Wars witnessed a continuing demand for local commuter services which resulted in the number of local trains operating between Kidderminster, Stourbridge Junction and Birmingham (Snow Hill) more than doubling. Amongst these local stopping trains was an interesting workmen's service which left Stourbridge Junction at 5.25 am for all stations to Old Hill arriving at 5.38 am. As this involved one of Stourbridge's steam railmotors, this machine would reverse at Old Hill to become the 5.50 am departure for Halesowen. The railmotor's return working would probably have been the 5.05 pm from Halesowen which reversed at Old Hill before leaving for Kidderminster (arrive 6.01 pm) at 5.20 pm. When the workmen's steam railmotor service was withdrawn on 31st March, 1928, a motor bus was provided between Old Hill and Halesowen.

A number of through workings were identified in the timetable for 1935, but by far the most interesting service at this time was the 9.42 am departure from Worcester (Shrub Hill)

'64XX' class 0-6-0PT No. 6418 with an auto-train working at Stourbridge Junction on 10th
September,1949.   *H.C. Casserley*

'Hall' class 4-6-0 No. 6936 *Breccles Hall* arrives at Stourbridge Junction with a Birmingham (Snow
Hill) to Hereford train on 24th March, 1951.   *B.W.L. Brooksbank*

'43XX' class 2-6-0 No. 6308 passes Stourbridge North Junction with a Wolverhampton (Low Level) to Stourbridge Junction local *c*. 1955.   *W.F. Deebank*

'57XX' class 0-6-0PT No. 9621 is seen with the 7.31 pm Stourbridge Junction to Wolverhampton (Low Level) near Stourbridge North Junction on 17th May, 1957.   *E.J. Dew*

'Modified Hall' class 4-6-0 No. 7908 *Henshall Hall* is seen at Old Hill receiving help from Stourbridge's '5100' class 2-6-2T No. 5199 on a heavy Birmingham-bound train on 15th September, 1956.   *H.C. Casserley*

An unidentified 2-6-2T is seen on Parkhead viaduct on a passenger train *c.* 1956.
C.B. Roberts/Dudley Libraries

which conveyed through carriages to Crewe calling at Kidderminster, Stourbridge Junction, Dudley and all other principal stations to Wolverhampton (Low Level). Actually, this train had quite a long history, for as far back as 1902 it had conveyed through carriages to the North of England. Then, the time of departure had been 9.55 am for Wolverhampton (Low Level) and the through carriages had been to Crewe and Manchester (London Road). The return working was the 11.50 am from Manchester arriving Wolverhampton at 3.23 pm, continuing via Dudley, Stourbridge Junction and Kidderminster to arrive at Worcester at 5.20 pm. By 1935, the Manchester through carriages had been withdrawn, although the service to Crewe continued on into the 1950s with through carriages on the 9.35 am departure from Worcester (Shrub Hill) over the ex-OWWR to Wolverhampton (Low Level) arriving at 11.13 am. Through carriages then went forward on the 11.22 am to Wellington, arriving at 12.07 pm. From there, the service continued to Crewe attached to the 12.15 pm via Market Drayton. This through train is only mentioned in Service Time Tables and earlier Public ones, postwar editions of the latter tending to suggest that passengers for the North of England change at Wolverhampton (Low Level) for the High Level station. Passengers taking this advice would usually arrive at Crewe approximately one hour before those travelling on the through service.

During the late 1930s a second through service was introduced linking stations on the Wellington to Wolverhampton line to Stourbridge Junction. An RAF establishment was to be built at Cosford to provide technical training facilities for air force personnel, however, the nearest railway station to the camp would be at Albrighton and therefore it was necessary to construct a local station (Cosford Halt) that would adequately serve the airfield's needs. On 31st March, 1938 Cosford Halt was opened to passenger traffic, whilst RAF Cosford became operational during the following August. The Working Timetable for 1939 indicates that a through service was in operation from Kidderminster, departing at 6.50 am (leaving Stourbridge at 7.10 am) calling at all stations, arriving Cosford at 8.19 am. This service was not solely confined to Service personnel as according to the October 1947 timetable, during the School term the train continued to Wellington arriving there at 8.44 am (Saturdays Excepted). During school holidays this service terminated at Cosford.

The GWR's Winter Timetable for 1947 showed an intensive local early morning service (5.15 am to 9.15 am) calling at all stations between Stourbridge Junction and Birmingham (Snow Hill) and an equally busy return service during the period 3.55 pm to 6.35 pm. Many of these trains, together with several off-peak services, began or terminated at Kidderminster. In addition, 11 local services ran each way between Wolverhampton (Low Level) and Stourbridge Junction (two ran to/from Kidderminster). There were also four 'stopping' trains, including the Crewe service, between Worcester-Wolverhampton and return. These included the 8.18 am departure from Wolverhampton which called at all stations to Oxford except Astwood Halt and Mickleton Halt and the 5.22 pm from Honeybourne which called at all stations to Wolverhampton except Astwood Halt and Cutnall Green.

The Summer timetable for 1951 showed a number of through services between Birmingham (Snow Hill) and the Malvern hills. In addition to the 7.10 pm departure from Birmingham to Great Malvern there was a 5.40 pm departure from Birmingham to Great Malvern which continued to Malvern Wells. On Saturdays, the 5.29 pm from Wolverhampton (Low Level) had through carriages for Ledbury, whilst through carriages to Birmingham were conveyed on the 7.10 am weekday train from Ledbury. Additional to these services were, of course, the workings between Birmingham (Snow Hill) and Hereford. There were four of these services to Birmingham and three in the opposite direction. Apart from some minor timing alterations this pattern of operation seemed to be maintained throughout the 1950s.

By the mid-1950s, the replacement of steam-hauled local services with diesel multiple units was close to becoming a reality. The Winter Timetable of 1954 had clearly taken this into account as the suburban services between Birmingham Snow Hill and Stourbridge Junction had been revised so that departures were to be at regularised intervals. These were as follows:

'Manor' class 4-6-0 No. 7806 *Cockington Manor* at Brierley Hill with the 1.00 pm Wolverhampton
to Stourbridge Junction on 21st January, 1961.   *E.J. Dew*

'5100' class 2-6-2T No. 4104 storms into Round Oak with a Stourbridge Junction-
Wolverhampton football excursion on 28th April, 1962.   *E.J. Dew*

'5100' class 2-6-2T No. 4179 at Round Oak station with a three-coach train from Wolverhampton to Stourbridge (the 3.57 pm). *Kidderminster Railway Museum*

'5100' class 2-6-2T No. 4173 arrives at Blower's Green with the 4.55 pm Wolverhampton to Stourbridge Junction train on 28th April, 1962. *E.J. Dew*

'Manor' class 4-6-0 No. 7817 *Garsington Manor* arrives at Dudley with the 4.10 pm Kidderminster-Birmingham (Snow Hill) on 28th April, 1962. The train now has to set back out of the platform to gain the Birmingham line in the background.   *E.J. Dew*

'9400' class 0-6-0PT No. 8426 arrives at Dudley with the 6.05 pm Wolverhampton to Stourbridge Junction train on 23rd July, 1962.   *E.J. Dew*

Birmingham Snow Hill-Stourbridge Junction: Hourly from 5.45 am to 10.45 pm
Stourbridge Junction-Birmingham Snow Hill: Hourly from 5.15 am to 8.15 am, then every hour
from 9.10am to 10.10pm.
(The above services will be supplemented by additional trains at Peak times.)

Dieselisation of local services coincided with the introduction of the Summer timetable on
17th June, 1957, although steam haulage of some peak time trains continued until well into
the 1960s. The 1957 timetable had 29 weekday up services and 27 down workings between
Snow Hill and Stourbridge, the majority of these were to/from Kidderminster including
several that originated/terminated at Worcester.
The early 1960s witnessed a drastic pruning of the rail network nationwide and as a result
Stourbridge found itself about to lose one of its oldest services. The axe fell on the local service
between Stourbridge Junction and Wolverhampton (Low Level) via Dudley on Monday 30th
July, 1962, the British Transport Commission announcing its decision with these words:

On and from Monday, 30th July, 1962, the passenger train service between Wolverhampton (Low
Level) and Stourbridge Junction will be withdrawn, and those passenger trains to and from
Birmingham Snow Hill, routed via Great Bridge South, which are extended to and from stations
south of Dudley over the Wolverhampton (Low Level)-Stourbridge Junction section of line, will
commence and terminate at Dudley

After the withdrawal of the passenger service, both Brettell Lane and Brierley Hill stations
remained open for a number of years to handle parcels traffic, as did Dudley after that station
was closed to passenger traffic on 6th July, 1964. However, by the end of 1966 all three
stations had lost this traffic and were closed completely, Dudley station being demolished
during the winter of 1966/67 to make way for a Freightliner terminal which was in turn
closed in September 1986. This site is due to be redeveloped and will either be 'Dudley
Castlegate' on the Dudley to Walsall heavy rail passenger service or 'Black Country World'
on the Midland Metro.
The virtual closure of Snow Hill led to the reinstatement of the curve from Smethwick Junction
to Galton Junction and passenger services to/from New Street over the Stourbridge line
commenced on 6th March, 1967. However, this was not quite the end of the Snow Hill to
Stourbridge Junction service. Snow Hill station finally closed on 4th March, 1972 and to mark
this rather poignant occasion the final train was something of an event. A 10-coach special, with
Pullman carriages for first class passengers, left for Stourbridge Junction at 6.05 pm hauled by
Brush type '4' (later class '47') No. D1543, returning to New Street at 9.20 pm. This was probably
the only passenger service to make the round trip between the two Birmingham stations.
In the first few years following the transfer of services to New Street, the Stourbridge line
seems to have been condemned to life as a suburban backwater with very few services
running through Stourbridge Junction outside of the peak periods. However, better times for
the Stourbridge line were just around the corner. By 1973, local services through the Junction
had been greatly improved by the introduction of a more frequent peak time service,
supplemented by hourly off-peak trains, running between Kidderminster, Birmingham (New
Street) and Lichfield City. The renaissance though really came about during the 1980s with
the growth of a very healthy suburban service that by May 1995 had expanded to more than
50 trains each way, running through the commuter corridor between Birmingham (New
Street), Stourbridge, Kidderminster and beyond. The line may not have its 'South Wales
Expresses' but with services to Worcester, Great Malvern and Hereford, the line has retained
some of its former importance and helped to ensure that the Junction, along with remaining
local stations, have not suffered the same fate as Dudley and Brierley Hill and those other
long-gone stations on the ex-OWWR north of Stourbridge.
The most local of trains is of course the 'Dodger' or shuttle service between Stourbridge
Junction and the Town station in Foster Street. At approximately ¾ mile, this train runs over

No. 4101 arrives at Dudley with a Wolverhampton to Worcester local on 24th March, 1951.
B.W.L. Brooksbank

'14XX' class 0-4-2T No. 1458 leaves Soho & Winson Green with a Dudley to Birmingham (Snow Hill) auto-train in October 1956. The service ran from Dudley over the South Staffs Railway to Horseley Fields Junction and then via Great Bridge to Swan Village.   *R.S. Carpenter Collection*

what is surely the shortest branch line in the country. In 1886, the service to the original Junction station numbered 17 trains each way between 7.42 am and 8.41 pm. However, by 1902 the new Junction station had opened and with it came an increase to 28 trains each way plus a restricted Sunday service. Today, although the Sunday service has long gone, the branch boasts a very demanding weekday operation which in 1995 numbered 74 trains each way between 6.01 am and 11.56 pm. Over the years the line has seen many changes in the motive power used, however, one thing that has not altered too much is the journey time between the two stations. In 1886 it was 3 minutes; today it is about 2½ minutes.

The shuttle service is usually thought of as being a single class train, operating exclusively from platform 1 at Stourbridge Junction to Stourbridge Town station in Foster Street, however, in the past, there have been some interesting variations. In 1886 for example, the 12.27 pm departure from Stourbridge Junction, which returned from the Town at 12.36 pm, was worked by the carriages and guard off the 11.40 am Birmingham (Snow Hill) to Stourbridge Junction service which had arrived at 12.24 pm. Later, these same carriages may have formed the 1.16 pm to the Town, returning at 1.28 pm, which then went forward as the 1.40 pm to Dudley. A second variation involved the steam railmotors which had taken over the Stourbridge Town services just after the turn of the century. By 1912, the first two early morning railmotors from the Town station would reverse at Stourbridge Junction and continue to Birmingham (Snow Hill) and Old Hill respectively. These services were undoubtedly provided for the convenience of local workers.

Before leaving the Town branch mention should be made of an interesting development that probably also occurred early in the 20th century. At this time first class carriage accommodation had been added to a number of early morning services over the line. One contemporary service timetable described these trains as 'Passenger' workings as distinct from the more usual 'Motor' which perhaps suggests that first class carriages were coupled to conventional third class stock to form additional loco-hauled trains that worked alongside the railmotors. Secondly, were these interlopers acting as through carriages between the branch and the main line? If this was the case then by the Winter of 1912 four such workings from Stourbridge Town (there were only two in the opposite direction) may have formed local services from Stourbridge Junction calling at all stations to Birmingham (Snow Hill). During the 1930s, first class carriages on the branch were withdrawn. If any readers have additional information on these workings then the author would only be too happy to hear from them.

So, what of the future? In September 1992 it was announced that the Passenger Transport Authority would be actively promoting proposals to establish a third cross-city line between Stourbridge and Dorridge via Birmingham (Snow Hill) and Moor Street. Known as 'Snow Hill Phase 2', this high priority scheme was submitted to the DoT in July 1992. Work began later that year on what had become known as the 'Jewellery Line' from Smethwick Junction along the former GWR track-bed to Birmingham (Snow Hill). This line opened to passenger traffic on 24th September, 1995.

The closure of the section of the freight-only line north of Round Oak from 22nd March, 1993, was seen locally as an opportunity to introduce a heavy rail passenger facility across the conurbation between Stourbridge Junction, Dudley and Walsall, with new 'Park & Ride' facilities at Silver End (Brierley Hill), Merry Hill/Round Oak and Castle Gate, Dudley. In April 1993 a feasibility study was carried out in respect of introducing a passenger service over the section and a report presented in June 1993. The draft Final report concluded that a service between Stourbridge and Walsall would not, at this time, be financially viable, although a service between Dudley and Walsall could be. However, since March 1995, the consultants commissioned by the Black Country consortium of local authorities have been reappraising the potential for services on the section between Dudley and Stourbridge and a report is to be submitted in the near future.

'14XX' class 0-4-2T No. 1414 stands at Stourbridge Town with auto-trailer No. 76 on 10th September, 1949.   *H.C. Casserley*

'14XX' class 0-4-2T No. 1458 heads towards Stourbridge Town on 3rd April, 1954 with Stourbridge Junction in the background.   *W.F. Deebank*

An ex-GWR railcar leaves Stourbridge Junction behind as it heads towards Stourbridge Town on 3rd August, 1957. *J.W. Gibbs*

Class '153' No. 153 375 is seen at Stourbridge Junction's platform 1 with the shuttle to Stourbridge Town on 21st September, 1995. *Author*

'2301' class Dean Goods 0-6-0 No. 2416 leaves Stourbridge Junction behind and is seen heading an up goods towards Hagley, past what appears to be an empty stock train waiting to gain access to Platform 4.   *Real Photographs*

'2301' class Dean Goods 0-6-0 No. 2381 with an up goods passes Pedmore just to the south of Stourbridge Junction.   *Real Photographs*

Freight Trains

Stourbridge was a very busy freight centre, well known for both its local and main line services. Running into the town was the Stourbridge Goods branch, a single line which left Stourbridge Junction on a 1 in 67 falling gradient. The branch actually ran parallel with the single passenger line as far as Stourbridge Town station before continuing on a 1 in 27 falling gradient to the goods yard in Amblecote. The branch was quite well used, sometimes seeing as many as eight trip workings per day. These would carry traffic to and from the goods yard, the local gas works and Bradley & Co.'s ironworks, the latter being reached via a level crossing across High Street. Locomotives though, were not permitted to cross the public road, so wagons for the private sidings serving the ironworks and mills had to be pushed across the level crossing by the shunting engine and allowed to roll to a standstill. However, this practice alone could not ensure that the locomotive would not encroach upon the highway so additional trucks had to be placed between the engine and those wagons to be put into or drawn out of Bradley's siding. This obviated the need for the locomotive to go on to the level crossing. Once the wagons of billets, scrap or fuel had been delivered, they would have to be hauled into, and the empties out of, the various departments. During the 1920s/30s, this was a task undertaken by Shire horses, although these were later replaced by a Fordson tractor. Coal was also delivered in large quantities and usually one load per day would be for the nearby gas works. The goods yard occupied three levels, the lowest level being in the vicinity of the canal, the highest occupying the large area to the south. As mentioned above, the yard was located at the bottom of a notoriously steep incline, a fact that had led to a number of accidents involving runaways, though the incline also made it very difficult for engines to haul their trains out of the yard. One technique that was employed by drivers anxious to ensure a good run involved reversing the train up against the siding stop block until all buffers were compressed. When sufficient steam pressure had been built-up in the locomotive's boiler, the brake would be released and with the aid of the energy at the buffers the train would thunder out of the yard and up the incline. With a clear road ahead, it continued on up through the Town station and into the Junction. This journey could often be quite a pyrotechnic affair which sometimes led to what has become the curse of modern steam specials, the lineside fire.

In view of the steepness of the line, in particular the 1 in 27 stretch, special instructions were devised for train crews working freight trains over the branch. For example, the last vehicle on every freight train entering or leaving the yard would be the brake van and under no circumstances was the guard allowed to leave the van whilst the train occupied any part of the 1 in 27 incline. In fact in all cases the guard had to ride outside the van compartment, at the hand brake, in order that instant braking could be given if a problem arose. All descending trains were required to stop at Angel Street stop board so that the wagon brakes could be pinned down. If the rails were wet or greasy, wheels would be spragged. A supply of sprags was always kept near the stop board and it was the responsibility of the head shunter at the goods yard to ensure that all sprags were returned. Moreover, the station master at Stourbridge Town station would check the supply of sprags daily to make certain that there was always sufficient numbers available. At the foot of the incline was fixed a second stop board and all trains and locomotives approaching the yard had to stop here before proceeding under the instructions of the head shunter.

Stourbridge Junction also had a large marshalling yard to the north of the station. The year after the opening of the new station, during September 1902, the old yard's handling capacity was substantially increased by the addition of sidings on both the down and up sides. Using land released by the removal of the original station platforms and the closure of the existing Town branch curve, together with land obtained to the west of the main line, the GWR was able to construct a yard that was approximately treble the size of the original. Also by 1902, traffic through the station had become particularly heavy and to reduce congestion in the platform area, two up freight only lines were brought into operation. The upgrading of the

'28XX' class 2-8-0 No. 2852 (a Stourbridge engine from 1947 to 1953) heads an up goods through Pedmore towards Hagley.   *Real Photographs*

'2181' class 0-6-0PT No. 2189 with shunter's truck, shunts the down goods yard on 10th September, 1949. This engine was formerly No. 2105 before being reclassified after being given increased braking power.   *H.C. Casserley*

marshalling facilities at the Junction prompted the local press to observe that the yard was now one of the best in the Midlands.

Further to the north were the sidings at Kingswinford Junction which were primarily used for the sorting of coal trains, several of which would originate on the Earl of Dudley's Pensnett Railway. Coal trains for Kingswinford Sidings would leave Baggeridge Junction, where the Pensnett Railway joined the GWR, and be brought down the Wombourn branch by local trip workings. At Kingswinford Junction the trains would reverse into the sidings to enable sorting to commence. As a matter of interest, the spelling of 'Wombourn' has generated much debate over the years. Lately, 'Wombourne' has tended to become the more usual spelling, however, until quite recently, both spellings were in common use and both the GWR and BR always used the spelling without the 'e' in their timetables and signs.

The reader will probably recall that the Wombourn branch opened for traffic in 1925 thereby enabling inter-regional freight traffic to and from Crewe and the North West of England to bypass the heavily congested Great Western lines around Dudley and Wolverhampton. The branch left the former OWWR main line at Kingswinford Junction and after passing through Brockmoor, Bromley, Pensnett and Gornal, would continue through Himley and Wombourn in rural Staffordshire and on towards Wolverhampton via Compton and Tettenhall. The branch joined the Wolverhampton to Shrewsbury main line by way of two junctions: Oxley North Junction was used by trains for the North West whilst Oxley Middle Junction was the destination for trains heading into or out of Oxley Sidings.

The Working Timetable for 3rd July to 24th September, 1939 showed that at this time there were three regular down workings and five regular up workings using the branch. In addition, a number of trains would 'run as required', or at weekends, as well as local workings calling at stations and sidings on the branch itself. However, traffic over the branch increased enormously during World War II when it was extensively used for armament and sugar beet shipments, the latter being grown locally for processing at the plant in Kidderminster.

An interesting story worth relating involved another local commodity, i.e. high quality foundry sand. This was extracted both in the Wombourn area and in the Wollaston area of Stourbridge and was shipped to South Wales from off the Wombourn branch and from Stourbridge Goods. It would appear that this sand was quite abrasive, a fact that had dramatic consequences for one particular freight train heading from Stourbridge to South Wales. Apparently, sand had percolated through the boards of the wagons and into the axle boxes bringing the train to a *grinding* halt at Withington station on the Worcester to Hereford line.

Summer on the Stourbridge line was the time of fruit trains destined for the North West of England. Due to the nature of the traffic, these fast through freight trains, which only ran during the growing season, operated as class 'C' Express Freight workings conveying perishables. The Working Timetable for the summer of 1939 (*see Appendix Three*) showed four such workings: the 6.00 pm departure from Worcester Goods; the 8.30 pm from Kidderminster; the 9.45 pm from Worcester Goods and the 11.29 pm out of Stourbridge Junction. All of these trains ran over the Wombourn branch and with one exception their destination was Crewe, the exception being the Stourbridge Junction departure which was for Shrewsbury.

The usefulness of the Wombourn branch as a means to move freight quickly to and from the North West of England was firmly established during the war years. As a result traffic over the line continued to flourish even after hostilities ceased in 1945, remaining healthy right up to the line's closure. By 1958, there were 13 up and 9 down daily through workings together with several that 'ran as required' or on a specific day. An interesting train was the class 'F' Round Oak-Market Drayton empties which had to reverse at Kingswinford Junction to gain access to the branch. Additionally, there was a local Trip working to and from Oxley Sidings which called at the various sidings on the line, plus an occasional coal train from Baggeridge Junction to Henwick and a class 'K' freight from Round Oak to Baggeridge. Unfortunately, the branch only had a relatively short working life for, despite the amount of traffic using the line, it was decided to close it as a through route from 1st March, 1965. The track between the junctions at Oxley and Pensnett was subsequently lifted, however, that

'Dukedog' class 4-4-0 No. 9010 stands at Stourbridge North Junction with a ballast train whilst the PW gang repack around the points on 5th June, 1949.   *W.F. Deebank*

'72XX' class 2-8-2T No. 7216 waits in the down sidings at the head of a ballast train on 19th June, 1954.   *W.F. Deebank*

Ex-LMS 0-8-0 No. 49099 brings a coal train from the Cannock area past Stourbridge North Junction on 20th April, 1954. The locomotive later returned to Bescot via Dudley with mineral empties.   *W.F. Deebank*

ROD 2-8-0 No. 3041 enters Stourbridge Junction yard up sidings with a freight from the Dudley direction.   *W.F. Deebank*

'28XX' class 2-8-0 No. 2858 on a northbound freight just north of Hagley on 2nd March, 1957.
J.W. Gibbs

Ex-LMS '8F' class 2-8-0 No. 48470 passes the cattle pens and signal box at Hagley on a mineral train on 2nd March, 1957.
J.W. Gibbs

between Pensnett Trading Estate and Kingswinford Junction was still in use until the early 1990s when the only regular service was withdrawn resulting in the branch being 'mothballed' in 1994.

Before leaving the subject of the Wombourn branch, there was one unusual incident worthy of special mention. The line between Baggeridge Junction and Wombourn, and Wombourn and Oxley Branch Junction, was single track and was therefore worked in accordance with the Electric Train Staff Regulations. Consequently, when a train left a single track section it was the fireman's responsibility to place the staff over the 'cow's horn' (this was a pole, similar in shape to a cow's horn, which was about 3 ft long and fixed in front of a rope net) located near to the signal box. One morning, the signalman at Baggeridge Junction went to retrieve the staff that should have been deposited on the 'cows horn' by the fireman of a Crewe to Worcester freight on its way to Kingswinford Junction. However, the unfortunate man could find no trace of it. This immediately led to the closure of the branch and a thorough search of the line and the surrounding area was carried out. Then, some eight hours after the disappearance had been reported, a telephone call was received from the goods yard at Worcester to say that the staff had been located hanging over the brake handle of a wagon! It would appear that unbeknown to the crew, the staff had bounced back off the 'cow's horn' and landed over the brake of the wagon immediately behind the engine. Undoubtedly, there would be one or two red faces around Worcester Shed when this little mishap became known, and perhaps a few questions were put to the crew as to how fast they were actually travelling at the time of the incident as the stipulated speed for locomotives during the transfer of the staff was just 15 mph.

Freight activity at Stourbridge Junction has declined enormously in recent years and by 1996 the number of trains passing through the district could just about be counted on the fingers of two hands. However, by turning back the clock to the days of steam a very different picture can be seen.

Prior to the advent of the railways, local industry had relied heavily on the canals for the shipment of essential raw materials such as coal, ironstone, sand and fire-clay. However, by the middle of the 19th century the barge's ascendency had been put under threat by the arrival in the Stourbridge area of the OWWR during 1852, and when the section between Stourbridge Junction and Dudley was opened on 16th November it was coal traffic that formed the first trains to use the line. Initially, freight services were confined to around three trains each way per day, one of which ran to and from Handborough where just to the south the Yarnton loop provided rail access to the LNWR and London. The opening of the Stourbridge Railway in the early 1860s enabled the railway to tap into nearby collieries and brickworks as well as the hollow-ware, chain-making and iron-working industries which could also be found in and around the Lye and Cradley area. During 1860 the OWWR and the Stourbridge Railway, together with the Worcester & Hereford Railway and the Newport, Abergavenny & Hereford Railway, amalgamated to form the West Midlands Railway, which in turn was absorbed by the GWR in 1863. The GWR completed its local network when direct access to Birmingham was gained when the Stourbridge Railway / Stourbridge Extension Railway opened throughout in 1867.

On 17th September, 1874 the Pontypool, Caerleon & Newport Railway was opened to goods traffic thereby finally linking the Great Western's South Wales main line to the Black Country and Birmingham via a route that passed through Pontypool Road, Hereford, Worcester and Stourbridge Junction. At the latter, trains would either take the OWWR to Dudley and Wolverhampton or the Stourbridge Extension which joined the Great Western's Wolverhampton to Birmingham main line at Handsworth Junction. The completion of this through route enabled the GWR to realise its ambition to compete successfully with the Midland Railway for the lucrative coal and goods traffic from South Wales to the populous West Midlands. At the same time, the conditions were created that were to lead to Stourbridge Junction becoming one of the region's major freight centres, a position it would retain until the end of steam.

The earliest GWR Working Timetable to hand dates from November 1876 and although it is not specific to the Oxford, Worcester & Wolverhampton Section, it does provide a useful guide to the type of traffic that flowed between South Wales and the industrial West

'56XX' class 0-6-2T No. 5612 passes Stourbridge Junction station with a mineral train on 14th April, 1960.   *E.J. Dew*

An ex-LNWR 0-8-0 has come of its train in Stourbridge up sidings and waits waits for the road on 3rd July, 1961.   *E.J. Dew*

Midlands. This Timetable has been used to construct *Table Seven* which shows freight traffic between South Wales and Worcester that was destined for or had arrived from Wolverhampton and Birmingham via Stourbridge Junction:

Table Seven

To the West Midlands
1.30 am Pontypool Road to Wolverhampton (Minerals)
3.45 am Pontypool Road to Bordesley Junction (Minerals)
7.00 am Pontypool Road to Bushbury near Wolverhampton (Goods & Minerals)
4.20 pm Pontypool Rd (ex-Newport) to Dudley & Wolverhampton(Goods & Minerals)
5.45 pm Newport to Wolverhampton (Live Stock) (1)
6.45 pm Swansea to Birmingham (Express Goods) (2)

From the West Midlands
1.35 am Wolverhampton (Victoria Basin) to Pontypool Road (Goods & Minerals)
2.15 am Bordesley Junction to Pontypool Road (Goods & Empties)
11.55 am Wolverhampton to Pontypool Road (Goods & Empties)
2.30 pm Wolverhampton to Pontypool Road (Goods & Minerals)
9.40 pm Wolverhampton to Pontypool Road (Empties)
11.40 pm Birmingham to Swansea (Goods)

Notes
(1) Shown also as conveying passenger traffic - perhaps carriages for the farm hands or drovers accompanying the cattle to market?
(2) This train went via the South Wales main line and the Caerleon line.

In addition to the details shown, there was a Wednesday-Only Cattle train taking livestock from Hereford to Birmingham and a return empty wagon working on the same day.

Moving forward 10 years to October 1886, the Working Timetable for the Oxford, Worcester & Wolverhampton Section indicates that a total of 60 regular freight services ran through or to/from Stourbridge Junction together with a number of trains that 'ran as required' or on particular days. Freight trains at this time were mainly designated as either 'Express Goods', 'Fast Goods', 'Ordinary Goods' or 'Goods/Branch Goods', and conveyed a wide range of commodities. Often these trains would carry mixed loads including livestock, minerals, coal, salt, vegetables and bricks, although some services conveyed just coal and slack, while Cattle trains transported livestock for the Birmingham area.

Stourbridge Junction in 1886 saw no less than six down 'Express Goods'. The first of these was the 12.00 midnight from Worcester to Wolverhampton, which was a continuation of the 5.45 pm from Newport and conveyed livestock for Birmingham and Wolverhampton, and South Wales traffic for South Staffordshire. This was followed by the 4.05 am from Worcester to Bordesley Junction which had originated at Swansea. Later in the day there were three through 'Express Goods' from Worcester to Crewe. The first of these was the 7.25 pm via Oxley Sidings and Wellington reaching Crewe by way of the Market Drayton line. This train took vegetable traffic for Manchester, stations in Yorkshire and destinations in the East Midlands. A 7.50 pm (Saturdays Excepted) conveyed traffic for Stockport, Manchester and stations on the Lancashire and Yorkshire Railway, whilst the 8.25 pm carried goods for Liverpool and the North. Finally, one other 'Express Goods' passed through the Junction. This was the 11.55 pm departure from Paddington to Victoria Basin, Wolverhampton.

In the opposite direction, there appears to have been only two trains designated 'Express Goods'. The first was the 11.55 pm departure from Bordesley Junction to Worcester and Swansea, whilst the other was the 2.55 am Oxley Sidings to Worcester, originating as the 11.10 pm from Crewe conveying traffic from the Manchester area. The first of these trains stopped

WD 'Austerity' 2-8-0 No. 90179 passes the down sidings at Stourbridge Junction.

W.F. Deebank

Stourbridge Shed's '57XX' class 0-6-0PT No. 9724 at Bewdley with a Kidderminster-Tenbury Wells freight on 2nd December, 1964.   *R.J. Buckley*

at Stourbridge Junction to detach vegetable empties for the Worcester area. These would subsequently go forward on the 4.50 am 'Fast Goods' from Oxley Sidings carrying traffic from Liverpool via Crewe. The second train was one of three which would leave wagons at the Junction for the Severn Valley line. The others were the 4.35 am Hockley to Worcester and the 6.05 am Dudley to Stoke Works (this ran as required). These wagons would then form the 9.10 am departure from Stourbridge Junction running over the Severn Valley line to Buildwas. Other traffic into the Junction included cattle from the Hereford area and Burton beer traffic from Dudley for Cheltenham and South Wales, the latter going forward on the 1.00 pm 'Fast Goods' from Dudley to Hereford. Finally, there was an interesting 'Goods' working which left Stourbridge Junction at 9.50 am for Woofferton. This train conveyed traffic from the West Midland Section to Leominster on the Shrewsbury to Hereford line and also did 'Roadside Work' between Bewdley and Woofferton on the Tenbury and Tenbury Wells branches.

During the dark days of World War I, there was a noticeable increase in the level of freight traffic passing through the area and by the middle of 1916 at least 70 goods services were due into or out of Stourbridge Junction on most weekdays. The principal long distance traffic flow was to and from Pontypool Road in South Wales and by July 1916 there were six daily up services supplemented by two which ran from Stourbridge Junction 'as required', and five, plus one which ran 'as required', in the opposite direction. Traffic for this major Welsh yard originated at Bordesley Junction, Dudley, Priestfield (2), Bilston and Oxley Sidings and with one exception, were all booked to be worked by a 'large engine'. Freight trains passing through Stourbridge Junction from Pontypool Road were mainly destined for Oxley Sidings although Victoria Basin, Bordesley Junction and Priestfield all received one service daily.

Express goods trains conveying fruit and vegetables for Crewe and the North of England were not new to Stourbridge Junction, although those shown in the Service Timetable for Summer 1916 show some interesting variations. Apart from the 'Fruit' trains, the 11.52 am ex-Toddington and the 6.55 pm from Worcester (Shrub Hill), there were four daily 'Vegetable' trains, i.e. the 7.50 pm, the 8.35 pm, the 9.20 pm and the 9.45 pm, plus a 5.45 pm departure which ran 'as required'. All of these originated at Worcester goods yard. The trains ran to different Schedules, namely A, B, C & D, although the Author must confess to knowing very little about them. However, this said, these Schedules do seem to be related to the final destination of the traffic, for example, Schedule A referred to Yorkshire and Manchester; Schedule B was Yorkshire and Schedules C & D Liverpool. Further information on this subject would be most welcome. These 'Vegetable' trains could also convey goods and where this was the case additional stops would be made, for example, between Stourbridge Junction and Oxley these would be at Dudley or Cannock Road Junction, or sometimes both. The most complex working was the 9.20 pm departure which could arrive at Stourbridge Junction at any one of three different times depending upon the particular Schedule. After Stourbridge Junction it would call at Cannock Road Junction if working to Schedule A; Dudley if Schedules C & D; Dudley and Cannock Road Junction if Schedule B!

Finally, there were two interesting services which arrived at Stourbridge Junction by unusual and very different routes. The first was the 7.00 pm departure from Crewe which ran via the Wolverhampton, Birmingham and Oxford line as far as Handsworth. Here the train would reverse and having left the main line at Handsworth Junction would continue over the Stourbridge Extension arriving at Stourbridge Junction at 4.00 am. A similar service ran in 1939 but this time the train started at Oxley Sidings. The second was one which originated at Bordesley Junction and ran 'as required', following a circular route which took the train back to Bordesley Junction via Old Hill, the Windmill End branch, Withymoor Basin, Netherton Junction, Round Oak, Stourbridge Junction and back through Cradley Heath. The locomotive would have had to run round its train four times during the journey which began at 4.25 pm and finished at 12.50 am.

Following the end of World War I in 1918 the number of freight trains using Stourbridge Junction fell by about 15 per cent, with the result that by the Summer of 1921 around 60 goods

Table Eight

Freight Trains Operating over the Stourbridge Line 11th, July, 1921 timetable

Depart	Down Services between	Arr.	Destination	Day	HC	Details of Train
6.30 pm	Pontypool Road	3.50 am	Oxley Sidings	MX	H	Booked for large engine; South Staffordshire goods and livestock; runs Tuesday-Sunday
1.50 am	Stourbridge Jn	4.27 am	Oxley Sidings	MX	F	Through goods to Crewe
3.35 am	Stourbridge Jn	4.35 am	Oxley Sidings	MO	F	Through goods to Crewe
1.30 am	Hartlebury	2.10 am	Stourbridge Jn	MX	F	Goods
3.15 am	Stourbridge Jn	5.45 am	Oxley Sidings	MX	J	Goods
3.50 am	Stourbridge Jn	6.10 am	Oxley Sidings	MX	K	Goods
9.10 pm	Reading	9.10 am	Oxley Sidings	MX	F	Goods; runs Tuesday-Sunday
5.50 am	Stourbridge Jn	10.15 am	Oxley Sidings	MX	K	Goods; on Sundays terminates at Stourbridge Jn 4.25 am
4.30 am	Worcester Goods	8.45 am	Oxley Sidings	MX	K	Goods and minerals
4.50 am	Worcester T. Jn	7.07 am	Dudley	MX	F	Goods and coal
10.25 pm	Cardiff	8.45 am	Oxley Sidings	MO	J	Goods and coal
10.25 pm	Cardiff	9.45 am	Oxley Sidings	MX	H	Goods, continuation of Saturday evening departure
9.35 am	Worcester Goods	2.10 pm	Stourbridge Jn	SO	H	Through goods and minerals
5.25 am	Pontypool Road	2.50 pm	Oxley Sidings		K	Goods
12.45 pm	Stourbridge Jn	5.40 pm	Bordesley Jn		H	Goods
3.15 pm	Worcester Goods		Netherton		K	Goods, runs via Windmill End
8.15 am	Pengam Sidings	9.00 pm	Priestfield		F	Goods and coal empties
3.30 pm	Littleton & Badsey		Crewe	SX	C	Passenger train fruit & veg. train, passes Oxley Sidings at 10.38 pm
4.22 pm	Kidderminster	6.05 pm	Stourbridge Jn	SX	K	Goods; engine and van from Droitwich
5.40 pm	Worcester FS	9.08 pm	Hockley	MO	E	Cattle; originates as 5.15 pm ex-Butt's Sidings
7.10 pm	Stourbridge Jn		Tipton	SX	F	Goods; starts 6.30 pm Saturdays and terminates at Dudley
7.15 pm	Kidderminster	11.15 pm	Bordesley Jn		E	Cattle; runs alternate Tuesdays
12.20 pm	Pontypool Road	10.50 pm	Oxley Sidings	WO	H	Goods
8.30 pm	Worcester T. Jn	10.40 pm	Bordesley Jn		E	Cattle; train originates at Hereford
8.35 pm	Worcester Goods		Oxley Sidings		E	Booked for class '43XX' haulage; Crewe vegetable train banked from Stourbridge Jn
5.45 pm	Stourbridge Jn	2.25 am	Stourbridge Jn		K	Goods
7.50 pm	Kingham		Cannock Road Jn	RR	H	Ironstone; banked from Churchill
9.50 pm	Worcester Goods	12.47 am	Oxley Sidings	SX	E	Booked for class '43XX' haulage; through goods to North via Crewe banked from Stourbridge Jn
9.50 pm	Worcester Goods	11.30 pm	Stourbridge Jn	SO	J	Goods
10.15 pm	Worcester Goods	1.15 am	Oxley Sidings	SXRR	E	Goods; banked from Stourbridge Jn
9.30 pm	Cradley	1.15 am	Oxley Sidings	SX	F	Through goods for Crewe; reaches Oxley 5 minutes later than stated if 10.15 pm ex-Worcester runs
11.30 pm	Worcester Goods		Moor Street		F	Carries 'E' headcode if conveying perishables
6.45 pm	Oxford	3.46 am	Stourbridge Jn	M-Su	K	Goods
6.50 pm	Banbury	5.30 am	Cannock Rd Jn	M-Su	H	Iron ore; arrives 5.35 pm Sundays; banked from Churchill
5.05 am	Stourbridge Jn	7.25 am	Oxley Sidings	Sun RR	K	Goods

Depart	Up services between		Arr. Destination	Day	HC	Details of Train
10.10 pm	Bordesley Jn	Neath		MX	C	Goods; attach Birmingham–Cardiff parcels van at Stourbridge, detach at Hereford; runs Tues–Sun.
11.35 pm	Bordesley Jn	Hereford		WO	H	Cattle empties
8.45 pm	Crewe	Stourbridge Jn	2.20 am		J	Goods
1.10 am	Dudley	Stourbridge Jn	2.45 am		K	Goods and minerals
9.50 pm	Crewe	Worcester Goods	5.00 am	MX	E	Goods
12.45 am	Cannock Road Jn	Stourbridge Jn	3.20 am	MX	K	Goods and minerals
11.45 pm	Bordesley Jn	Honeybourne	5.26 am	MX	F	Goods
2.20 am	Cannock Road Jn	Adderbury		MO	F	Load 60 ironstone empties plus goods; starts 11.10 pm (MSX), ROD engine.
1.30 am	Bordesley Jn	Pontypool Road		MX	J	Goods and empties
3.00 am	Bordesley Jn	Honeybourne	7.25 am	MO	F	Goods
12.50 am	Crewe	Worcester Goods	7.30 am	MX	F	Goods
2.15 am	Crewe	Worcester Goods	7.30 am	MO	E	Goods
3.15 am	Moor Street	Worcester Goods	9.12 am	MX	E	Goods
7.30 am	Priestfield	Pontypool Road			F	Worked by large engine on through goods
4.00 am	Crewe	Stourbridge Jn	9.50 am	MX	H	Goods
8.40 am	Stourbridge Jn	Tenbury Wells			F	Runs via Tenbury and Bewdley line
9.35 am	Priestfield	Cardiff			F	Through goods
10.30 am	Stourbridge Jn	Droitwich	2.30 pm	SX	F	Goods
10.25 am	Dudley	Worcester Goods	2.45 pm		K	Goods
11.00 am	Bilston	Pontypool Road			J	Worked by large engine
3.00 pm	Bordesley Jn	Kidderminster	3.15 pm		H	Cattle empties; runs alternate Tuesdays
3.20 pm	Stourbridge Jn	Worcester Goods	4.30 pm	SO	E	Goods
5.20 pm	Crewe	Worcester Goods	7.25 pm	RR	E	Return fruit & veg. empties
6.45 pm	Oxley Sidings	Pontypool Road		RR	C	Goods; requires banking assistance in Dudley area
6.55 pm	Oxley Sidings	Stourbridge Jn	7.30 pm	SX	F	Goods
	Netherton	Worcester Goods	10.50 pm		E	Goods
	Priestfield	Pontypool Road			F	Goods and coal
8.15 pm	Cannock Road Jn	Reading		SX	F	Booked for class '43XX' haulage; goods
9.40 pm	Oxley Sidings	Worcester Goods	2.00 am	SX	F	Goods; requires banking assistance in Dudley area; class 'J' from Stourbridge Jn
9.55 pm	Tipton	Stourbridge Jn	1.40 am		F	On Saturdays train originates at Dudley
9.20 pm	Hockley	Worcester Goods	1.35 am	MO	J	Cattle empties
10.05 pm	Victoria Basin	Cardiff		MO	F	Worked by large engine
11.10 pm	Cannock Road Jn	Adderbury		SX	F	Load of 60 ironstone empties, ROD engine.
11.15 pm	Oxley Sidings	Stourbridge Jn	2.00 am	SX	K	Goods
2.30 am	Stourbridge Jn	Worcester Goods	4.20 am	Sun	J	Goods and empties
1.10 am	Dudley	Stourbridge Jn	2.45 am	Sun	K	Goods and minerals
12.10 am	Cannock Road Jn	Stourbridge Jn	3.05 am	SunRR	J	Goods

These details do not include trains starting or terminating at Stourbridge Jn that ran over the Stourbridge Extension e.g. the Bordesley Jn pick-up freights.

Ex-LMS '8F' class 2-8-0 No. 48733 passes Engine Shed sidings with mineral empties from Stourport power station on 19th June, 1954. The locomotive had earlier delivered a full load to Stourport.   *W.F. Deebank*

Ex-LMS 'Black Five' 4-6-0 No. 44914 with a freight at Round Oak sidings *c.* 1965.   *V. Morgan*

services were regularly operating over Stourbridge lines; still quite a considerable amount of traffic! One of these was a class 'C' Express Freight forming the 3.30 pm departure from Littleton & Badsey which carried fruit and vegetables to Crewe. This service was the only goods train to pass Stourbridge Junction non-stop, having first called at a number of stations along the route presumably to attach additional vans. After Stourbridge, the train called at both Dudley and Wolverhampton (Low Level) before continuing north over the Shrewsbury line. Also during 1921, ironstone from the Banbury area was being carried in large quantities to blast furnaces in the Black Country by the daily Banbury to Cannock Road Junction class 'H' freight which departed at 6.50 pm. A second train, the 7.50 pm from Kingham, ran 'as required'. Both services called at Stourbridge Junction, Round Oak, Hartshill & Woodside, Dudley and Bilston West. Ironstone trains from Banbury for the Stourbridge area followed quite an interesting route. Having left Banbury, trains would run over the Banbury & Cheltenham branch via Adderbury and Bloxham Ironstone Sidings to Kingham where they passed along the Chipping Norton loop. At Kingham West Junction they presumably reversed over the Banbury & Cheltenham line into Kingham in order to gain access to the OWWR for the journey north. Iron ore empties were returned to Adderbury via Kingham and Kingham East Junction. The outward trains must have been particularly heavy as they were booked for a large brake van and needed banking assistance from Churchill which is just to the north of Kidderminster. Later, a change in the pattern of demand in the district may have led to a reduction in the amount of ironstone required as by 1927 this traffic was no longer working over the OWWR to the Stourbridge area. However, ironstone continued to be delivered to the West Midlands, much of it destined for the steel works in Bilston. In 1939 these heavy freights originated at Banbury and Ironstone Sidings and ran via Leamington Spa to the Black Country where the majority terminated at either Stow Heath or Priestfield. The loaded hoppers were then 'tripped' over the OWWR to Bilston West. Returning to the 1920s, a number of the GWR's more prestigious freight services received names. Of particular interest to readers of this book would be 'The Stour', a fast goods which operated between Park Royal and Stourbridge Junction and the 8.35 pm Worcester Goods to Crewe express vegetable train which was known by the more imaginative nickname 'The Sparagrass'.

By the end of the 1930s, the pattern and number of freight train workings was not too dissimilar to that of earlier years. A major part of traffic through or to Stourbridge Junction was of course directed along the south-west corridor to Worcester, Hereford and South Wales, whilst in the opposite direction, a large part of the traffic was destined either for Bordesley Junction, Birmingham or destinations in the Wolverhampton area and the North of England. The Wombourn branch had now been operational for some 14 years and was proving particularly useful for the movement of class 'C' Express Freights conveying perishables from the Worcester and Stourbridge areas to such destinations as Crewe and Shrewsbury. Services from the South for Stourbridge and beyond were confined to two trains; the first was a class 'F' through fast freight which left Reading at 8.15 pm for Oxley Sidings. The second was the 6.45 pm departure from Oxford to Stourbridge Junction running under a class 'J' headcode conveying mineral empties. In the opposite direction a class 'F' freight left Cannock Road Junction for Reading at 7.50 pm. Cattle still formed a small part of the traffic into the Junction with trains from Butts Siding, Worcester (Mondays only); Hereford (for Bordesley Junction running Wednesdays only); Tenbury Wells and a Kidderminster to Bordesley Junction service, the last two operating on alternate Tuesdays. In addition to freight was an interesting Sunday working catering for the pigeon fanciers of the area. Running as required, this train would leave Wolverhampton (Low Level) at 8.25 am under a class 'C' headcode and would call at most stations to Stourbridge Junction and Evesham where it terminated. Once the birds had flown, the train departed Evesham at 12.25 pm conveying empty pigeon baskets to Wolverhampton and various stations in between.

Freight originating from stations and branches on the Stourbridge Extension Railway to the west of Old Hill was largely 'pick-up' work with trains travelling in the Bordesley Junction direction collecting traffic from Lye and Cradley as required. Much of this traffic would

'28XX' class 2-8-0 No. 3861 on a class 'F' southbound freight arriving at Stourbridge Junction on 24th March, 1951.   *B.W.L. Brooksbank*

'Hall' class 4-6-0 No. 5959 *Mawley Hall* on an up class 'C' express freight at Stourbridge Junction on 31st March, 1958.   *B.W.L. Brooksbank*

consist of bricks from off the Hayes Lane branch; metals, bricks and clay from the Corngreaves branch, and chain and general merchandise from the Spinners End branch serving Old Hill Goods Depot. In the opposite direction, goods train would normally only stop at Cradley and Lye to detach traffic, wagons waiting in the yards and sidings for dispatch to Stourbridge Junction and beyond being disposed of via the appropriate Bank Train. However, not all freight from the Cradley area was handled by the Bank Trains and over the years some traffic for the North West in particular was formed into designated freight services, e.g. in 1886 a 'fast goods' departed Cradley for Oxley Sidings at 7.40 pm, whilst during and after World War I a through freight bound for Crewe was booked to leave Cradley at 9.30 pm under class 'F' headlamps. Later, this service became the 8.05 pm departure reaching Crewe by way of the Wombourn branch. This continued to run until at least May 1947. Incidentally, down trains did have to negotiate a very steep descending gradient between Rowley Regis and Cradley necessitating many freights having to halt at Rowley Regis stop board. Here the wagon brakes would be pinned down for the run into Cradley where the brakes would then be picked up.

At the outbreak of World War II on 3rd September, 1939, at least 60 goods trains were operating into or out of Stourbridge Junction each weekday (Mondays excepted). Of these, about 20 ran over the Stourbridge Extension, the majority to/from Bordesley Junction. Unfortunately, details of actual wartime freight services in the area have been difficult to come by, although it would probably be accurate to assume that the demands generated by the conflict resulted in substantial growth; this was certainly the case during World War I. The cessation of hostilities in 1945 resulted in a slow return to normal and by 1946 the number of freight trains using Stourbridge Junction was just slightly below that of the immediate pre-war period. However, the post-war reconstruction programme required the movement of large quantities of goods and raw materials, with the result that, by the early 1950s, traffic flowing through the district had increased by approximately 30 per cent. By the middle of the decade freight traffic using Stourbridge Junction had probably reached its peak with the Wombourn branch in particular playing a major role in facilitating the movement of goods to and from the North of England.

Whilst the majority of trains either called or started/terminated at the yards, certain 'Express Goods' and 'Through Freights' did pass non-stop, the destination for several of these being the sizeable and important Kingswinford Sidings located adjacent to Kingswinford Junction and branch. The expansion of freight services in the area after the war meant that these sidings were required to handle a considerable amount of traffic, in fact by September 1951 almost 30 goods trains were using the sidings on most working days (*see Appendix Four*). Many of these were long distance class 'H' through goods, although two class 'F' unfitted express freights did terminate there. A significant proportion of the traffic handled at Kingswinford arrived from off the nearby branch, the sidings acting as a marshalling facility for mineral traffic from Baggeridge Junction in particular, a location which at its post-war peak required as many as four trips per day to clear. At the yard wagons would be sorted and dispatched by way of the Bank Trains, to local destinations such as Round Oak, Blower's Green sidings, Dudley Goods Yard, Priestfield, Bilston and by 1955 Cannock Road Junction. Additionally, traffic for Oxley Sidings, Tipton and Stourbridge Junction would often be forwarded via class 'K' local freight services. Unfortunately, the onset of a new decade was accompanied by a decline and by 1962 only three regular services apart from the Bank Trains were using the yard. These included two class 'H' workings from Round Oak; one to Paddington, the other to Crewe.

Freight trains that did halt at Stourbridge yard did not do so just to deliver or pick-up traffic. For example, during September 1951 the 7.43 pm ex-Bristol class 'E' inter-regional freight to Bescot was scheduled to have a banking engine attached to help it overcome the stiff climb to Dudley. Altogether, there were seven down trains scheduled for banking from Stourbridge. These were the following departures (from Stourbridge):

'7400' class 0-6-0PT No. 7402 shunts Stourbridge Junction up sidings on 24th March, 1951.

B.W.L. Brooksbank

Ex-LMS '8F' class 2-8-0 No. 48705 enters Stourbridge Junction on a class 'J' freight on 9th February, 1957.   *J.W. Gibbs*

12.33 am	Class 'E' Bristol to Bescot	
2.57 am	Class 'H' Gloucester to Bescot	(SX)
9.50 pm	Class 'D' Worcester to Crewe	(SX)
10.02 pm	Class 'F' Worcester to Crewe	(SO)
11.07 pm	Class 'D' Worcester to Crewe	(Runs as Required SX)
11.20 pm	Class 'F' Worcester to Crewe	
12.03 am	Class 'F' Worcester to Oxley Sidings	(Runs as Required SX)

The need to supply a banker was not necessarily confined to those trains actually scheduled for assistance and it has been suggested that at times almost all freight workings heading to Dudley or in the Bordesley Junction direction required banking, hence the fact that four banking engines were provided by the shed at night and three during the day. Traffic bound for Dudley would be assisted as far as Blower's Green where the engine would 'drop off', whilst freights using the Stourbridge Extension Railway had to overcome the notorious Old Hill Bank where a rising gradient of 1 in 51 from Old Hill to Rowley Regis presented a stiff test for train crews and locomotives alike. The assisting engine would be uncoupled at Rowley Regis.

On the subject of banking, several of the heavier passenger trains also required assistance, especially holiday excursion traffic from places such as Weston-super-Mare and Barry Island. Passenger traffic though was not actually 'banked', the assisting engine being attached to the train engine instead. However, what this meant was that an engine such as an 0-6-2T for example, could not be used for these duties as the absence of a leading bogie meant that the engine ran the risk of being pushed off the track on a sharp curve by the more powerful train engine. Consequently, the pilot engine would usually be a '51XX' class 2-6-2T, although if it were necessary to use an 0-6-2T due to the unavailability of more suitable motive power, these engines would have to be coupled inside the train engine. In the case of passenger trains heading north over the former OWWR, assistance would be given as far as Dudley.

The falling gradient of 1 in 75 between Round Oak and Brettell Lane led to crews on nearly all freight trains heading south from Dudley to Stourbridge Junction having to pin down the wagon brakes at Round Oak North stop board. The descent completed, brakes would then be released at Engine Shed signal box. This gradient also posed problems for up freights bound for Kingswinford Junction sidings or Moor Lane Depot which had to reverse at Brettell Lane and cross over to the down side. As will be seen later, at least one crew got into difficulties carrying out this move. Some services stopped at Stourbridge Junction or Engine Shed box to change crews whilst those for the Stourbridge Extension Railway from the North would usually halt on the up (to Worcester) side, in or near the station, to enable the engine to be uncoupled. The locomotive would then run round its train and after being re-attached at the other end would proceed tender first towards Stourbridge North Junction, at some point crossing over to gain the up line to Birmingham. This manoeuvre was necessary as there was no direct access to the Stourbridge Extension Railway from the OWWR main line for trains arriving from the North. The reader will have noticed that the Stourbridge Extension Railway up line is to Birmingham and the down to Stourbridge. Consequently, trains running from the Birmingham direction, for example, would follow the down line as far as Stourbridge North Junction where they would join the up line from Wolverhampton to Worcester and London.

The post-war freight scene in the Stourbridge area saw the growth of one particular type of traffic - fuel oil, although by 1951 this traffic had still to make a real impact on an already substantial flow of goods which passed through the area on a daily basis. At the time there appeared to be two daily weekday departures and one Sunday departure for oil trains from Stanlow to Rowley Regis via the Wombourn branch. However, by 1962, this traffic had experienced a significant increase, representing a major slice of the still considerable freight traffic that continued to use the Junction at this time.

Fuel oil traffic departing Stourbridge Junction during the period 18th June-9th September, 1962 was as follows:

An unidentified pannier tank thunders up the bank from Amblecote goods yard on 8th April, 1961.   *E.J. Dew*

'57XX' class 0-6-0PT No. 9613 begins the climb from Amblecote goods yard with the Saturday afternoon trip to Stourbridge Junction on 25th July, 1964.   *J.C. Haydon*

Table Nine

Dept		From	To	Dep. Stour. Jn	Loaded/Empty	Notes
10.38 pm	MX	Soho Pool	Cardiff	12.40 am	E	CC
6.00 pm	SX	Cardiff	Soho Pool	1.15 am	F	AE/CC
12.05 am	MX	Rowley Regis	Thames Haven	1.23 am	E	
1.55 am	MX	Rowley Regis	Stanlow	2.57 am	E	R
8.20 pm	SO	Thames Haven	Rowley Regis	5.35 am (Sun)	F	AE
12.20 pm	WFO	Cardiff	Soho Pool	7.35 am	F	AE/CC
10.40 pm	MX	Thames Haven	Rowley Regis	10.01 am	F	AE
8.35 am	SX	Rowley Regis	Ripple Lane	9.25 am	E	
9.35 am	SO	Rowley Regis	Thames Haven	10.47 am	E	
4.40 am	SX	Acton	Old Hill	11.41 am (12.01 (SO))	F	AE
2.35 pm	SXQ	Rowley Regis	Hooton	3.29 pm	E	R
6.45 pm	SO	Rowley Regis	Ripple Lane	7.28 pm	E	
8.23 pm	SX	Rowley Regis	Thames Haven	9.50 pm	E	
8.00 pm	SO	Soho Pool	Cardiff	10.05 pm	E	CC
9.40 am	SX	Thames Haven	Rowley Regis	10.15 pm	F	AE/CC
3.50 pm	SO	Cardiff	Soho Pool	11.10 pm	F	AE/CC
1.08 pm	SO	Ripple Lane	Rowley Regis	11.25 pm	F	CC

Key: M Monday, S Saturday, W Wednesday, F Friday, O Only, X Excepted, Q As required, CC Change Crew, AE Assisting Engine required, R Reverse at Stourbridge
Note: Several Oil Trains to and from Stanlow or Ellesmere Port were routed over the branch between Blower's Green and Old Hill via Windmill End.

The 18th April, 1955 saw the introduction of the Longbridge car parts train, a 50 wagon fully-fitted freight which left Morris Cowley at 9.50 am, arriving at Stourbridge Junction at about 12.30 pm. This service ran with a brake van attached to both front and rear; normal practice for freight trains working to the Halesowen branch from Stourbridge. At Stourbridge Junction yards, the 4-6-0 locomotive would be replaced by two Pannier tanks, one at each end. This arrangement provided both banking assistance and additional braking power on the steep gradients encountered on the line. On arrival at Old Hill the complete ensemble would reverse on to the Halesowen branch, the engine formerly at the rear now leading. Having reached Longbridge, the engines and brake vans would be uncoupled and attached to 50 empties in the adjacent siding in readiness for a 3.25 pm departure. Back at Stourbridge Junction, the tank engines would be replaced by the original locomotive.

One of the least publicised areas of freight handling work was that which involved the Bank Trains. Between 1939 and 1955, for example, Stourbridge shed operated no less than 16 schedules daily. Each Bank Train was numbered, each number representing a specific service, whilst the engine itself would carry a corresponding target. Bank Trains were used to clear and shunt traffic at Stourbridge Junction and Amblecote goods yard, as well as the sidings and yards on the main line to Dudley and the Stourbridge Extension Railway up to Old Hill, Rowley Regis and Oldbury & Langley Green. They would also convey wagons between them. The Brettell Lane and Dudley service was also booked to call at Bilston West and Priestfield, whilst in 1955, Bank Train No. 9 worked beyond Priestfield to Cannock Road, Wolverhampton. Stourbridge's Bank Trains also operated over the Windmill End branch, calling at Cox's Lane sidings and Netherton goods depot. Netherton was also the destination for Wolverhampton's No. 31 Bank Train which originated at Oxley Sidings. The locomotive would shunt the depot yard until early evening before taking a train back to Dudley, and the Old Hill to Halesowen line shunting Halesowen goods yard and Canal Junction sidings, as well as carrying out trips to the Canal Basin. The engines would also haul the workmen's specials to and from Longbridge. The Halesowen evening engine even worked services as far

An unidentified class '56' enters Hagley station with the Brierley Hill to Cardiff Tidal empty steel wagons *c.* 1993.   *G. Angell*

Class '31s' Nos. 31 439 and 31 465 race through Stourbridge Junction with empty mineral wagons on 12th August, 1995   *Author*

as Handsworth and Queen's Head. On the Kingswinford branch, the trip workings between Kingswinford Junction and Baggeridge Junction were worked by both an 'early' and 'late' service, with the former also clearing Pensnett, whilst the latter handled traffic at Bromley. By June 1955, the late service had been discontinued. Presumably all Bromley traffic was now dealt with by No. 1 Bank Train - Blower's Green and Bromley early service which shunted both the Basin and the Private sidings. In 1947, Bank Train No. 7 was booked to work to Hartlebury and Elmley Lovett sidings although by 1955 this trip had been terminated at Hartlebury.

The decline of Stourbridge Junction as an important freight centre began with the closure of the Town Goods branch in 1965 and continued throughout the rest of the 1960s with the rationalisation of the track layout and the shutdown of the yards, a process which, together with the closure of the engines sheds, resulted in a large number of jobs being lost in the district. *Table Ten* shows the position for 1991 and 1994.

Table Ten

Freight trains through Stourbridge Junction and/or Brierley Hill, 14th May, 1990 to 11th May, 1991

Dept	Type	Day	Train		Pass Stourbridge Jn	Note
17.10	SLK	MX	Carmarthen Jn to Bescot Yard		00.39	
15.00	SLK	MX	Coatbridge FLT to Tavistock Jn		00.56	
19.45	SLK	MX	Belmont to Gloucester NY		02.04	
01.15	COY		Cardiff Tidal to Wednesbury Ex TC*		06.30	AE
07.00	SLK	MO	Gloucester NY to Cliffe Vale		08.25	
22.25	SLK	MX	St Blazey SS to Cliffe Vale		08.25	
04.28	COY		Scunthorpe W. TC to Brierley Hill	(arr.)	09.20	
09.50	COY		Wednesbury Ex TC to Cardiff Tidal†		11.30	
11.40	COY		Brierley Hill to Scunthorpe W TC		#	
07.22	DEPT		Radyr Jn SS to Bescot Yard		13.04	VB
14.52	DEPT		Bescot Yard to Gloucester NY		15.34	VB
12.40	COY	WX	Cardiff Tidal TC to Wednesbury Ex TC*		17.04	VB/AE
09.45	COY	MX	Tees NY to Margam TC*		18.35	
14.00	SLK		Taunton Goods to Walton Old Jn		18.40	
17.02	SLK		Cliffe Vale to Exeter Riverside		19.50	
19.33	COY	WX	Wednesbury Ex TC to Cardiff Tidal*		20.34	VB

24th January, 1994 to 28th May, 1994

Dept	Type	Day	Train	Pass Stourbridge Jn	Note
22.07	DEPT	SX	Swindon Cocklebury to Bescot	00.42	
02.30	DEPT	MX	Bescot Yard to Swindon Cocklebury	03.20	VB
00.05	MET	FSX	Margam TC to Round Oak	05.15	
02.35	MET	WO	Cardiff Tidal TC to Coopers Metals	05.24	
22.10	UKC	SO	St Blazey SS to Bescot	05.34	
02.52	MET	MWFO	Cardiff Tidal TC to Brierley Hill	05.48	
08.55	MET	MWFO	Brierley Hill to Cardiff Tidal TC	09.05	
08.22	UKC	SO	Bescot Yard to St Blazey SS	09.07	
10.08	MET	FSX	Round Oak to Margam TC	10.32	
17.16	MET	WO	Coopers Metals to Cardiff Tidal TC	19.25	

Notes: AE Assisting Engine attached; VB Vacuum braked train; SLK Speedlink; COY Company train; DEPT Departmental; SS Sorting sidings; Ex TC Exchange terminal complex; TC Terminal complex; FLT Freightliner terminal; MET Trainload Freight Metals; UKC Railfreight Distribution-UK Contracts; * Via Brierley Hill; † Via Round Oak & Brierley Hill; # Via Great Bridge.

Class '60' No. 60 092 heads the late-running 6V05 Round Oak to Margam steel empties at Pedmore on 1st December, 1995.   *Author*

Class '37' No. 37 680 reverses its train off the down line into the adjacent sidings where the locomotive will run round. The train is the return trip working from Moor Street Depot to Bescot on 27th February, 1998.   *Author*

Future Prospects for Freight in the Area?

Is there a future for freight services in the Stourbridge area? In 1992 BR Railfreight announced that it was considering options to sever the Stourbridge to Walsall freight line either north of Round Oak (Trainload Freight's preferred option), or from a point south of Kingswinford Junction, due to the continuing decline in the movement of freight traffic through the area. At this time the line was used by freight trains to and from Bescot yard requiring access to the depot at Round Oak, Moor Lane Freight Terminal (now known as Transrail Steel Terminal, Moor Street), Brierley Hill and the Pensnett Trading Estate, together with the Wednesbury Steel Terminal. However, the latter was due for closure and a scrap metal yard at Bilston that also used the line was also to be closed and perhaps relocated. By early 1993 Trainload Freight's preferred option was implemented and the line north of Round Oak was closed to traffic on 22nd March, 1993. This decision did not effect the three freight terminals in the Brierley Hill area as these could still be reached from the remaining section of track between Stourbridge Junction and Round Oak.

During 1993 there were some strong arguments put forward by the West Midlands Regional Rail Forum in support of a Regional European Freight Terminal to be developed at Bescot. At the same time, the development proposals put forward for Hams Hall and Daventry were being opposed, especially with regard to the latter, which was seen as having severe economic disadvantages for the West Midlands region in general and the Black Country in particular. However, British Rail rejected the Bescot proposal on the grounds that there was insufficient space to accommodate a viable Channel Tunnel Terminal and declared that the options to develop Hams Hall, or extend the facilities at Landor Street freight terminal in Birmingham, were to be considered instead. Despite this decision, the West Midland local authorities continued actively to support development at Bescot as this was seen as central to the process of economic regeneration in the area. At the same time, the rail companies were urged to protect the terminals at Pensnett, Round Oak and Moor Street whose survival had been threatened by proposals to expand facilities at BR depots elsewhere. The under-utilisation of the remaining section of the Kingswinford branch to Pensnett Trading Estate had encouraged Railfreight Distribution to seek closure of the depot should the major freight user, FDB Distribution, decide to relocate. Sadly, by 1994 the line had fallen into disuse and in view of Railtrack's estimate to maintain the branch it was decided to 'mothball' the line until such time new users could be found. However, it is understood that there are plans to promote the terminal with Round Oak Rail being identified as one company that may be interested in the move to Pensnett. Hopefully, these plans will be successful in breathing new life into the branch. Meanwhile, Round Oak Rail continued to import South Wales steel to its Depot in Brierley Hill via a daily service from Margam, while Transrail in Moor Street, Brierley Hill received a shipment of steel wire from Cardiff on Mondays, Wednesdays and Fridays. Both terminals are also served by a regular Railfreight Distribution 'Connectrail' service. *(See 'Postcript' on page 236, for an update.)*

Transrail class '60' No. 60 063 *James Murray* heads the 6V05 Round Oak-Margam steel empties on the 18th January, 1996.   *Author*

A freight is seen crossing Stambermill viaduct. *R. Walker Collection/Wolverhampton Express & Star*

'57XX' class 0-6-0PT No. 9646 approaches Brettell Lane with a class '9' freight on 12th September, 1963. *R.J. Buckley*

Chapter Five

Branches and Sidings

The Former OWWR to Dudley

Leaving Stourbridge Junction station, trains bound for Dudley and Wolverhampton would cross the viaduct at Stambermill before travelling over Amblecote embankment, through Brettell Lane station and on towards Brierley Hill. This stretch of line was characterised by a landscape dominated by fireclay excavations and brickworks, some of which possessed direct rail connections with the main line.

Just beyond the junction with the Stourbridge Extension Railway, on the western side of the main line, was 'Rufford's Pottery and Brickworks' siding which came into use on 23rd August, 1882. This siding was served by a tramway that passed behind the North signal box before joining the main tramway which ran north to terminate at a fireclay and brickworks, and east under the main line at Junction Road to pass through Hungary Hill firebrick works, terminating in the fireclay mines of Hungary Hill colliery. Branch tramways from the shafts to the north and from New Farm colliery to the south, joined the main tramway in the vicinity of the works. On 7th December, 1949 Rufford's siding was withdrawn from use although the original agreement had terminated much earlier in 1936.

An agreement dated 29th April, 1899 led to the construction of a siding opposite the junction to Stourbridge locomotive sheds. This siding handled traffic from a mineral railway and tramway that was used to carry bricks from the works of John Hall located just to the south of Amblecote Road. The works itself was also served by two other tramways, these being used to transport raw materials from nearby excavations. Presumably, the mineral railway ceased operation when the BR siding closed in March 1961. Further on along the line, at a point just short of the Stourbridge canal on the approach to Brettell Lane station, a siding left the down main line and continued into Brettell Lane firebrick works. Built around 1870, this line was eventually linked to a substantial tramway network that was developed around the works and nearby canal basin. This network was probably constructed about the turn of the century and connected to a lengthy tramway that passed under Brettell Lane and continued to Nagersfield firebrick works in the Hawbush district of Brierley Hill.

Entering Brettell Lane goods yard from the east was a tramway from a fireclay and brick works located just to the south east of Plants Hollow. In 1884 this tramway ran directly into Brettell Lane goods yard, but by 1919 it had been diverted in a north-westerly direction possibly to link in with a second tramway which may have been used to transport minerals from nearby fireclay workings to a wharf on the Stourbridge canal. Having passed the canal, the tramway returned to its original path into the down yard. By 1938 the tramway and works had disappeared, the only evidence to suggest its existence being a footpath which followed the line of the track-bed. Near the site of these old workings was a later tramway which brought fireclay to the brickworks of E.J. & J. Pearson. The finished product was then shipped by a tramway using the continuous rope system, to the Stourbridge canal in Lower Delph. Just to the north of Brettell Lane station, a siding once joined the down main line from Harris & Pearson's brickworks.

Continuing towards Brierley Hill, the line divides at Kingswinford Junction. There, the Kingswinford branch diverges to the west to terminate in Pensnett. As explained elsewhere, this branch was once a through route between the ex-OWWR route and the Shrewsbury to Wolverhampton main line at Oxley. In 1884 there was evidence to suggest that just beyond the junction there existed a short siding to a bottle works located on the up side of the branch. However, by the early 20th century the works and siding had disappeared and in its place was built the longer Moor Lane goods branch and Depot. Opened on 14th August, 1922, this branch was sited immediately adjacent to Kingswinford marshalling yard. On 16th

Class '56XX' 0-6-2T No. 6677 hurries through Brettell Lane station towards Stourbridge with a
class 'K' freight *c.* 1950s.   *Black Country Museum*

Brettell Lane station looking towards Brierley Hill.   *Black Country Museum*

'28XX' class 2-8-0 No. 2817 passes Kingswinford Sidings with a down freight on 8th May, 1957.
E.J. Dew

'57XX' class 0-6-0PT No. 9646 at Kingswinford Sidings with a class '9' freight for Stourbridge Junction on 12th September, 1963. *R.J. Buckley*

Round Oak station looking north. Round Oak South signal box can be seen beyond the bridge.
Black Country Museum

'56XX' class 0-6-2T No. 6678 leaves Round Oak sidings for Stourbridge *c.* 1963.   In the foreground is Round Oak crossing.   *V. Morgan*

September, 1963, the marshalling facility was withdrawn, although part of the site was used to accommodate Moor Lane Concentration Depot which opened on 31st May, 1965. Today, Moor Lane Depot is no more, the site being occupied by EWS's steel terminal whose main function is handling steel wire imported from South Wales. On the up side of the yard a goods loop came into use during February 1916. From this loop was constructed a siding to a loading dock and cattle pens belonging to Marsh & Baxter. This facility was withdrawn on the termination of the Private Siding Agreement on 13th March, 1967.

By 1903 a short tramway from High Ercal colliery had been built which terminated near to Kingswinford Junction. The colliery had originally fallen into disuse during the latter part of the 19th century, however on reopening it may not have proved to be a viable proposition as it was again shown as 'disused' by 1919, the tramway probably being taken out of use c. 1912. Further to the north, there may have been a tramway leading from Belle Isle colliery which ended at or near the main line just to the south of Brierley Hill station. By 1884 little could be detected to suggest that this ever existed.

Beyond Brierley Hill was to be found the major iron producing district of Round Oak which came to be dominated by the huge Round Oak works that had been founded in 1857 by William, 11th Lord Ward (later to become Earl of Dudley). Round Oak had been associated with iron production since the late 18th century with the Earl of Dudley's Old Level and Level New Furnaces being located close to the nearby Dudley canal. To the north of Round Oak lay the rest of the Dudley estate including the mineral rich Pensnett Chase and the Himley coalfield. Following the death in 1833 of John William, Fourth Viscount Ward and First Earl of Dudley, the estate was placed in trust and it was during this period, between 1833-45, that a standard gauge railway (the Pensnett Railway) was constructed linking the collieries of the Himley coalfield just to the north of Shut End with the Level New Furnaces at Round Oak. By the mid-1840s this railway was at work supplying these furnaces with the necessary raw materials. Both the Dudley Estate and the Pensnett Railway were to prove troublesome to the promoters of the then broad gauge Oxford, Worcester and Wolverhampton Railway.

On 29th May, 1845, a Parliamentary Select Committee was set up to examine the OWWR Bill. Opposing the Bill was the Dudley estate, in particular Richard Smith the estate's mineral agent who, for various reasons, supported the rival narrow gauge London, Worcester & South Staffordshire Railway (LW&SSR) sponsored by the London & Birmingham Railway. Smith's argument focused on two main areas; the gauge, which the LW&SSR had in common with the Pensnett Railway, and the route. The LW&SSR promised a branch line that would diverge from the main line near Dudley and run to Brierley Hill via Sedgley, an arrangement, it was argued, that would be more appropriate given the existing transport structure and the volume of goods to be carried. These views, together with those of others opposed to the OWWR, failed to convince the Committee.

The second thorn in the side of the OWWR was the Pensnett Railway itself. At the time of the Inquiry this railway was probably at an advanced stage of construction, although it had yet to reach Round Oak where it was to cross the planned route of the OWWR. The problem was that at Round Oak the level of the Pensnett Railway would be several feet higher than that of the OWWR. This matter was addressed at the Inquiry when Isambard Kingdom Brunel, the OWWR's Engineer, was asked : 'Is it your intention to adopt your Railway to the level of my Lord Ward's Railway?', to which Brunel replied : 'If Lord Ward will not alter his railway an inch, we must come to his'. It has subsequently been assumed that when the builders of the OWWR arrived at Round Oak late in 1852 they found the Pensnett Railway made to the original levels. Paragraph 54 of the OWWR Act states:

. . . that the Railway hereby authorised to be made, shall be constructed so as to pass on a level across the said Pensnett Railway, and so as not alter the intended line of the said Pensnett Railway as now being made, without the consent of the said William Baron Ward in writing . . .

Above: An unidentified 0-8-0 is seen at Blower's Green Junction with a mineral working *c.* 1954. The line to Old Hill can be seen on the left, and Blower's Green sidings are in the distance.
Below: '61XX' class 2-6-2T No. 6118 is seen with a southbound mineral working as it passes through Blower's Green station *c.* 1954. *(Both) W.R. Lait/Dudley Library*

Clearly, the railway company and the Dudley Estate were able to reach an agreement which both satisfied the provisions of the Act and enabled any variation between the levels of the two lines to be eliminated. As a result, a flat crossing (the almost legendary 'Round Oak Crossing') was subsequently built which enabled the single line of the Pensnett Railway to intersect the double OWWR track at virtually 90 degrees. Secondly, despite a persistent view to the contrary, trains running along the OWWR have always had priority at this crossing. Sidings were duly added to both up and down main lines, the former serving Round Oak works whilst the latter connected with the Pensnett Railway. The existence of this crossing has been widely documented, however, R.A. Cooke's research suggests that this was not the only crossing to be found at Round Oak during the 19th century. A survey carried out by the GWR in 1878 shows a second line intersecting the OWWR about 50 yards further to the east. This line continued behind the works, passed the canal basin and rejoined the 'main' section just to the north of the Old Level Furnaces. This second crossing though may only have had a fairly short working life, possibly being taken out of use in the early 1880s? It clearly does not appear on the OS map of 1884, although the alignment of certain sidings on each side of the main line does seem to support the view that a second crossing co-existed alongside the more well known example. Returning to the story of the main crossing, this lay undisturbed for almost 120 years until in January 1971 a modernisation scheme carried out at the works necessitated its repositioning some 60 yards further up the main line. Sadly, a few years later in December 1982, Round Oak steel works closed dealing a severe blow to the local economy and ending the district's association with iron and steel making that had lasted for approximately 200 years.

Running into Round Oak sidings from the north-east was the Woodside branch which had been constructed in 1852, the branch serving the large Woodside ironworks of Bramah and Cochrane. These works were also connected into a system of tramways that brought raw materials from the Old Level colliery (and later the Hurst colliery) located to the south of the works, whilst another originated at Woodside colliery and ran under the OWW main line and over the Pensnett canal before dividing to feed several sites within the works itself. In 1882 the Pensnett Railway constructed an extension to the branch enabling firebricks to be transported over the line from Mobberley and Perry's 'Hurst' brickworks. Although Woodside ironworks had closed down by the late 1930s, the branch itself, albeit much reduced, continued in use up to, and probably beyond 1960.

About halfway between Harts Hill & Woodside station and Parkhead viaduct, were the Parkhead sidings with a branch leading to Parkhead colliery. By 1903 the colliery branch had fallen into disuse, however, the sidings survived until 23rd May, 1965. After crossing Parkhead viaduct the line passes through Blower's Green sidings and station before disappearing into Dudley tunnel. Between the station and the sidings is Blower's Green Junction (formerly Netherton Junction) where a branch line left the main line to gently curve away towards the quaintly named Bumble Hole and on into Old Hill. Blower's Green sidings were located just to the south-west of this junction, the principal use being to accommodate traffic for or off the branch, or generated from nearby rail-connected works and collieries. On the up side a siding had been made to serve a standard gauge mineral railway which had been built during the 1870s to Grazebrook's Netherton Old Furnaces, situated beside the Dudley canal in Peartree Lane. This railway ran parallel with a lengthy tramway that brought raw materials to the ironworks from Yorkspark colliery. The works was also served by tramways running from Netherton Old colliery. By 1903 Yorkspark colliery had closed and the tramway taken out of use, as was the short siding from the down main line to the colliery. However, Grazebrook's siding was still in use as late as 1955. By 1921 a private siding to the South Staffs Wagon Company in Shaw Road was built from the down main line and this lasted in use for 30 years until the Private Siding Agreement was terminated in 1951. A short branch, also from the up sidings, was constructed around the 1890s, possibly to carry coal traffic from the Cabbagehall pit. By 1904, the pit had closed, however, the sidings themselves remained until at least 1919. In the years that followed, the sidings to the old colliery were

An early postcard view of the south end of Dudley station.   *Lens of Sutton*

A mineral train is seen passing through Dudley station *c.* 1954.

C.B. Roberts/Dudley Library

The south end of Dudley station *c.* 1957 with '57XX' class 0-6-0PT No. 8742 in the bay.

R.S. Carpenter Collection

Dudley goods yard *c.* 1954 with '56XX' class 0-6-2T No. 6698 passing with a mineral train. A '57XX' class 0-6-0PT can be seen in the yard.

I.S. Moseley/Dudley Library

An early view of Lye station looking towards Birmingham. The line off to the left ran behind the signal box joining the brickworks siding of J. Foulkes.   *Lens of Sutton*

A later view of Lye station *c.* 1970 again looking towards Birmingham. The signal box closed on 30th December, 1973. The brickworks connection had been removed on 17th February, 1952. The goods shed is on the right.   *Lens of Sutton*

partially lifted, the site being developed as a railhead serving a number of works (including the South Staffs Wagon Works) on the Cabbagehall Industrial site located off New Road, Netherton. This railhead probably remained in use until the closure of Blower's Green sidings in the late 1960s.

Traffic for Round Oak, Kingswinford Junction, Stourbridge Junction and beyond was accommodated in the larger up sidings at Blower's Green and trains wishing to run to the up main line would leave these sidings at either Blower's Green Sidings signal box, or further along the loop line at the site of Blower's Green Crossing signal box which had controlled a nearby level crossing. This crossing and box were closed around June 1897. On the down side of this level crossing there had been built a series of sidings serving Blower's Green colliery and brickworks (later to become known as Thornleigh brickworks). The down sidings at Blower's Green, together with the goods shed, were taken out of use on 3rd December, 1967. By 1st January, 1968 the Old Hill branch was closed thereby virtually making the up sidings redundant. The process was completed with the closure of the Blower's Green Sidings signal box on 12th January, 1969 and the Junction signal box on 30th March of the same year.

The Stourbridge Extension Railway to Old Hill

The Stourbridge Extension Railway joins the ex-OWWR route at Junction Road just to the north of the site of the original main line station. Trains for Birmingham would leave the station and cross in a north-easterly direction towards Old Hill, the route between the two being noted for extensive industrialisation and mining operations. On this section of line there are two intermediate stations at Lye and Cradley. Heading towards the former the line crosses the Stourbridge Road and passes a fireclay and brick works located to the left in Stambermill. Known in 1920 as the River Stour works, this was connected to the up main line via Timmis's siding which had been constructed by August 1882 together with a controlling signal box and a siding from the down line which led to the Regina Works in Hay Green. Timmis's sidings survived until 1964 although the signal box was probably closed early in 1952, the Regina Works siding being taken out of use in 1951.

The first station on the line is at Lye. Here, a small goods yard could be found just beyond the down platform. In 1884, the yard had a modest goods shed that was subsequently rebuilt and enlarged at least twice with the 1920 version being approximately 320 ft in length. The yard seemed to comprise of three through sidings and a dead-end siding to the rear of the shed. By 1919, further sidings had been added together with two cranes, one of which being a travelling type. By 1884 the large fireclay and brickworks just to the north of Lye station had been provided with a rail connection, although this was probably taken out of use early in the 20th century.

Moving on towards Hayes Lane, a branch had been constructed which left the main line in an easterly direction. Opened in June 1863, the Cradley Park branch (also known as the Hayes Lane branch) was to serve two different sites. Having passed under Hayes Lane, the line continued in a south-easterly direction until at Cradley Park sidings the line divided with one line swinging southwards towards The Hayes, whilst the other continued in a south-easterly direction to terminate near the junction of Park Lane and Park Road, Colley Gate. The former terminated near a number of tramways which served brickworks in both Hayes Lane and Balds Lane, as well as Hayes colliery and Oldnall colliery, the latter being located more than ¼ mile from the sidings. Cradley Park sidings were closed c. 1946/47.

The Colley Gate section was used to move bricks etc. from the Netherend and Lower Delph fireclay and brickworks. There were also several tramways leading into the branch; two served Cradley Park and Cradley collieries, whilst a third ran from the Chapel brick, tile and terra cotta works and the Old Netherend colliery in Park Lane, the latter running alongside the road before crossing over to terminate near the branch. The Cradley Park branch closed

A view facing towards the level crossing from the up platform at Cradley station *c.* 1962.
Lens of Sutton

Cradley station *c.* 1962 from the down platform looking towards the level crossing. Note the Lambretta scooter parked outside the signal box.   *Lens of Sutton*

to traffic on 10th August, 1964, although by this time only part of the branch still appeared to be in use, the track from just beyond the site of Cradley Park sidings having been closed in April 1962.

Having passed the Cradley Park branch the line swings north-east towards Cradley Heath. On this stretch of line there had been built three sets of sidings. The first served the fireclay excavations at Old Netherend colliery which in 1884 may have been connected to the works by a tramway. By 1900 the tramway had disappeared and by 1919 the rail connection had also been removed. Near to Maypole Hill road bridge, Netherend reception sidings had been built on the down side of the main line at Lanes End (by the 1920s renamed 'Two Lanes End'). These sidings were in existence prior to 1884 and were used to accommodate traffic to and from nearby collieries and brickworks. Adjoining these sidings were those for Homer Hill which had come into use during April 1867. By 1884 these sidings were handling traffic off a tramway serving Homerhill colliery and although there was a brickworks nearby, it is not clear if the works used this facility. However, by 1903, the original brickworks had gone and the tramway had been extended to include Homerhill fireclay and brickworks which had been built adjacent the colliery. These sidings, though, were not to enjoy a long life and by 1919, if not earlier, both sets had been taken out of use.

Crossing the River Stour the line enters the heavily industrialised district of Cradley/Cradley Heath. To the left stood Cradley Forge ironworks just before the goods yard at Cradley Forge itself. In the 1880s, the yard was equipped with a small goods shed, crane and four sidings. Trailing in from the north, crossing Forge Lane via a level crossing, was the single line of the Earl of Dudley's Pensnett Railway running down from Saltwells colliery to connect into the main line. Known as the Saltwells Railway the line stretched 8.78 miles from Level Street to Cradley station. By 1903 three more sidings had been added and by 1919 the yard contained 10 sidings and a new goods shed had been erected to the east of the mineral railway adjacent to Forge Lane. Saltwells colliery had closed some years earlier although the mineral railway itself was still in use much later, probably up to the end of World War II. To the south of the station stood the Stour works, home, in 1865, of the Staffordshire Public Chain and Anchor Testing Company Limited. This works was linked to the main line by a siding some 100 yards to the south east of the station. Cradley station was at one time comprised of two staggered platforms divided by a level crossing. The up platform was later rebuilt opposite the down platform, the new configuration coming into use during January 1984.

Moving on through Cradley station (the station was renamed 'Cradley Heath and Cradley' on 1st July, 1899 but subsequently reverted to 'Cradley') the line passes through Cradley Heath where, approximately 150 yards beyond the bridge over Cradley Road, the Corngreaves branch was constructed. Opened on 1st April, 1863, this branch left the main line in a south-easterly direction heading for the huge Corngreaves ironworks. In addition to the ironworks and adjacent factories, the branch served four collieries: the Stour colliery (later to achieve notoriety in respect of the 1914 High Street disaster), Codsall, Timbertree and New Hawne collieries, the last three all employing tramways leading to the branch. By 1919, the branch also served Corngreaves colliery situated just to the south of the Stour colliery. However, in addition to the branch, and predating it, was a narrow gauge (3 ft 2½ in.) mineral railway that left the works complex due north, crossing Graingers Lane before passing under the Stourbridge to Birmingham main line and carrying on along Corngreaves Road before veering north-east towards Reddall Hill. The line terminated to the east of Old Hill at two canal basins on the Dudley canal, passing over the Netherton and Halesowen branch about 150 yards to the south of Garratts Lane on the way. This mineral railway served the Bearmore colliery, the Black Waggon and Old Lion collieries in Old Hill and the Fly colliery off Garratts Lane as well as the works complex at Corngreaves. Originally, wagons on the tramways and mineral railway were horse drawn although steam haulage was introduced from the middle to late 1860s. Later, locomotive haulage on the New Hawne and Timbertree tramways was replaced by a continuous rope system. The tramway to New Hawne colliery was noted for

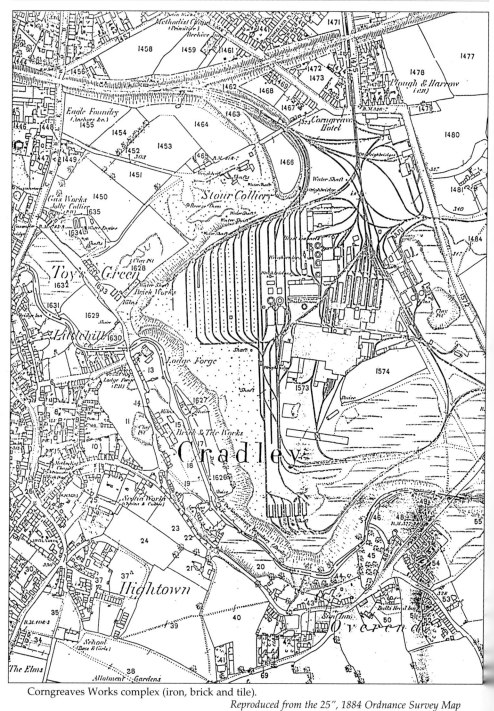

Corngreaves Works complex (iron, brick and tile).

Reproduced from the 25", 1884 Ordnance Survey Map

the viaduct which carried the line over the River Stour and even today traces of the brick pillars can still be seen on the river bank.

During 1885 the New British Iron Company entered into an agreement with the Witley Colliery Company to supply coal to the Corngreaves works and as a result a mineral railway was constructed to Witley colliery in Belle Vale, about one mile to the west of Halesowen. This steam-operated standard gauge railway served both the ironworks and the Corngreaves branch itself. By the end of 1921 mining operations ceased at Witley and the line was abandoned and dismantled, although it is still possible to see remains of the bridge which carried the line over the road leading to Cradley Heath. The site of the colliery buildings was to become the local authority depot, however, a few years ago this was demolished and today is occupied by a housing estate. The Corngreaves branch closed on 12th April, 1965.

As mentioned above, the Corngreaves branch originally left the main line just beyond the Cradley Road bridge. However, by June 1890 this junction, together with the signal box, had been closed and a new layout introduced at Cradley Junction, just to the east of the level crossing by the up platform of Cradley station. This layout was then subsequently modified during the early years of the 20th century to accommodate the Spinners End branch. Authorised in August 1904, the line probably opened to traffic on 1st July, 1907. The branch ran parallel to the main line for approximately two-thirds of a mile before dropping down to pass under it about 220 yards to the east of Corngreaves Road, terminating at Spinners End itself. The branch was built to serve the inaccurately named Old Hill goods depot which was actually located in Cradley Heath. Early in the 20th century a number of sidings had been added, one gave access to Lloyd's Proving House, added c. 1906, whilst another came in from Fellows Bros. Clyde Chain works situated on the Corngreaves side of the main line, opened c. 1907/08. During July 1923, additional sidings were constructed on the western side of the yard to serve Cox and Danks. The Spinners End branch was officially closed to traffic on 10th August, 1964, although it may have been taken out of use as early as April that same year.

The Kingswinford Branch

The Kingswinford branch leaves the former OWWR main line at Kingswinford Junction situated just to the south of Moor Street steel terminal which today occupies the site of the old marshalling yard. Opened on 14th November, 1858, the branch originally served Bromley Basin, although by 1860 the line had been extended in a northerly direction towards the Himley coalfield where at Oak Farm Junction the branch divided. One line turned west to terminate at Oak Farm in Shut End, whilst the other (probably the more important of the two) continued northwards initially terminating near to the lane leading from the Himley to Dudley turnpike road to the Glynne Arms (more commonly known as the 'Crooked House'). This section was later extended to Askew Bridge, the terminus being referred to in Great Western Working Timetables simply as Himley. Originally, the branch was constructed as a single line throughout with passing points near Kingswinford Junction, Cricketfields, Tiledhouse colliery and Shut End Works. By February 1916 the line between Kingswinford Junction and Brockmoor had been doubled although it is likely that it continued to be worked as a single line section. By January 1925 the branch had been doubled throughout as far as Oak Farm brickworks, coinciding with the opening of the through route to Wolverhampton which joined the main line to Shrewsbury at Oxley Middle and Oxley North Junctions. However, the story of what became known as the Wombourn branch has been extensively covered by Ned Williams in his book *The Railway to Wombourn* and therefore only the Kingswinford Branch itself will be dealt with here.

It should not come as a surprise to learn that the branch passed through an area whose industrial landscape was dominated in true Black Country style by ironworks, collieries and brickworks, and it was these industries which supplied virtually all of the traffic for the line. Unfortunately, the nature of the industries along the branch meant that works opened and

Above: Bromley Basin on the Stourbridge Extension canal on 16th June, 1962. The photographer has his back to the junction where the Stourbridge Extension canal joins the Stourbridge canal. The Stourbridge canal passes under the Kingswinford branch at right-angles.

Below: The north end of Bromley canal basin in June 1962. Staunches hold back water from the abandoned section of the Stourbridge Extension canal beyond the sluice.

(Both) Kidderminster Railway Museum

A view of Bromley Halt from the road overbridge looking north. On the left, running parallel with the railway can be seen the bed of the abandoned section of the Stourbridge Extension canal. *Kidderminster Railway Museum*

closed at fairly regular intervals and therefore it has been particularly difficult to pin down precisely when associated rail connections were built or abandoned, and whether these were sidings or standard / narrow gauge tramways.

When, in 1925 the line became a through route there was introduced a fairly short-lived passenger service. Four stations were constructed on the former Kingswinford branch, the first of these being located approximately 600 yards beyond Kingswinford Junction. Opened on 11th May, 1925 Brockmoor Halt was built just to the south of Moor Lane road bridge and the up platform can still be seen today, although it is very overgrown and only close inspection reveals its existence. On the underside of the road bridge is painted the distance from Paddington: 144 miles 61 chains. In the early 1880s, just beyond the Halt on either side of the running line, was Cricketfields colliery which possessed a short siding connecting into the down side of the branch. Immediately adjacent to the colliery was an ironworks, this too was linked to the down side. By the early 20th century the ironworks had fallen into disuse and a brickworks had been built on the colliery site utilising the former siding. The brickworks remained at work for some years (this may have been the siding referred to as Brown & Freer's siding in the 1921 Timetable). Intersecting the ironworks siding before joining the down running line was another connection which led from a tramway serving an ironworks (Brockmoor Foundry?), located on the banks of the Stourbridge canal in the fork of Leys Junction where the Fens branch joined the main cut. The Fens branch was a navigable feeder forming the main water supply to the Stourbridge canal from the three reservoirs at Fens Pool. The tramway appeared to be still in use after World War I. An entry in the 1921 Timetable refers to the Kingswinford Branch 'Pick-up' service calling at Cricketfield to clear the Tin Shed. Unfortunately, it has been difficult to determine precisely where this was and its use.

Continuing under High Street (Brockmoor) road bridge the branch passed the Cookley Iron and Tin Plate Works which over the years possessed sidings on both sides of the branch; a scrap dock remained in use on the down side until the 1970s. It was near here that the line crossed the Stourbridge canal and ran alongside the Stourbridge Extension canal, which had opened in 1840 and had become one of the OWWR's few profitable ventures when the railway purchased the canal in March 1847. The Extension canal joined the Fens branch at Brockmoor Junction and here was located Bromley Basin sidings where goods brought along the canal were transferred to the railway. In 1921 a major traffic flow into the Basin was pig iron, some of which may have originated at the blast furnaces of the nearby Lays ironworks. Bromley Basin sidings closed at the end of 1967.

Further along the Extension canal were two short canal branches that had served a number of old collieries such as Crablane, Burrows and Leasowes in Bromley and Standhills, Horton and Ketley in Kingswinford, all of which were disused by 1882. However, the Ketley branch canal still carried traffic (probably to Bromley Basin) in the form of bricks produced at the Ketley works and perhaps the Tiledhouse works. By the beginning of the 20th century a tramway had been built which ran from the New Bromley colliery to the Stourbridge canal via the Bromley colliery. This tramway was in turn connected to one from Bridgend colliery and Himley colliery's 'Fish' pit located just to the south of the Grove Pool which was one of the Stourbridge canal's feeder reservoirs, via a loop near Bluck's Lane (the Bryce Road of today), which ran direct to a siding on the Kingswinford branch located opposite the Bromley canal branch. By the beginning of the 20th century the 'Fish' pit had closed and the tramway removed. A few years later both the Bridgend and New Bromley tramway sections had been abandoned, and Bromley colliery closed, although the remaining tramway to the now disused Bromley colliery was diverted and extended to run to Bromley Lane ironworks located on the Stourbridge canal about ¼ mile to the north-east of Bromley Basin.

Leaving Bromley Basin behind, the branch ran parallel to the Extension canal, under Bromley Lane road bridge to Bromley Halt which was also opened in May 1925. In common with Brockmoor the up platform can still be seen today. Approximately ½ mile beyond the Halt, was the large Corbyn's Hall colliery and ironworks founded by Benjamin Gibbons in

Pensnett Halt looking north on 16th June, 1962. Note the subsidence of the track.
Kidderminster Railway Museum

Pensnett Halt looking south towards Brettell Lane from the road overbridge. The platforms are overgrown and the only remaining structure is the signal box. *Kidderminster Railway Museum*

what is thought to have been 1824. Predating the arrival of the railway was of course the Stourbridge Extension canal and from this a short branch had been constructed to serve the works and colliery. This basin and also the main cut, were the termini for a number of tramways that formed part of a complex internal system. With the advent of the railway, the tramway network was extended to sidings which had been provided on the down side of the branch. Just beyond the canal branch there was another short siding or tramway that ran to Coppice colliery. This siding had been abandoned *c.* 1900. Corbyn's Hall Works possibly closed during 1868; certainly by 1884 the tramways had been removed and the canal branch filled in.

During the early 1840s, on a site located almost opposite the Corbyn's Hall Works, on the west bank of the Stourbridge Extension canal, Benjamin Gibbons founded Corbyn's Hall New Works which, with three blast furnaces, was one of the biggest producers of pig-iron on the branch. The building of the railway enabled sidings to be laid to the works, these crossed the canal and joined the down side of the branch midway between Gibbons bridge and the Kingswinford-Dudley road bridge. The works later moved into steel making although by 1938 these had closed down. It is believed that the company also developed mining operations in the area with several pits being worked by the firm of Bradley & Foster. This probably explains why the sidings were known as Foster's sidings. As a matter of interest the Gibbons' family home was Corbyn's Hall located on the outskirts of Pensnett village.

Although closure of the 'New' works led to much of the trackwork being removed, one short siding did survive. This left the down running line just to the south of Pensnett signal box to terminate in Gibbons' Lenches Bridge Steel Works. Later, probably after World War II, a lengthy siding was constructed which ran alongside the Lenches Bridge Works line, parallel to the Kingswinford branch, before curving off to the west. It then crossed the Stourbridge Extension canal before terminating near the site of the old Standhills colliery alongside a section of the disused branch canal that had originally run as far as Ketley brickworks. This mineral line became known as the Ketley branch and served Bromley brickworks which was connected to the railway by a short siding.

Switching back to the east side of the Kingswinford branch, Corbyn's Hall brickworks had been built near to the site of the former ironworks and had been connected to the up side of the branch via a short siding. The brickworks also employed a tramway which had been added by 1919 and ran from nearby excavations to the up side of the branch near Gibbons bridge. The tramway passed the site of sidings that appear to have served the northernmost end of Corbyn's Hall colliery and terminated at Gibbons bridge. However, the precise use that these were put to has been difficult to establish. Near the brickworks was later built Corbyn's Hall steelworks and these were provided with a rail connection known as Gibbons sidings. These were taken out of use on 11th June, 1961 when presumably the steelworks closed down.

Beyond Gibbons bridge stood Pensnett Halt built just to the south of the bridge carrying the main Dudley-Kingswinford road. Although very similar to other stations on the branch, it did possess a goods loop which ran behind the up platform. Pensnett in the 19th century was a very heavily industrialised area, much of this activity being focused upon James Foster's Shut End ironworks, although originally the manufacturing and mining activities in the area had been developed by John Bradley & Co. With four blast furnaces, this works was the largest producer of pig-iron on the branch and required a network of internal tramways to move materials around the site and from nearby brickworks and collieries. The network was linked to the Earl of Dudley's Shut End Railway which had been built to the west of the works and had as its terminus Ashwood Basin on the Staffs and Worcester canal. Shut End also possessed two short canal branches that had been built into the works from the Stourbridge Extension canal; these too were served by tramways. When the OWWR arrived at Pensnett in the early 1860s the company provided a rail connection to the ironworks (Bradley's siding), which left the down side of the branch just to the north of the main road bridge before joining the southern section of the Shut End Works railway. Later, the GWR

'Modified Hall' class 4-6-0 No. 6965 *Thirlestaine Hall* approaches Gornal Halt with a through freight *c*. 1960.   *V. Morgan*

'57XX' class 0-6-0PT No. 4696 is seen on a short freight between Pensnett and Gornal Halt *c*. 1959. The line to the right of the locomotive leads to the Dreadnought Tileworks. *R. Williams*

Beyond the bridge Gornal Halt can be seen in this view from October 1930.

Ned Williams Collection

Gornal Halt looking south. Both of the overgrown platforms still have their dilapidated 'pagoda' style shelters. *Kidderminster Railway Museum*

Baggeridge Junction signal box on 16th June, 1962. The line to Baggeridge colliery and Round Oak steelworks is behind the signal box.   *Kidderminster Railway Museum*

NCB 'Austerity' 0-6-0ST No. 9 is seen on the Earl of Dudley's Pensnett Railway *c.* 1960.
                                                                                    V. Morgan

constructed a siding to Shut End New colliery at Tansey Green. This siding left the up side of the branch near Fosters bridge which carried one of the Shut End Works' lines to a local brickworks also in Tansey Green. By the 1930s Shut End New colliery had been abandoned with the result that the rail connection was shortened so as to terminate just to the north of Dreadnought Road off the main Kingswinford-Dudley Road, the surviving two sidings becoming known as the Sand sidings. By the end of 1900 the Shut End Works' siding to the adjacent brickworks had been replaced by one provided by the GWR and this remained in use serving the Dreadnought Tileworks until the early 1960s when this, together with the Sand sidings, were removed. Although iron-making at Shut End had ceased altogether by the 1890s, the site was later to become home to Stourbridge Refractories. These works continued to use the branch via Bradleys sidings.

Looking north over the parapet of the road bridge at Pensnett today, there is little to remind the visitor that here was an area that once was alive with the sights, sounds and smells of those industries which had given the Black Country its name. All that survives are the stark remains of the Coal Concentration Depot (opened 1st May, 1964) and several disused and overgrown sidings which once also served the nearby Pensnett Trading Estate. By the early 1990s these sidings had fallen into disuse and despite hopes that services to the area would be reinstated, at the time of writing none had materialised.

Moving a little way north, past Pensnett North signal box (built during the early part of the 20th century) to a point near to where the road to Tansey Green crossed the 'main' line, a lengthy branch had once existed that ran to a brickworks located adjacent to the Pensnett Railway at Barrow Hill colliery. This branch also possessed a short siding to Tansey Green colliery. However, by 1884 the siding had been abandoned, although the bulk of the branch survived into the 20th century, having been removed by 1919. Continuing in a northerly direction, the main line passed under Tansey Green road bridge where Gornal Halt was opened in 1925. Here the line swung west, originally passing across the road between Kingswinford and Lower Gornal via a level crossing. However, in the early 1920s the line was lowered and a new road bridge constructed. A little further on the line divided at Oak Farm Junction, where one section continued towards Oak Farm at which sidings were constructed for Walker's brickworks and Oak Farm colliery. In the 1860s, when the branch reached the area, there must also have existed Oak Farm ironworks as this was mentioned in the Minutes of the Evidence to the OWWR Inquiry in 1845. This works possessed two blast furnaces and an adjacent foundry. Walker's brickworks was also served by a tramway which crossed Oak Lane and ran to a basin off the Stourbridge Extension canal, just to the north of the Stourbridge Extension colliery and brickworks.

Returning to Oak Farm Junction, the Askew Bridge branch swung north towards the Himley coalfields. Almost immediately the branch crossed the Earl of Dudley's Pensnett Railway, a connection to this being made in 1875. Originally, the branch terminated to the south of the main Himley to Dudley turnpike at a lane that led to Himley colliery's Pit No. 4 and the Glynne Arms. However, by the 1880s, the branch had been extended to Askew Bridge itself where it terminated adjacent to a narrow gauge tramway that ran from Straits Green colliery located approximately ½ mile to the north-east. Early in the 20th century both the tramway and the branch extension appear to have been abandoned, although by the 1930s the latter seems to have been reinstated as part of the Earl of Dudley's railway network. Whilst Askew Bridge represented the limit of the GWR's operation in the Himley coalfields, the development of Baggeridge colliery led to the company constructing a new line to be worked by the Pensnett Railway. This line ran in a north-westerly direction from the original terminus of the Askew Bridge branch, before swinging north to pass under the Himley-Dudley main road and on to the new, high output, pit at Baggeridge Wood. This extension came into use during the early years of the 20th century, together with a spur which connected the line to the former Shut End Railway at Himley Wood, thereby enabling coal to be transported direct to Ashwood Basin on the Staffs & Worcester canal. During the early development of the pit at Baggeridge in the 1890s, coal was taken to a reception point on the Shut End Railway via a narrow gauge

Himley station looking towards Wombourn on 16th June, 1962. The red brick buildings were still in good condition at this time. Although two platforms were built track was never laid to the up platform.   *Kidderminster Railway Museum*

'Hall' class 4-6-0 No. 6933 *Birtles Hall* approaches Himley with an express freight (class '4' or 'C') from Crewe to Bristol West Depot on 3rd October, 1963.   *R.J. Buckley*

tramway. The tramway was taken out of use when the standard gauge line was completed. On 11th January, 1925, when the Kingswinford branch was opened as through route to Wolverhampton, Oak Farm Junction became known as Baggeridge Junction and a signal box was built to control traffic movements. By 1956 the junction had been singled, the connection from the Pensnett Railway to the down main line being removed on 1st July. On 16th July, 1967 the down line from the site of Pensnett North signal box (closed in 1932) to Baggeridge Junction signal box was taken out of use, the burnt-out remains of the latter being officially closed at the same time. The ground frame which replaced the box at Baggeridge Junction continued in use until 1st April, 1968 when traffic to this point was withdrawn.

The Netherton and Halesowen Railway

The Netherton and Halesowen Railway consisted of two distinct sections, both opening to traffic on the same day, 1st March, 1878. The northern section ran from Netherton Junction (later Blower's Green Junction) to the Stourbridge-Birmingham main line at Old Hill becoming known as the Windmill End branch early in the 20th century. The southern part of the railway linked Old Hill to Halesowen and to gain access to this line traffic off the Windmill End branch needed to reverse at Old Hill. On 10th September, 1883 the Halesowen Railway opened, thereby extending the branch to Northfield via Halesowen Junction on the Midland main line. The two sections are geographically quite different with the Windmill End branch passing through a typical Black Country landscape. On the other hand the route from Old Hill to Halesowen and beyond was far less industrialised with much of the line passing through unspoilt countryside.

The Windmill End Branch

The branch was double track throughout and served four intermediate stations, Baptist End Halt (nearest to Dudley), Windmill End, Darby End Halt and Old Hill (High Street) Halt. Upon opening the branch had just one station, Windmill End, and it was not until August 1905 that the Halts were added. Windmill End was a more substantial station than the Halts which were made up of simple wooden platforms and corrugated iron huts, although during 1957 these were replaced by prefabricated concrete structures and bus-stop type shelters. Windmill End also possessed a footbridge and it is believed that this came from the original Stourbridge Junction station after closure in 1901. From the start of the Winter Timetable of 1952 Windmill End lost its 'station' status and became Windmill End Halt.

Leaving the main line at Netherton Junction (later Blower's Green Junction) the branch headed towards Old Hill and after passing Baptist End Halt reached Windmill End Junction and the start of the Withymoor Basin branch (renamed the Netherton Goods branch on 1st August, 1921). The branch left the main line in a southerly direction by way of a double track junction, however, after 200 yards the lines converged. The branch opened on 10th March, 1879 and terminated at a small goods shed which had been erected next to a basin off the Dudley canal at Bishton's Bridge.

In the 1880s the Withymoor Basin branch passed the disused Baptist End colliery and then over Netherton Brook which ran into the Bumble Hole canal loop (part of the original Dudley No. 2 canal). This loop had been made redundant when the straight approach to Netherton tunnel was cut in 1858. Virtually opposite the brook was Buffery Furnaces although this, and Baptist End colliery, were ever connected to the railway. Beyond Buffery Furnaces lay the Northfield Road level crossing and the adjacent Netherton Furnaces which was served by a tramway from nearby pits. The branch continued to the goods depot past a siding which curved away in a north-easterly direction, crossing Northfield Road on its way towards some disused pits that at one time were probably part of Windmill End colliery. By the early 1880s this siding terminated just before Bumble Hole Road (now St Peter's Road) where it was met

Blower's Green Junction with a '57XX' class 0-6-0PT on the Old Hill line *c.* 1963. Blower's Green sidings are in the distance. *W.H. Massey/Dudley Libraries*

Windmill End Junction *c.* 1963. *K. Poole/Dudley Libraries*

by a tramway from Netherton Furnaces. At this time Withymoor Goods Depot possessed seven dead-end sidings, two of these being added to the original lines *c.* 1880.

The early years of the 20th century saw the Withymoor branch develop considerably. By 1904 a new siding had been added approximately halfway down the branch; this headed in a south-easterly direction before curving south to terminate near the tramway on the eastern side of Netherton Furnaces. A few years later this siding had been extended to the remains of the siding that had originally terminated at Bumble Hole Road, thereby forming a continuous loop from the branch to Withymoor goods depot. From this loop sidings were constructed to Netherton Furnaces and also to the canal basin and wharf near Northfield Road. The original tramways terminating to the west and east of the Furnaces had by this time been removed. Further to the north, not far from the lane leading to Bumble Hole Road, several sidings had been laid from the loop, through the nearby colliery area to terminate at Netherton Furnaces; one even continued to a small goods shed close to Northfield Road. However, by the 1930s the ironworks had closed and the loop severed at Northfield Road. The line which had formed the northern section of the loop continued in use and, after dividing near St Peter's Road, several sidings ran to a nearby corn mill and, presumably, also the Northfield Road canal basin. In order to assist the reader in his/her understanding of the complex nature of this particular line a map has been included on page 147 showing the situation as at 1919.

Further along the branch, just beyond the small road bridge which carried a lane from Bumble Hole Road, a number of sidings had been constructed on each side of the running line just to the north of Northfield Road level crossing. At the Goods Depot itself, siding capacity had been increased and a more substantial goods shed had been built; this replaced the original. Heading away from the depot were also several sidings serving Withymoor Tool Works, as well as the shorter section of the former loop line. The branch closed on 5th July, 1965, although it was 1967 before the track was lifted and the goods shed demolished.

Returning to the Windmill End branch, the line continued past the Junction signal box opposite to which had been built a temporary siding *c.* 1915. This had been removed by 1919. On the approach to Windmill End station the line was crossed in the early 1900s by two tramways. The first ran from Buffery colliery to a canal basin on the Bumble Hole canal branch, whilst the second originated at Mudhall colliery and served Bournes Hill Basin which had been built at the point where the Bumble Hole canal loop had been severed.

The reader will have noticed that 'Bumble Hole' has been mentioned several times and therefore the origins of this unusual name may provide an interesting diversion from the main thrust of the story. The nearby Windmill End Furnaces had for many years fed upon minerals extracted from land around which the Bumble Hole canal loop passed. Legend has it that the owner of these furnaces installed a steam driven hammer housed in an iron-clad building at the bottom of the pit. When the hammer was operated, the noise it made sounded like 'bum-hul bum-hul' and was referred to by locals as 'bum-hul in the hole'. By the 1880s this had been shortened to Bumble Hole.

By the end of the century the ironworks had been abandoned although an alternative use was found for the Bumble Hole pits. *Circa* April 1904, a new siding was added to the branch which ran parallel to the down running line for some 350 yards and was controlled by a ground frame. Off this line ran another siding southwards to the old clay pit at the Bumble Hole. At the pit the siding was supplied by a number of tramways. This siding became known as the Ballast siding and remained in use until the late 1930s. The ground frame and parallel siding were subsequently taken out of use during February 1946.

After the Ballast sidings, the branch crossed both the Netherton Tunnel branch of the Dudley canal and Dudley No. 2 canal which used to link with the Worcester & Birmingham canal at Selly Oak. Today this terminates near the Hawne Basin in Halesowen. More on this Basin later. In between the two canals was a level crossing which took the branch over a lane which ran between Windmill End village and Windmill End colliery's No. 3 pit. By 1919 this colliery operated a tramway from nearby coal shafts to a wharf on the Boshboil Arm of the canal. The name 'Boshboil' originates from the practice of cooling hot ashes from the adjacent coke ovens

'57XX' class 0-6-0PT No. 3605 is seen at Withymoor goods yard *c.* 1962.

W.H. Massey/Dudley Libraries

Ex-GWR railcar No. W22W is stands at Windmill End station on 15th September, 1956. This vehicle is now preserved at Didcot Railway Centre.   *H.C. Casserley*

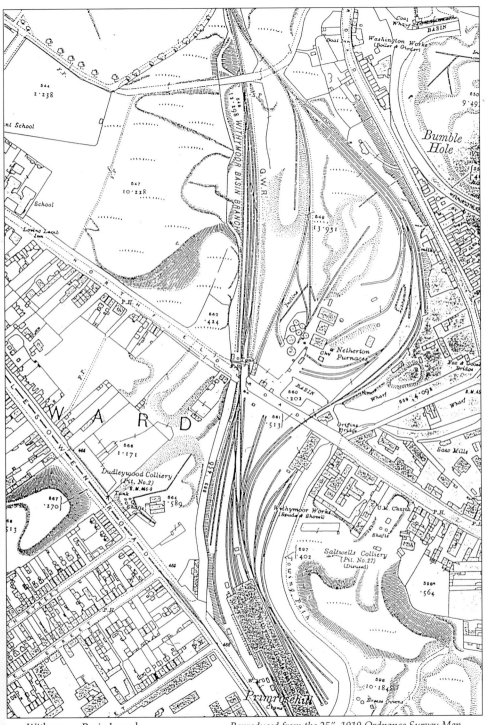

Withymoor Basin branch.   *Reproduced from the 25", 1919 Ordnance Survey Map*

Cobb's engine house and the Dudley canal in January 1998. *Author*

A postcard view of the station frontage at Old Hill. *Lens of Sutton*

in bosh tubs. Originally, this and the Bumble Hole canal branch were linked to form the Bumble Hole canal loop. However, with the construction of the straight section of canal the loop was abandoned and severed at what later became Bournes Hill Basin. Just to the north of the level crossing Cobb's Engine House Bridge crossed the Netherton Tunnel branch canal and by 1903 was used to carry a tramway conveying coal from Windmill End colliery to the pumping engine located in Cobb's Engine House itself. This pumping engine was used to drain nearby pits into Dudley No. 2 canal. The engine house was built in 1831 and worked right up to 1928, whilst the shell of the building and the chimney stack still stand today and is a scheduled ancient monument. The Watt beam engine was purchased by Henry Ford and resides in the USA.

Between Windmill End station and Darby End Halt the branch passed a number of collieries and works, none of which had any direct connection to the railway. However, to the east of Windmill End station, Warrens Hall colliery tramway transported minerals to the nearby Dudley No. 2 canal. Further east was the large Hailstones quarry in Rowley which operated a tramway that ran to an arm off the Dudley canal, located near the Birmingham Pottery, via a 175 yds-long tunnel under the main Dudley to Birmingham road.

Beyond Darby End Halt the branch arrived at Cox's Lane sidings having first passed over a level crossing at Cox's Lane and under a tramway from Ashtree Colliery to a basin on the Dudley canal. The area around the sidings was dominated by the large Old Hill ironworks which stood on both sides of Powke Lane. The ironworks possessed a tramway network which ran at various times to a nearby canal basin; the Bluebell Pit; Gawn colliery Pit No. 8; Old Hill colliery's Garratt's Lane Pit and Cox's Lane sidings themselves which connected to the branch at a point on the up running line. From this same point Garratt's Lane Pit was served by two sidings which ran parallel to the branch. By the 1930s the pit had been abandoned, the third parallel siding laid in the 1920s being used by a Tarmacadam works. The three sidings were taken out of use on 23rd June, 1954. Having reached Old Hill, the branch passed under a narrow gauge mineral railway from Corngreaves ironworks to a basin on the Dudley canal and over a tramway from Haden Hill colliery (abandoned by 1919) to Pit No. 2, before curving east into the platforms of Old Hill station itself.

The Old Hill to Halesowen Branch

The Halesowen branch left the Stourbridge Junction-Birmingham main line by way of a double track junction sited immediately to the east of Old Hill station, whilst Old Hill's down platform outer face curved away with the branch to accommodate passenger services. In the 1880s, near to the crossover point, a tramway originating at the Granville and Gorsty Hill colliery passed under the main line to terminate at an arm on the Dudley canal, as well as serving the sidings adjacent the down running line. Several of these sidings continued alongside the branch and in later years served a timber yard. Another siding formed a goods loop with the branch. The single line of the branch commenced about 100 yards before Haden Hill tunnel (151 yards long) and opposite this point was Haden Hill colliery Pit No. 2. A tramway from this pit ran under both the main line and Windmill End branch to Haden Hill colliery Pit No. 1. Haden Hill tunnel was constructed with a slight curve and when the branch emerged it was heading in a south-easterly direction.

Leaving the tunnel behind, the branch reached the only intermediate station between Old Hill and Halesowen. Not far from the branch was Coombes Wood colliery and this was one of the main reasons why Coombes Holloway Halt was opened on 1st July, 1905. The single platform was initially located on the down side of the branch, however, in 1914 the platform was moved to the opposite side. This relocation was the result of a plan to build a short connecting line from the down side of the branch to the Halesowen Basin branch thereby giving direct access to the canal basin from Old Hill. Known as the 'Halesowen Loop' the work was authorised by the GWR Traffic Committee on 8th August, 1912 and confirmed by Act of Parliament in 1913. Although there have been doubts expressed as to whether the line and the accompanying sidings were actually built, R.A. Cooke has confirmed that the work was carried out immediately after the Act was passed. Additionally, a new Private Siding Agreement was signed with Sir George

Old Hill station with the Windmill End branch curving away to the right.   *Lens of Sutton*

Old Hill station looking towards Birmingham. A class '57XX' is seen arriving with a local train.
H.C. Casserley

A passenger train at Halesowen. The locomotive is possibly a '517' class 0-4-2T on a train for Old Hill *c*. 1920.   *Lens of Sutton*

A steam railmotor at Halesowen *c*. 1920.   *Lens of Sutton*

Halesowen station *c.* 1950 with an ex-Midland Railway 0-6-0 heading a London Midland Region freight train.   *Dudley Libraries*

Halesowen station *c.* 1959 with '57XX' 0-6-0PT No. 3658 in the platform.   *Lens of Sutton*

Hingley relating to modified connections to Coombes Wood colliery. Apparently, these lines were never actually brought into full use due to mining subsidence and were eventually removed in 1928, a year after the signal box controlling the junction (Halesowen Basin Junction) closed. However, the earthworks which carried the loop remained visible for many years.

The approach to Halesowen saw the branch pass Canal Basin Junction and its controlling ground frame which was opened on 2nd April, 1902. Here, the Halesowen Basin branch left the down side on a long semi-circular path to the Dudley canal. In fact the line almost arrived back at Halesowen station. Just before the station on the up side of the branch was the goods yard, shed and some cattle pens, whilst opposite were several other sidings, one of which was used by Walter Somers & Company to remove waste metal and swarf. Interestingly, the Ordnance Survey map for 1884 shows a signal box located on the down side opposite the goods yard, although, by 1904, this was shown on another plan as the Halesowen Joint Station ground frame. This ground frame was taken out of use in September 1945.

Halesowen station was 1 mile 34 chains from Old Hill, the branch being some 2 miles 43 chains shorter than the Windmill End branch. Halesowen was originally the terminus for the branch and in the early days only possessed one platform. However, when the GWR entered into an agreement with the Halesowen Railway to share station facilities, a second platform was built probably in the 1880s. The station signal box could be found on the down platform, which also had a waiting room and office. This building contrasted sharply to that on the opposite platform being quite basic by comparison. The station track layout was modified several times during the early years of operation. One of these changes resulted in a short siding being created in between the two running lines. This siding had a stop block at each end. Just beyond the station, the single line from Old Hill and the Halesowen Railway converged to pass under a bridge carrying the road down Mucklow Hill. Just to the south of the bridge stood the water tank (located on the left-hand side). Apparently, the GWR was charged by the Midland Railway each time one of its engines used the facility. From Mucklow Hill the Halesowen Railway continued to Halesowen Junction via Hunnington, over Dowery Dell viaduct, past Frankley sidings, Rubery and Longbridge. Readers interested in this railway might like to refer to *By Rail to Halesowen* by M. Hale and N. Williams.

Returning to the Halesowen Basin branch, a number of sidings had been built at the junction which ran parallel to the main line. However, by 1948, the triangle of land in the mouth of the junction accommodated a fan-like array of sidings whilst the original parallel lines now formed a loop with the Halesowen branch. At this time a brickworks could be found nearby, although there was no evidence of a rail connection at or near the junction. The Basin branch initially headed north before curving east under a footbridge and past a group of sidings which came off the inside of the curve to terminate adjacent to Coombes Wood colliery. These sidings were all removed by September 1937. The colliery also had its own tramway and this may have run to a basin on the Dudley canal. The colliery had closed by 1948. Swinging south the line continued to rise steadily as it passed a number of sidings to Walter Somers & Company before arriving at the basin itself. This canal basin is also known as Hawne Basin although the area known as 'Hawne' is about ½ mile to the north-west. Possibly the name was derived from a tramway that once ran from the long abandoned Old Hawne colliery, over the River Stour, through 'The Furnace' to terminate at the canal. Over the years the amount of traffic handled at the basin grew considerably with the result that the number of sidings had to be increased accordingly. One of the main uses of the basin was to handle steel tubes that had been transported down the Dudley canal from Coombes Wood Tube Works. At the basin the tubes were transferred from barges to wagons in Stewart & Lloyds sidings, these having been added by 1925. Nearby was a siding which served Hickman's Brick & Tile Company and Coombes Wood colliery. The branch eventually terminated near Walter Somer's Haywood Forge sidings. Sadly, competition from road transport sounded the death knell for the branch and by the late 1960s the only regular traffic was the movement of large steel ingots. However, it was Halesowen goods yard that was the first to go on 9th September, 1968, the Halesowen Basin branch soldiering on for another year before it too closed on 1st October, 1969.

'57XX' class 0-6-0PT No. 3658 stands outside Halesowen signal box *c.* 1959.   *Lens of Sutton*

An unidentified '57XX' class 0-6-0PT shunts Halesowen Basin *c.* 1961.   *Ray Kendrick*

Pannier tank No. 2718 on Dowery Dell viaduct with a train for Longbridge on 12th July, 1939.
H.C. Casserley

Class '655' 0-6-0PT No. 2718 crosses Dowery Dell viaduct with an evening workmen's train from Longbridge to Old Hill on 12th July, 1939.   *H.C. Casserley*

An outside-framed ex-Midland Railway 0-6-0 is seen with a train near Rubery on 12th July, 1939.
H.C. Casserley

'74XX' class 0-6-0PT No. 7432 was photographed at Longbridge with a train for Old Hill on 8th
April, 1957.   *H.C. Casserley*

Chapter Six

Major Reconstruction Work on the OWWR

The Three Viaducts

The year 1882 saw a major construction work carried out on the former OWWR when Stambermill viaduct, located just to the north of Stourbridge Junction station, was rebuilt. Originally, the Oxford, Worcester and Wolverhampton Railway between Stourbridge and Dudley had boasted three large wooden viaducts. Parkhead viaduct was rebuilt *c.* 1877-78, an announcement in the *Brierley Hill Advertiser* during June 1877 indicating what work was to be carried out:

> A new large viaduct is to be erected by the Great Western Railway at Parkhead, near Dudley. The wood supports which carry the present structure over the Birmingham canal and Lord Dudley's and Messrs Grazebrooks's branches, are to be built in with bricks. A contract to supply 1, 000,000 of the latter has been secured by Messrs Phillips and McEwen, of Dudley. The contractor for the work is Mr C.J. Smith of Westminster. The viaduct is to be finished by the end of December next.

A second, and lesser known viaduct, situated just beyond the southern end of Brettell Lane station, had been filled in some years earlier by a Worcester contractor by the name of Dixon. This viaduct was 130 yards long and stood approximately 55 feet high. The filling in had been carried out using cinder and other materials from Brierley Hill, Corbyns Hall and Kingswinford and had taken 30 men per day, 12 months to complete at a cost of £4,000 (this was not the last to be heard of this viaduct-see later). However, it was Stambermill viaduct that principally occupied the thoughts of local people.

Stambermill viaduct had for many years been the subject of much concern due to a number of accidents that had occurred there. Such was the unease, that by February 1871 there was talk of partially filling in this viaduct also. Stourbridge Commissioners had for some time been enquiring of the Board of Trade as to when this viaduct had last been inspected. At a meeting at the beginning of March the clerk read out the first reply to his letter which stated that 'Stoobrook [*sic*] Viaduct' near Kidderminster had been inspected in January 1872. The clerk's second letter had however, received a more convincing reply which informed them that Stambermill viaduct had not been inspected since the opening of the line in 1852. It was agreed that the matter be taken up with the GWR with some urgency.

On 12th December, 1876, Captain Tyler, representing the Board of Trade, carried out an inspection of the viaduct. The 15th October had witnessed another accident on the viaduct when a luggage train suffered a broken coupling causing the train to divide on the Brettell Lane side. The driver of the locomotive, unaware of what had happened, continued to the viaduct where he reduced speed. The detached part of the train running uncontrolled and at an increasing speed caught up and collided with the front portion causing vans to be propelled into the valley below. Thankfully, no one appears to have been seriously hurt, but had the accident involved a passenger train the consequences would have been horrendous, a fact not lost on those living locally who renewed their demands for the viaduct to be filled in. However, it was not until early in 1882 that the problem of the viaduct was finally resolved. The *Brierley Hill Advertiser* reported the event as follows:

The New Viaduct at Stamber Mill

A handsome viaduct has been built by the Great Western Railway Company to replace the old timber structure at Stamber Mill, which has stood about thirty years, and was constantly in need of repairs. The new viaduct is built on the west side of the old one, and the railway diverted onto

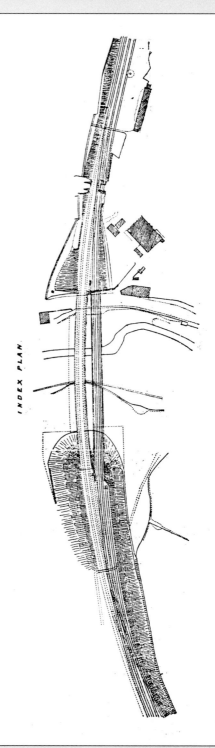

VIADUCT AT STOURBRIDGE, GREAT WESTERN RAILWAY.

571' 0"

RAIL LEVEL

INDEX PLAN.

Plan of Stambermill viaduct, 1882.

The Engineer

it. It is 571 feet long, and 98 feet high at the highest point. There are ten semicircular arches of 44 ft 6 in. clear span, faced with blue pressed bricks, and the arches spring from massive Derbyshire stone springers, 2 ft 9 in. high and 7 ft across. The piers are 6 ft thick under these springers and batter 1 in 40 to the plinth, which is 31 ft below the springers. This plinth is of blue pressed brick 9 in. high, and 6 in. projection. Below the plinth the same batter to the piers is preserved. The viaduct is built of brindled bricks, of which four million bricks were used, a large portion of them . having been made in the immediate neighbourhood. To relieve the parapets there are bold string courses and copings of Derbyshire stone, and on the pilasters at each end of the viaduct are set large ornamental caps. The deepest foundation is that of the abutment at the north or Brettell Lane end, which is carried down to a depth of 46 ft below the ground, and was a difficult piece of work, owing to its contiguity to the abutment of the old viaduct and the main line. Over one thousand tons of concrete were put into this foundation. The other foundations vary from 36 ft to 18 ft in depth, and are either on sandstone rock or hard fireclay marl. Of an uncommon design were the centres on which the arches were turned, inasmuch as they were constructed on the principle of a complicated roof-truss of the 'A' type, the members in tension were of iron, the rest timber. They were supported on beams resting on the piers, holes being left in the brickwork for their removal after completion of arches. The advantages of this type of centre was its elasticity as compared with the old-fashioned rigid centre. The arches took their form while the centre was yet under it. By thus making provisions for the settlement of the arch as observed in the case of the first one turned, all the others were arranged so as to be perfectly level. On September 20th, 1881, the first excavation was commenced. On October 13th of the same year the first brick was laid, and the last coping stone was bedded on January 11th, 1882, the viaduct having been under 6 months in course of construction. Messrs Kellet and Bentley carried out the work in a very efficient manner, and the same firm are also constructing a similar viaduct at Blakedown, near Kidderminster, for the same railway company. The cost of the viaduct was £13,835. Mr W.D. Robotham, the engineer, was represented on the ground by Mr C.R. Williams.

The work on the new viaduct seems to have been officially completed by 14th April, 1882, however, it was to be almost a month before it was actually brought into use, the date being 10th May, 1882.

The original timber-built Stambermill viaduct c. 1865.   *Dudley Libraries*

The Amblecote Bank Deviation

Early in 1972 a decision was taken to reconstruct the embankment between Vicarage Road, Amblecote and the Stourbridge canal at Brettell Lane. British Rail had been attempting to resolve the subsidence problems associated with this stretch of line for some 15 years but to no avail. The source of the trouble had been identified as being settlement of the old mine workings in the area, although the old wooden viaduct which had been filled-in about 100 years earlier, may have started to give way thereby contributing to the disturbance. In view of the above it was agreed that the best solution was to remove the existing embankment and the underlying minerals, consolidate thoroughly the ensuing back-fill and rebuild the embankment and relay the track to the original line and levels.

In February 1972, planning permission was given to construct a temporary embankment and railway line and Murphy Bros were given the task of winning from the whole area all remnant clay and associated coal seams left unworked by previous deep mining operations. The temporary embankment was built from a point near Old Hall Close and followed a curve of 700 feet radius, eventually to rejoin the main line near the Stourbridge canal. The path of the temporary line approximately halved the distance between the original line and the houses located in Dennis Hall Road.

On completion of the opencast mining operation, which went down approximately 150 feet in places, the temporary embankment was removed and the track returned to its former line, although the new embankment differed slightly from its predecessor in one important detail. Originally, there had been a public footpath that ran from Withymoor to Brettell Lane through a small tunnel that had been specially constructed in the embankment. In later years a local farmer used this pathway to move cattle from one field to another. However, during the extraction process the footpath disappeared and when it came to the time to return the site to its former condition the contractors, who either did not see the necessity of restoring the walkway or were ignorant of its existence, failed to reinstate the tunnel through the newly built embankment. As a matter of interest, the tunnel had associated with it its own piece of gruesome history.

Known to local people as the 'Murder Bridge', after the body of a young woman was found nearby, this grisly sobriquet probably owes its origins to the events of June and July 1906. On Tuesday 26th June a Cradley chain-maker, Enoch Cox, stabbed and shot his estranged wife Amy at her parents' home in Cradley Heath. Cox then committed suicide by shooting himself through the head, the bullet passing straight through the skull, narrowly missing a pursuing policeman. The next day, the parents of Caroline Pearson, an employee at Messrs Harris & Pearson, in Brettell Lane, reported her missing. Apparently she had been friendly with Cox and was seen in his company on the night of the attack. A witness stated that Cox was acting very strangely showing Caroline a pistol and some cartridges saying 'how should you like some of these in you'. At the same time he also threatened to kill both his wife and Caroline's sister Annie. Despite these warnings, Caroline accompanied Cox to the Birch Tree public house in Amblecote. When she left at about 9.30 pm that was the last time Caroline was seen alive.

Notwithstanding a widespread search the police were unable to find any trace of Caroline Pearson. However, on the evening of Tuesday 10th July, a Mrs Cooper entered the Birch Tree public house and complained to her nephew Joseph Woolridge of an awful odour emanating from a nearby field of rye and suggested that the body of 'Carrie' Pearson might be lying there. Woolridge, accompanied by Harry Wilcox and Arthur Skelding, together with the pub dog, went to investigate and it was the dog that led the men to the unfortunate woman's remains. By this time Caroline's body was so badly decomposed that the cause of death could not be determined, causing the jury at the subsequent inquest to enter a verdict of 'Found dead'. However, it has never been disputed that she died at the hands of Enoch Cox.

Chapter Seven

Schemes Proposed but not Constructed

Lines to the South of Stourbridge and through Kinver

It has already been shown that a number of schemes promoting railways to Stourbridge were, for one reason or another, never constructed. The proposals so far examined have concerned railways either arriving at Stourbridge from the east of the region or located within the town itself. However, there were, in addition to these, a number of other railways that were promoted that would have linked Stourbridge to the iron-making towns of the Stour Valley; to Bewdley on the Severn Valley Railway; and one that proposed an alternative route to Kidderminster, linking in with a number of towns in the South Midlands. Furthermore, there were others which, although not directly connected with Stourbridge itself, did fall within the general area so far described. It is to these schemes that the story will now turn.

The Birmingham, Wolverhampton and Stour Valley Railway Bill, 1846 has already been mentioned in connection with the line from Smethwick to Stourbridge. However, the Bill also proposed that the line would continue through Stourbridge, along the Stour Valley and the iron-making communities associated with it, namely Kinver and Cookley, through Kidderminster to terminate at a basin of the Staffs & Worcester canal at Stourport. It is believed that although the line was supported in the districts it was to serve, the Bill met strong opposition from landowners and the OWWR with the result that the scheme was withdrawn without even being debated in Parliament. This proposal was the first of several that involved the towns of Kidderminster and/or Bewdley, but of particular interest is that it would have included on its route Kinver, a village that was to be mentioned many times in schemes involving proposals to construct railways on the western side of Stourbridge.

Although the picturesque village of Kinver was served by the Staffordshire & Worcester canal, the community, along with others in the area, held a burning desire to be linked into the local rail network. Consequently, throughout the second half of the 19th century, there were a number of campaigns aimed at securing support for a standard gauge railway for the district. Unfortunately, despite the fact that several schemes were promoted over a period of almost 80 years, all efforts were to prove unsuccessful. However, by the early 20th century, the famous Kinver Light Railway had been constructed thereby fulfiling at least part of the community's dream.

In 1865 the Stourbridge Railway promoted the Stour Valley Extension Railway. Originally conceived as an extension to the company's 'Branch Railway to Stourbridge' as authorised by the Stourbridge Railway Act, 1865, the line would have passed through Wollaston before swinging west towards the Stewponey and Stourton. Beyond Stourton, the line continued along the Stour Valley through Kinver to Cookley and Wolverley, by-passing Kidderminster the line would terminate at a junction with the Severn Valley Railway some 880 yards north of Bewdley station. As there was no east to south connection, there was clearly no intention to actually communicate with Bewdley itself, the principal idea being to link with the Tenbury-Bewdley Railway, opened on 13th August, 1864, thereby creating the potential for a through route between the Black Country and South Wales.

The GWR was also anxious to pursue a scheme to the Severn Valley Railway and in 1872 promoted a railway between Stourbridge and Bewdley. The proposed route between Stourbridge and Cookley appeared to follow a very similar direction to that outlined in the 1865 Stour Valley Extension scheme. However, after passing through Wolverley, the line continued southwards to Kidderminster before swinging west to join the Severn Valley Railway to the south of Bewdley, therefore serving Bewdley station as well as gaining access to the Tenbury line.

At the time of this proposal there was already an authorised route to Bewdley from Kidderminster, the so-called 'Kidderminster-Bewdley curve' the construction of which had been strongly supported by the London & North Western who also recognised the benefits of obtaining access to South Wales via the Bewdley-Tenbury route. Consequently, the LNWR had no desire to see this latest scheme succeed as this would in effect cause the GWR to abandon the proposal to construct the 'curve'. The Stourbridge-Bewdley Railway was also to be strongly opposed by such notables as Mr H.F. Foley; the Earl of Stamford and Warrington; Mr F.W. Knight MP and the Earl of Dudley, all major landowners and influential voices in Parliament, to which, by March 1872, 33 petitions against the Bill had already been lodged. It was apparent that the major opposition to the plan would be from those strongly in favour of the construction of the Bewdley 'curve' and such fierce opposition was seen at the time as virtually an automatic veto on the project; a victory for the self-interest of the few at the expense of the many.

Amongst the petitioners against the Bill were the Stourbridge Improvement Commissioners, a fact that did not escape the notice of local supporters of the Bill. The Chairman, Mr H. Hughes, was at pains to point out that the Board was not against the construction of the line, quite the opposite in fact. The petition was filed principally to ensure that a 'locus standi' would be obtained in Parliament thereby ensuring the voice of the ratepayers would be heard. As in the past, the communities to be served by the line were strongly in favour, however, continued opposition from the principal landowners, railway companies, in particular the LNWR, and the Staffs & Worcester Canal Company ensured the rejection of the plan in the 1873 session of Parliament.

During 1874, a proposal was prepared entitled the West Staffordshire Railway Bill, which promoted a railway that would commence at a junction on the western side of the Stour Valley Railway, belonging to the LNWR, at a bridge approximately 500 yards south of Monmore Green station, itself situated just to the south of Wolverhampton (High Level) station. The line would pass through Wolverhampton in a south-westerly direction, continuing on to the west of Sedgley, near Sedgley Hall Farm, through Gornal and Gornal Wood, Shut End, Kingswinford and Wollaston. Passing to the west of Stourbridge, the line swung west towards Whittington and Kinver, then south past Cookley Forge, Wolverley and Kidderminster (West). Here the line veered towards the Severn Valley Railway to terminate by a junction with the Tenbury and Bewdley Railway near Dowles, at or near the eastern abutment of the bridge carrying that railway over the River Severn. Again, this project had the route to South Wales very much in mind.

The main line of the railway, 19 miles and 1 furlong in length, was planned to give a far more direct route between Stourbridge and Kidderminster (although there was not a connection proposed with Stourbridge itself). It was certainly argued at the Select Committee of the House of Commons which had been appointed to enquire into the merits of the Bill that this would be the case, the reduction in route mileage being achieved by building a number of branches to nearby towns and works rather than attempting to connect them all with the main line. This approach led to a route between Stourbridge and Kidderminster that was 3 miles less than the 1872 proposal.

The Bill proposed five branches; one leading into Wordsley; another which would reach Kinver terminating at the Hyde ironworks; a third leading to the ironworks at Cookley; the fourth terminated at the Broadwaters Forge, Wolverley whilst the last joined the Severn Valley Railway approximately 460 yards to the north of Bewdley station thereby giving access to the town and Stourport. The estimate for the construction of the main line, which unlike the 1872 proposal would be double track, was quoted as £550,000, the branches costing an additional £184,525, giving an overall estimate for the project of £734,525 or £32,000 per mile. The 1872 plan had been costed at £17,000 per mile, or £26,500 if double track were employed, a figure, it was claimed, that underestimated the true cost of the project. The Bill was backed by the LNWR however, it was reported that the LNWR General Traffic Manager, Mr Findley, in evidence to the Select Committee, argued that the powers sought by the promoters to run over the Stour Valley line and into the LNW station and wharves at Wolverhampton were excessive and highly objectionable to the company. The strongest opposition though was from the GWR and the canal companies and, although the Bill was supported by no less a person than Lord Dudley, the Select Committee took heed of the objections and rejected the Bill on the grounds that the preamble was not proven.

A second, less ambitious scheme, was proposed a year later in 1875. The Stourbridge Western Railway project, prepared for presentation to Parliament in the session of 1876, promoted the construction of a railway from Stourbridge to Kingswinford, Cookley and Kinver, with several branches. Consisting of five railways, Railway No. 1 commenced by a junction with the branch authorised by the GWR Act of 1874, approximately 10 chains (220 yards) from the main line station at Chawn Hill, Stourbridge. The line would then continue west beyond the town before swinging north to Kingswinford where it joined the Shut End Railway at the bottom of the first inclined plane, probably very close to where *Agenoria* began her historic journey some 47 years before. The second railway left No. 1 at a junction at Bowling Green Lane and after heading in a westerly direction towards Whittington, swung sharply south very near to the ironworks located near the village before terminating on the north side of Cookley at the ironworks there. Railway Nos. 1 and 2 could probably be described as the main line, whilst Railway No. 3 was the branch to Kinver. Leaving via a junction with Railway No. 2 near Whittington ironworks, the branch passed through Kinver to the east of the High Street before terminating just to the south of Hyde ironworks. The remaining two railways, Nos. 4 and 5, were in effect short connections to existing lines. Railway No. 4 connected Railway No. 1 to the existing Great Western branch that currently terminated to the west of Stourbridge High Street in the ironworks complex located adjacent to the canal. Railway No. 5 was to connect Railway No. 1 to the GWR main line by a junction at or near Stourbridge station. This was included as a precautionary measure to ensure a connection could be made to the main line in the event of the Great Western branch, authorised by the 1874 Act, not being constructed. At the time, the promoters of this scheme seemed confident that the plan would receive Parliamentary approval as it did not appear to conflict with the interests of either the Midland Railway or the LNWR. However, lack of coverage in the local press suggests that the Bill was withdrawn quite early on. Possibly the fact that the Great Western had decided to commence construction of the 'Kidderminster-Bewdley curve' may have influenced the promoters to take this course of action; it certainly must have played a part in the rejection of the West Staffordshire proposal. The 'curve' was subsequently opened to traffic on 1st June, 1878.

Of all the lines covered by this section, probably the most ambitious was that promoted as the Kidderminster, Stourbridge, Redditch and Hampton Junction Railway in the Parliamentary session of 1883. Comprised of eight railways, the scheme commenced, as the title suggests, at Kidderminster and would terminate at Hampton-in-Arden. Railways 1, 5, 6 and 8 represented a line that went eastwards from Kidderminster, through Chaddesley Corbett, Bromsgrove, Redditch, Henley-in-Arden before swinging north to join the LNWR at Hampton-in-Arden. At Bromsgrove, Railway No. 7 formed a junction with the Birmingham and Gloucester Railway, while at Chaddesley Corbett, Railway No. 3 headed north towards Stourbridge terminating at Pedmore Hall where the line divided into Railways 2 and 4. The former was to continue north where it would terminate to the east of Stourbridge Junction station, whilst the latter left Railway No. 3 to form a junction with the Great Western (the ex-OWWR main line) near the bridge carrying the road from Pedmore to Oldswinford. However, this too was destined not to be constructed.

During October 1884 a number of meetings were held in and around the Stourbridge area seeking support for an enterprising scheme that would promote a new railway between Wolverhampton and Bromsgrove. The plan for the route seems to have originated at Cookley and was presented by a Mr J. Wetherell of that village. Although floated as an independent railway, there were concerns that such a scheme would undoubtedly meet stiff opposition from both railway and canal companies and it was therefore suggested that one of the major railway companies be approached with a view to generating support for a joint venture. Some disenchantment was expressed with the Great Western Railway and the consensus appeared to favour an alliance with the Midland Railway. As it was planned to join the Midland at Bromsgrove this course of action would not be inappropriate.

A description of the route appeared in the *County Express*. It was proposed to begin the line near Wolverhampton where it would head south through Upper Penn, where a station would be built, over Penn Common to Sedgley and Upper and Lower Gornal. Continuing south the line would open up the coalfields on Pensnett Chase owned by the Earl of Dudley before continuing on through Kingswinford and Wordsley. After crossing the Stourbridge canal the line would pass through Wollaston. To the west of Stourbridge, a branch would be built to connect into the Stourbridge Town and Goods branch. Leaving Stourbridge the line would turn west between the 'Ridge' and Whittington Common to cross both the Staffs & Worcester canal and the Stour near Penhold in the south-east corner of the Parish of Kinver (no mention was actually made though of running a line to Kinver. However, by now the Hyde ironworks had in fact ceased production making a line into Kinver less attractive in terms of freight traffic, although when in full operation the Hyde's output of finished goods and its input of raw materials amounted to approximately 50,000 tons per annum). From Penhold, the line would head towards Cookley via the Whittington Iron Works and then on to Wolverley and Kidderminster. At Kidderminster it was proposed that a new centrally located 'Low Level' station be constructed. Leaving Kidderminster under the Hoo Brook viaduct, the line would continue to the south of Stone and eastwards to Chaddesley Corbett and on to Bromsgrove where another new station would be constructed about 1½ miles nearer to the town than the present Midland station. The line would then join the Midland Railway giving a total route length of approximately 26 miles serving a population of some 200,000 people.

A public meeting held at Kinver during October 1884 underlined the mood of the community. The village had been hit hard by the closure of the Hyde ironworks and residents saw as their only salvation from economic ruin, a rail link into the village which would enable the district to be opened up as a leisure resort. It was suggested that with the proper transport facilities Kinver, with its scenic beauty and nearby river and canal, could become a second Malvern. Prophetically, the Reverend J. Hodgson advocated the construction of a tramway or light railway between Stourbridge and Kinver, a suggestion that was at the time unpopular with advocates of a conventional rail link.

Despite widespread support, a Wolverhampton & Bromsgrove Railway Bill failed to materialise. Instead, 'The Stourbridge (Western) Railway Bill', which proposed a railway commencing just to the south of John Bradley's ironworks in Amblecote, terminating near Penhold in the Parish of Kinver, was deposited in the Private Bill Office of the House of Commons on 20th December, 1884. This proposal for what was a short and isolated line, corresponded with part of the much grander Wolverhampton & Bromsgrove scheme, although why this was the only section submitted remains a mystery. The Bill faced stiff opposition in Parliament, especially from the Staffs & Worcester Canal Co., the Stourbridge Navigation Co and the trustees under the Will of the late Earl of Stamford & Warrington. The Bill was withdrawn in March 1885.

In the 22nd December, 1894 edition of the *County Express*, a letter from G. Addenbrooke of Leamington made interesting reading. What was suggested was an extension to the Shut End Railway taking it beyond Ashwood basin, on the Staffs & Worcester canal, three miles south to Kinver, access to the railway being from the Great Western's Kingswinford branch. Intermediate stations could be erected at the Stewponey; also at a place where the mineral railway crosses the Wolverhampton to Stourbridge main road, i.e. just north of Kingswinford near Wall Heath; at Pensnett and by Bromley Lane bridge, the latter two being on the Kingswinford branch itself. Being a very circuitous route probably precluded it from really being taken too seriously, although Kingswinford Rural Council did consider applying for a Light Railway Order under the Light Railway Act, 1896 that would have possibly utilised part of the Earl of Dudley's railway in a line from Kingswinford to Kinver, Cookley and Kidderminster. Certainly the Council looked at the possibility of running passenger trains on the Pensnett Railway, although the scheme for Kinver, etc. may have been planned along similar lines to the 1875 Stourbridge Western project. Nothing, though, came of this plan.

The year 1897 saw a further determined effort to bring the railway to Kinver, plans being drawn up once again to pursue a line from the bottom of Stourbridge town along the Stour Valley. It was considered that the railway could be justified in terms of revenue from passenger and excursion traffic supported by the movement of agricultural produce. The Stour Valley iron industry had declined enormously by the late 19th century with the works at The Hyde, Gothersley, Whittington, Cookley, Cookley Forge and Wolverley all being forced to close (this may explain in part why the 1885 project was truncated). Consequently, it would not be revenue from the carriage of freight that would attract the railway to the Stour Valley, and only Kinver seemed to offer the kind of attractions that would bring the public in sufficient numbers to make any railway project viable. However, persuading the Great Western to promote a Bill on the strength of passenger traffic alone was seen by some as a major obstacle, especially as all earlier projects had failed at a time when the district's industrial capacity was fully operational.

During September 1897 there was a development that was to give the supporters of a railway line between Stourbridge and Kinver a much needed boost. Viscount Emlyn, the Chairman of the GWR was reported as saying in a speech to the half-yearly meeting of shareholders: 'With regard to these light railways, we are glad to meet any light railway schemes founded on sound commercial lines, but we are not inclined to dabble in those which have not that aspect, so far as we can gauge it'.

The *County Express* saw this statement as a challenge to the advocates of the railway to demonstrate to the GWR that their scheme had been founded on sound commercial lines based on passenger and goods traffic which would yield a reasonable return on investment. Needless to say the challenge was accepted and members of the Joint Railway Committee (members of both Stourbridge and Kinver Councils were on this committee) formally took the project to Paddington to place before the Directors of the Great Western (it should be remembered that plans for promoting the Kinver Light Railway were by now quite well advanced). However, despite the efforts of Messrs Jones, Collis, Foley, Punchard, Goddard and Fiddian, the GWR Directors informed the Joint Committee that their proposal had been rejected.

The Great Western though, did suggest that the line be constructed using funds raised by private subscription and if built, and if the terms were favourable, the company would then be prepared to operate it. The company also suggested that the local authorities and interested land owners approach the Light Railway Commissioners for permission to apply for a grant under the Act towards making the line. The first grant made under the Light Railways Act had been made to the Tanat Valley Railway which would join Oswestry to Llangynog. It was decided that Mr Foley and Mr Collis would represent the Joint Committee at a meeting to discuss this point with Mr Wilkinson of the GWR. However, the outcome of the meeting was clearly unsatisfactory and the Joint Committee decided not to recommend this course of action, and instead would support the application for an electric light railway made by BET Company Limited.

It might be thought that the decision to support the building of the Kinver Light Railway would have signalled the end for plans to construct a conventional railway to the village. This, however, was not the case. In the early 1920s, the GWR promoted the Great Western (Additional Powers) Railway Bill, 1923 which included Railway No. 1 between Stourbridge and Kinver. Commencing at a junction with the Great Western main line just to the south of the Junction station, the railway would have terminated near the bottom of Kinver High Street. Why the Great Western proposed this scheme so late is not known, especially with the nearby Kinver Light Railway, admittedly well past its heyday, and local buses providing stiff competition for the holiday traffic, which by now was probably a lot less than when the Kinver Light Railway was at its peak in the early years of the 20th century. The scheme did not go ahead thereby ending once and for all the dream of a 'main line railway to Kinver'.

Schemes for Cradley, Old Hill, Netherton and the Stourbridge Railway

In addition to the schemes involving the 'Cradley Loop' mentioned earlier, there were several other proposals for the Cradley area that were promoted but not constructed. During 1854 the Oxford, Worcester and Wolverhampton Railway promoted the Dudley and Old Hill Railway, notice of the company's intention to apply to Parliament during the 1855 Session appearing in the *Wolverhampton Chronicle* on 29th November. The company requested leave to bring in a Bill to make a railway:

> Commencing by a junction with the Oxford, Worcester and Wolverhampton Railway, at or near the Netherton Station of such Railway . . . and terminating at or near to the public highway leading from Netherton through Withymoor to Black Heath . . . and near to certain iron blast furnaces, called the Old Hill Furnaces, belonging to Messieurs Thomas and Isaac Badger.

In effect, the above was the northern half of the 'Outer Loop' of the OWWR's Cradley Loop proposal of the previous year.

On 30th November, 1860, the Cradley Heath and Dudley Railway submitted plans to Parliament for a railway from The Five Ways, Cradley Heath to Dudley, for consideration during the session of 1861. The railway was to commence by a junction with the Stourbridge Railway at or near a highway leading from Cradley to Five Ways and would then head in a north-easterly direction towards Reddall Hill before swinging round Old Hill and heading north-west, in the direction of Withymoor Mill. The line would then pass close to Netherton, through Bumble Hole, Baptist End and near to the Buffery ironworks, where it would cross the OWWR main line at Blower's Green. It was also proposed to construct a branch at this point that would join the OWWR main line at or near Netherton station. From Blower's Green, the line passed to the west of Dudley, near to the Old Park ironworks and Russells Hall, before swinging east, giving the route a characteristic 'S' shape, to terminate at a junction with the South Staffordshire Railway just to the north of Dudley station at a point near to the Dudley Port Furnaces. The proposed route between Cradley Heath and Blower's Green/Netherton appeared to be broadly similar to that described by the 'Outer loop' of the 1853/54 Cradley Loop project and was to suffer a similar fate.

In 1876, the GWR promoted a Bill which, along with other purposes, proposed the construction of three Railways. Railway No. 1 was to have commenced by a junction with the Netherton and Halesowen Railway (then in the course of construction) to the east of Furnace Hill and would terminate just to the north of Lutley Mill. From here, Railway No. 2 continued west terminating at a coal and fire-clay colliery in Foxcote Lane, between Lower Lutley and Parkside, near Two Gates. Railway No. 3 headed north from a junction with Railways 1 and 2, where it would have joined the Corngreaves branch near the bridge carrying the branch over the New British Iron Company's tramway.

Several years later, the Clent Railway scheme was prepared for presentation before Parliament during the Session 1888. As the name suggests, this scheme was designed to bring a railway into the Clent Hills at St Kenelms. The proposal comprised six railways; Railway No. 1 leaving the Halesowen and Bromsgrove Railway at Hunnington to terminate at Lutley. Here, Railway No. 2 would then continue southwards to terminate at St Kenelms. Railway No. 3, 4 and 5 left No. 1 to run north where it was to have joined the Stourbridge Railway some 427 yards east of the Corngreaves Road bridge. Incidentally, Railway No. 6 provided the south connection between Railway No. 2 and Railways 3, 4 and 5.

Schemes to the north and south of Dudley and the Welsh connection

Although Craven Arms is a village near the Welsh border it did have considerable significance for Black Country railway promoters. Located on the Shrewsbury & Hereford Railway near a junction with the Knighton Railway, Craven Arms was seen as the gateway to the vital, mineral rich areas around Llanelly and Swansea in South Wales. In Central Wales, the Knighton Railway was one of three railways that were built during the 1860s which combined to form a through route from Shrewsbury to Llandovery and the Great Western line to Llanelly. However, in order that the West Midlands might benefit from this new route it was proposed to build a line of railway from the Black Country to Craven Arms via Bridgnorth.

In 1861 an application was made to Parliament in the name of the South Staffordshire and Central Wales Railway, for an Act to incorporate a company to make a railway from Craven Arms to Dudley with branches to Ludlow, Much Wenlock, Bridgnorth and the Kingswinford branch of the West Midland Railway. Commencing by a junction with the Knighton Railway, the line terminated by a junction with the South Staffordshire Railway on the north-east side of Dudley Goods station. The proposed branch to the Kingswinford branch was to have left the main line just to the east of the village of Himley, terminating by a junction with the branch at its terminus near to Oak Farm Furnaces and ironworks. A year later, the Parliamentary session of 1862 saw a similar but less ambitious plan put forward under the title of the South Staffordshire and Central Wales (Dudley and Bridgnorth Railway). This line of railway would have commenced on the east bank of the River Severn to the south of Bridgnorth and, after taking a slightly more southerly route than its predecessor, would have joined the South Staffordshire Railway just to the north of Dudley station. However, this plan included a proposal for an additional junction which would enable trains to access the northern end of Dudley station and powers were sought to allow the company to use the station. It was also proposed to construct a short connection to the West Midland Railway at the north end of the WMR engine shed. The scheme also proposed a branch from the main line to the small Staffordshire village of Swindon. As this line would have begun at Bridgnorth it is thought that a separate scheme may have been proposed to take the railway across the Severn to Craven Arms.

Between 1863 and 1865 three very similar schemes were proposed which, if built, would have brought a railway to Wolverhampton and to Dudley via the West Midland Railway between Round Oak and Blower's Green. The plans, made in the names of the 'Welsh & Midland Counties Junction Railway' (1863) and the 'Central Wales & Staffordshire Junction Railway' (1864 and 1865), all included a branch to the Staffordshire & Worcestershire canal at Swindon, although only the CW&SJR variants seemed to make a connection with the Kingswinford branch, this being at or near Shut End. One major difference between the plans involved the route to Wolverhampton. In the 1865 version the line would have gone in a northerly direction, terminating by a junction with the Shrewsbury & Birmingham line near Oxley, whereas the others would have joined the Birmingham, Wolverhampton & Stour Valley Railway (the LNWR) south of Wolverhampton near Ettingshall Road & Bilston station.

Chapter Eight

Accidents and Unusual Events

This Chapter highlights some of the lighter, and darker moments of the railway's history. The early days of the lines' operations were notable for a number of fatal and harrowing accidents. Some of these were the result of poor working practices and/or faulty railway equipment, whilst others were due to the negligence of the railway personnel involved. Several incidents were caused through irresponsible behaviour and, on at least one occasion, through the stresses of working on the railway itself. There were, of course, less tragic, perhaps unusual incidents to recall, as well as some more heartening moments. It is hoped that the following will have achieved a reasonable balance between them all.

Faulty Couplings

On Tuesday 3rd May, 1853, a number of empty carriages, which were being shunted down the main line between Dudley and Netherton stations, were involved in a runaway incident after six carriages became detached when a coupling parted. The runaways headed at an ever increasing speed towards Stourbridge and at the far side of Brierley Hill & Round Oak station collided with a down passenger train. The driver of the train, on seeing the uncontrolled approach of the carriages, immediately shut off steam, applied the brake and put the locomotive into reverse gear. However, the impact was still sufficient to reduce the leading three carriages to matchwood. Thankfully, injuries to passengers (including a certain Michael Grazebrook, a Director of the OWWR) were slight, although two ladies did require further medical treatment. This was the first accident to happen on the stretch of track between Stourbridge and Dudley since the line opened; unfortunately, five years later, a similar accident was to occur that was to have far more tragic consequences.

Disaster struck on 23rd August, 1858, on the section of track between Brettell Lane and Round Oak stations. Earlier in the day a packed excursion, ostensibly a special for schoolchildren, teachers and friends, had left Wolverhampton for Worcester three minutes late at 9.18 am. The heavily laden train was equipped with a brake van at each end, the guards being George Cording in the leading van and Frederick Cook in the rear. In charge of the engine was driver Jonas Lockwood. The special called at all intermediate stations and at Dudley a further eight carriages were added as well as a second locomotive driven by Thomas Benson. At Stourbridge Junction three more carriages were attached and by the time the train reached Worcester there were more than 1,500 people on board, many of whom were children. Not unnaturally, a festive air persisted throughout the outward journey and this relaxed atmosphere seems to have spread to the brake van where Cook spent much of the time smoking and allowing accompanying passengers to take turns operating the screw brake. This irresponsible behaviour resulted in several severe jolts which led to the parting of central couplings and side chains on three separate occasions: at Brettell Lane, Hagley and Droitwich! Each time Cook was able to carry out temporary repairs.

Having enjoyed their day out the excursionists arrived back at Worcester station to find that the train home had been divided into two: this was to enable the steep gradient between Brettell Lane and Round Oak to be tackled more easily. The leading train, consisting of 29 carriages and a brake van at each end, departed Worcester at 6.25 pm and was hauled by an 0-6-0 goods engine driven by John Birt; the second train of 16 carriages and two brake vans left about 15 minutes later. At Stourbridge Junction a second locomotive, driven by Robert McGee, was attached to assist the 0-6-0 on the gruelling climb to Round Oak. Cook, accompanied by six or seven passengers, occupied the rear van. The second train was hauled by just one 0-4-0 locomotive throughout the journey. At 8.10 pm, as the first train drew to a halt at Round Oak station there was a loud snap as a coupling parted between the twelfth and thirteenth carriages together with the side chains - the evening's dreadful events were about to unfold! Immediately, 17 carriages (including a carriage brake) packed with 450 men, women and children, plus Cook's brake van, began to roll back towards Brettell Lane. By this time the following train was slowly inching its way up the gradient to Round Oak and had almost reached Moor Lane bridge when it was hit by the runaway. The impact was so great that Cook's brake van and two adjoining wooden-bodied carriages were smashed to pieces instantly killing 11 and injuring scores more; sadly three more passengers were to die later from their injuries. Amazingly, the locomotive on the second train only suffered minor damage.

At the subsequent Inquest, Cook stated that despite screwing down the handbrake hard thereby fully locking all four wheels of the van, he was unable to halt the train. Consequently he had no choice but to jump for his life, shouting a warning at the same time. This statement was corroborated by two men, Joseph Williams and Thomas Brett who said they were in the van with Cook at the time. Moreover, Jonas Lockwood, the engine driver of the second train, saw sparks flying from the wheels of the van (implying that the brake must have been put on). However, evidence was to be laid before the Inquest which was to cast substantial doubt on Cook's testimony.

On 28th August, at Round Oak, the Board of Trade Inspector, Captain Tyler, carried out an elaborate experiment. Seventeen carriages, similar to those involved in the accident, were assembled together with a brake van. Each carriage was then loaded with iron weighing 22 cwt, this being about 5 cwt more than that computed by Tyler as representing the laden weight at the time of the accident. The train was then released down the bank. This experiment was conducted several times, the carriages being allowed to run from varying distances to allow different velocities to be achieved before attempts were made to bring them to a halt. On each occasion the train was stopped by the application of the handbrake in the brake van. Some days later, officers of the OWWR conducted a similar experiment in front of the Inquest jury. Once again the train was stopped by screwing down the brake. To further undermine the guard's testimony, quite damning evidence was found in the wreckage of Cook's brake van.

Although the coupling was certainly defective, it was the guard, Frederick Cook, who was to become the villain of the piece. On the outward journey Cook had allowed others to operate the handbrake. This irresponsible behaviour had probably weakened the couplings with the result that at Round Oak the most fragile had simply given away. Cook also claimed to have applied the brake when the two parts of the train were only about six yards apart. The experiments at Round Oak seemed to indicate that such a prompt response would have halted the runaway quite quickly, yet Cook was unable to do so, in fact, the brakescrew recovered from the remains of the van indicated that the brake had not even been applied! Furthermore, Charles Markham, locomotive engineer on the Midland Railway, suggested that the sparks from the van's wheels were caused, not by the application of the brake, but by friction due to the wheel flanges rubbing against the outer rail of the curve. So was Cook guilty of dereliction of duty (was he indeed even in his van when the carriages separated)? The Inquest jury had no doubts and unanimously returned a verdict of manslaughter against him.

A faulty coupling was again the cause of an accident at Brettell Lane in December 1869. A freight train from Wolverhampton to Oxford was approaching Brettell Lane station when a coupling parted causing the derailment of at least one wagon and the separation of the train into two parts. The locomotive, together with a number of wagons, was successfully halted in the station but not before the derailed wagon(s), which had remained attached to the locomotive, had caused considerable damage to the permanent way. The arrival of the locomotive and some of its wagons was quickly followed by the appearance of the remaining vehicles which had continued to roll down the incline. The resulting collision completely blocked both main lines, however, what made things worse for those attending the accident was the imminent arrival of a Wolverhampton-bound express. It was at this point though, that Lady Luck offered a helping hand. Apparently, the express, driven by John Gilroy, was running two minutes late due to an enforced stop at Hagley to drop off Lord Lyttleton.

'County' class 4-6-0 No. 1009 *County of Carmarthen* has become derailed alongside Stourbridge
Junction South signal box on 27th May, 1961.   *E.J. Dew*

A close-up of the derailed locomotive No. 1009 *County of Carmarthen* on 27th May, 1961.
R. Walker Collection/Wolverhampton Express & Star

Consequently, by the time the express reached Brettell Lane someone was in position by the trackside to warn the driver of the accident. The express was able to pull-up with 100 yards to spare thereby avoiding a possible major disaster.

Trouble on the Main Line

In June 1861, a quite spectacular event lit up the sky around Hagley. Apparently, a goods train making its way to Stourbridge was found to be on fire. It was subsequently necessary to uncouple the unaffected rear portion of the train at Hagley and take the burning wagons on to Stourbridge where water was available to extinguish the blaze. Also at Hagley, in March 1865, an attempt was made to derail a train by placing two fish plates onto the track. Luckily, a passing employee noticed the obstruction and immediately removed them before any damage could be done. During September of that same year, there occurred a collision in the Hagley area between a passenger train and a freight. The 10.15 pm arrival at Stourbridge was following some five minutes behind a 40-wagon goods train. The freight was due to be shunted out of the path of the express at Stourbridge; unfortunately, the gradient from Hagley slowed the freight down sufficiently for the express to catch it up and at Whitehall, just south of Stourbridge, the two collided. The guard on the freight saw the approach of the express and was able to jump clear just moments before the impact shattered his van completely. Strangely, little of the impact was in fact felt on the freight engine and the crew continued blissfully along until told of the incident at Stourbridge. Although the express engine was derailed and several wagons damaged, no one appears to have been killed or even seriously injured.

On 11th November, 1867 an accident occurred between two trains at Smethwick Junction which was a direct result of the working arrangements which were then in force. Passengers for stations on the Stourbridge Extension and beyond could travel from either Birmingham New Street or Snow Hill stations via Smethwick Junction. Apparently, LNWR trains from New Street bound for Stourbridge were required to come to a halt before Smethwick Junction where the engine would be detached. The carriages would then be moved forward and coupled up to a waiting Great Western train. Inexplicably, on this occasion, the driver of the LNW locomotive did not stop short and continued instead into the rear of the stationary GWR train. Luckily, it appears that there were no serious injuries.

An accident at Stourbridge station late in 1870 brought about by signal failure prompted the authorities to take unusual action. One of the distant signals controlled from the station box could not be seen by the signalman and therefore if it malfunctioned, as it must have done earlier, the box would not be aware of the failure until it had been reported or, much worse, in the event of an accident. To provide the signalman with a better view of his 'distant' the company installed a flight of steps early in 1871.

A signal was the cause of a collision on 13th January, 1875 outside Lye station. The 7.40 pm from Birmingham (Snow Hill) was held at Lye. The station master subsequently instructed the driver to proceed although the distant signal was still at caution. Approaching the Stourbridge home signal, the driver saw it come 'off' and mistakenly thinking it was for him, began to accelerate round the bend towards the station. However, as he rounded the curve, the truth dawned upon him. The home signal was giving permission to proceed to an earlier luggage train which had been delayed to carry out repairs to the draw-bar on the locomotive, hence the Lye distant being set at 'caution'. Thankfully, the ensuing collision resulted in only minor injuries and no serious damage.

It would appear that the OWWR's original rails and longitudinal sleepers that made up the section of track between Stourbridge and Brierley Hill were removed c. 1875, for on 18th July of that year a derailment occurred which was directly attributable to this work. The local permanent way gang had been working on the down line between Brettell Lane station and the old viaduct and, having prepared the longitudinal track for lifting, moved aside to allow a slow moving passenger train from Stourbridge to pass by. Unfortunately, one of the rails that had been made ready for removal, slipped under the weight of the train causing the locomotive to leave the track. Thankfully, none of the carriages were derailed and they were hauled back to Stourbridge where they were switched to the up line for the journey back to Brettell Lane.

On 17th July, 1936 a fatal accident, involving an auto-train and a southbound freight train, occurred on the main line some 600 yards to the north of Stourbridge Junction station. The auto-train formed the 11.30 pm departure from Dudley and was due to arrive at Stourbridge Junction at 11.49 pm. According to reports, departure from Dudley was on time, the auto-train leaving some 10 minutes behind the freight train that was booked to precede it to Stourbridge (this was possibly the Victoria Basin to Cardiff express goods). On arrival at Stourbridge Junction, the freight was held at a signal just outside the yard. The fireman alighted from the engine and walked to the North signal box where he was told that the signal, which may not have been operating correctly, was in his favour. However, before the freight train was able to clear the main line, the auto-train crashed into the rear, demolishing the brake van and derailing several vans. Two passengers travelling in the trailer received minor injuries, although the driver, William Meredith, who had been trapped in the driving compartment, was found to be very seriously hurt. Sadly Mr Meredith was to succumb to his injuries early the next morning. The line remained closed until 5.30 am.

The Fortunate and the not so Fortunate

The pressures of working on the railway were not without their consequences. On 28th May, 1865, Mr William Rigby, one of two station masters employed at Stourbridge (the other was Mr J. Phillips who worked on the Passenger Department) took his own life. It was reported at the inquest that the strain imposed upon him by the amalgamation of the Great Western and the West Midland Railway was undoubtedly a contributory factor leading to the suicide. 'A committee of respectable and responsible gentlemen' was subsequently formed to raise a 'subscription' to aid his wife and five children. A second, alleged, suicide, was that of Mr James Corfield, the station master at Brierley Hill, on 25th August, 1876. Mr Corfield's body was found in the Stourbridge canal at Wordsley, although the circumstances surrounding the death were less obvious and the jury at the inquest were unable to confirm that the unfortunate man took his own life.

On 6th May, 1871 both lucky escape and tragedy were reported. The former involved a yardsman at Stourbridge who jumped from a freight train onto the adjacent line right into the path of an oncoming passenger train. Luckily the man was able to scramble clear, the train only removing the coat that he was wearing. Tragically, fireman Charles Spiers was not so lucky. Apparently, he was attempting to uncouple two wagons at Chapel Bridge Salt works in Droitwich while the train was still in motion. While standing astride the couplings his foot must have slipped and he died under the wheels of the wagons. What aggravated the tragedy was the fact that his father was driving the train.

Passengers on Stourbridge station witnessed a remarkable escape on Thursday 6th December, 1873. Ticket collector John Locke, whose father was also employed by the company as a district inspector, was involved in an incident with a locomotive and brake van. Crossing the line to the opposite platform to collect tickets from passengers who had just arrived, he failed to notice an oncoming locomotive propelling the van. Unable to stop the van hit Mr Locke, knocking the hapless man directly onto the track. Miraculously, the van then passed over him without causing injury, but he then became wedged under the locomotive's firebox. In order to free him, the ballast under him had to be excavated to facilitate his release. Burned and scalded, he was eventually freed and sent immediately to the Guest Hospital.

A similar, if not even more remarkable incident happened to father and son George Hussey (69) and Arthur Hussey (34) on 14th March, 1903 at Round Oak station. Employed at the chain works, the two men were on their way home to Stourbridge. Arriving at the station they purchased tickets for the 4.34 pm and crossed the footbridge to the down platform. Realising their error, they decided to cross by way of the track. On reaching the up line the father stumbled and both men fell onto the track. Before they could recover an engine and brake van passed over them and continued on to Stourbridge. The father then rose from the track, apparently none the worse for what must have been a terrifying experience. However, his son lay still, but to the relief of all, on being carried to the platform, he regained consciousness. Amazingly, both men were sufficiently recovered to catch the train they had obtained tickets for, the whole incident being over in a matter of nine minutes. It later transpired that the escape was even more surprising due to the fact that the tender of the locomotive involved was fitted with a water scoop, which meant that no more than 12 inches of space existed between this and the ballast below.

On Tuesday 12th December, 1905, Mr Alfred Pearson of Quarry Bank endured a frightful ordeal whilst taking a short cut home along the Stourbridge Extension. Approaching Old Hill station, Mr Pearson was passed by a Birmingham to Stourbridge local service. The turbulence caused by the train dragged the helpless man into the gap between the carriages and onto the buffers and couplings where he managed to hang on for some 70 yards until the train came to a halt at Old Hill station. Hearing his cries for help, amazed railway staff were able to extricate the man from his perilous position. Luckily, Mr Pearson was found not to be seriously injured.

In October 1882, a certain Mr Charles Moody of the well known establishment Messrs Mark and Moody was to make the headlines when he survived a fall from Stambermill viaduct. A keen photographer, he had presumably climbed onto the old wooden viaduct to obtain a better view of the new structure recently constructed alongside. However, in this endeavour he must have slipped and fell into the River Stour below. It was suggested that the fall was of the full 102 feet from the top of the viaduct to the river which at this location was only two feet deep at the time. He was rescued alive but unconscious by a Mr Weston and one other passer-by and taken to a nearby brick-kiln to dry out and recover. Shortly after the incident Mr Moody was able to return home.

There is a well known adage in show business: 'never work with animals and children'. On the morning of 11th August, 1898, working with animals certainly took on a new dimension at Stourbridge Junction for the freight handlers concerned. By 9 am, several attempts had been made to remove a bull from a cattle truck. The animal had been consigned to a Mr Norris of Lye and perhaps wary of the fate that awaited him, the bull was none too keen to go and resisted all efforts to unload it, fiercely attacking anyone foolhardy enough to try. The animal's stiff resistance, however, came to an abrupt end at 9.30 am when a single shot to the head dispatched the unfortunate animal to the great green pasture in the sky.

Fare avoidance was quite a common practice and two incidents are worth relating here. The first involved a passenger by the name of Palmer who in June 1887 was accused of travelling in a first class compartment on the 8.03 from Dudley to Stourbridge when only being in possession of a second class ticket. Unremarkable in itself perhaps, but it would appear that this individual made a habit of such action. On an earlier occasion, his predilection for first class travel resulted in a porter at Dudley station, who was in the process of removing him from a first class compartment, losing his legs in a terrible accident. This tragedy clearly left Palmer unrepentant.

On the 25th March, 1865 it was reported in the local press (84 column lines in fact) that a police officer had been charged with failing to pay the fare on a journey from Worcester to Stourbridge on 23rd February. Interestingly, the case was dismissed on the grounds that a railway employee had allowed him to enter the carriage even when knowing the officer did not have a ticket. Apparently, the officer was an acquaintance of the porter and it had been said that the fare would be paid at Stourbridge. Although the journey had been made in contravention of the relevant clause in the railway company's Act, the Bench ruled that the journey had been made in the full knowledge of a company official and that the responsibility lay with him to ensure that the passenger had obtained the relevant ticket prior to commencement of the journey.

There was a very bizarre incident at the Junction station at the end of December 1898. The heavily laden South Wales express had just begun to depart after having a pilot engine attached to assist the train up the steeply graded Extension on its non-stop run to Birmingham (Snow Hill) - passengers could leave the train at Smethwick Junction if prior arrangements had been made with the guard at Stourbridge Junction. Suddenly, a man rushed onto the platform, chased after the train and jumped aboard the last carriage. Holding onto the carriage grab handle with one hand, the man frantically tried to open the carriage door with the other. Two porters, seeing the incident, rushed forward and tried to remove him from his precarious foothold by grabbing hold of his coat. However, what the porters succeeded in doing was merely to remove the tails of the coat from the rest of the garment and in so doing collided with another passenger standing on the platform knocking him to the ground. By now the man had safely boarded the train and was on his way to Birmingham. However, the authorities at Stourbridge did not intend to let the matter drop and telegraphed Snow Hill informing them of the incident. On arrival the compartment was searched but no such man was discovered. Even stranger, not one of the passengers in the compartment seemed to have even witnessed the event. Annoyed officials promptly telegraphed Stourbridge ridiculing the message, however, the reply came back 'we have the coat tails to prove what we say'. A search of the tails revealed several items amongst which were papers signed by a Pygmalion Potts - was this the mysterious stranger?

Runaway Trains Over the OWWR

Incidents involving 'runaways' were certainly not unknown in the district and a number were reported in the local press. One such incident occurred on the night of 2nd September, 1891. At approximately midnight, a heavily laden freight consisting of 14 wagons was shunted into the refuge sidings at Round Oak to enable what would probably be the 11.05 pm departure from Birmingham (Snow Hill), which would be routed via Dudley onto the ex-OWWR main line to Stourbridge, to pass. After the passenger train had passed, the freight train left the siding and proceeded along the up line towards Brierley Hill. However, unbeknown to the train crew, a rake of 12 wagons which had also occupied the siding, some of which were full of pig-iron from the nearby works, also inexplicably trundled out onto the main line in the wake of the freight. At Kingswinford Junction, between Brettell Lane and Brierley Hill stations, the freight train was hit in the rear by these wagons which had picked-up considerable momentum on the incline from Round Oak. Major damage to the brake van and several wagons ensued although the guard managed to escape with only minor injuries. The Stourbridge breakdown gang attended the scene and eventually what remained of the freight train was allowed to get under way.

As the 19th century drew to a close, local arguments in favour of a new station layout were given a considerable boost by a potentially very serious collision which occurred at the Junction on the evening of 12th December, 1898. The 7.30 pm arrival from the Town had moved forward empty towards the viaduct in preparation to cross onto the up line for the return journey. Once the manoeuvre had been completed, the carriages were detached and the locomotive returned to the down line so that it could run round its train. The South Wales express was due to arrive at 7.40 pm which just about gave sufficient time to carry out this movement. However, a Dudley-bound freight came off the Town branch onto the down line, the driver unaware that the line was now occupied by the Town locomotive. The driver and fireman on the latter, seeing the freight heading towards them promptly jumped for their lives. The resulting impact seemed to cause the regulator to open and as the locomotive must have been in gear with the brake off, it began to move away under its own power. The engine steamed on across the viaduct, through Brettell Lane station and on towards Kingswinford Junction. Here, with the gradient against it, the engine slowed sufficiently for it to be boarded and brought to a halt.

The scene of '57XX' 0-6-0PT No. 3788's accident at Stambermill viaduct on 6th September, 1965.
R. Walker Collection/Wolverhampton Express & Star

On 6th September, 1965 a class '57XX' 0-6-0PT No. 3788 was in charge of a freight train consisting of 22 wagons loaded with steel pipes and plates from Oxley Sidings to Moor Lane Goods Depot. According to local newspaper reports the crew were unable to halt the train after it had begun to run away from Brettell Lane station in the direction of Stourbridge Junction. The signalman manning the box at Stourbridge Engine Shed, apparently acting in accordance with the normal procedure for this stretch of line, switched the runaway into the up loop. The train continued along the loop and crashed through the stop block, the locomotive and about 12 wagons finishing up at the bottom of the bank adjacent to the viaduct. Thankfully, both driver and fireman had earlier jumped clear.

The Stourbridge Town Branch - A Notorious Incline

On 15th June, 1897 an accident occurred on the steeply graded Town branch. A train of empty cattle trucks and horse boxes which was being assembled to carry animals from the annual livestock show, was being reversed down the incline, probably towards the cattle pens

Two commercial postcard views of the accident at Amblecote goods depot on 24th April, 1905.
Stourbridge Library and Author's Collection

to the north of the canal basin, when the locomotive's vacuum brake failed. The wagons and locomotive, unable to stop, ploughed into a line of stationary wagons driving them into the offices of a local coal merchant by the name of Newman. Luckily, both Mr Newman and his clerk had just left or both would have been seriously injured if not killed by the crash. The wagons also collided with the stables belonging to Messrs Bantock & Co., bringing the slate roof crashing to the ground. The horses, however, were saved by the substantial timber framework, although a carter, Thomas Mulliner, was unfortunately injured.

At noon on Easter Monday, 24th April, 1905, the Goods branch once again was the scene of a major accident. It would appear that an 0-6-0 saddle tank was descending the branch bunker first at the head of 32 wagons, the combined weight of which probably being in excess of 400 tons, when the driver lost control. Although the brakes were on and the engine was in reverse, adhesion was lost and the whole train slid towards the goods office at the foot of the siding. The fireman jumped from the cab and attempted to 'sprag' the wheels on the wagons. He was quickly joined by shunters Freeman and Price who managed to drop the brakes on several wagons (should this not have been done prior to the train's descent?). However, it became clear, very quickly, that nothing could be done to halt the train and just before it crashed into the wooden stop block the driver jumped clear. The train, now travelling at about 10 mph, demolished the stop block, cleared the 15 foot roadway beyond and smashed into and through the goods office, reducing to rubble 20 feet of walling on either side of the building. Amazingly, the roof remained in place. The two trucks immediately behind the locomotive careered up to form a ' / \ ' shape against the skyline, a scene which was to be captured by a local photographer and published in the *County Express*. A 25-man breakdown gang attended the accident under the supervision of locomotive inspector Lodge and permanent way inspector Simpson. Happily, no one was seriously injured, the offices being empty at the time. There were three sidings terminating near the goods office and it was reported in the local press that 'arrangements are in progress for the elimination of all possibility of a similar accident occurring in the future'. Unfortunately, almost 43 years later, an almost identical incident was to occur.

Tuesday 10th February, 1948 had begun with continuous heavy rain which lasted throughout most of the early morning. At about 6.15 am, a heavily laden freight (possibly No 3 Bank Train - Stourbridge Goods Depot Engine) eased out of Stourbridge Junction over the branch towards Stourbridge Town station. In the cab of the 0-6-0PT, the normal motive

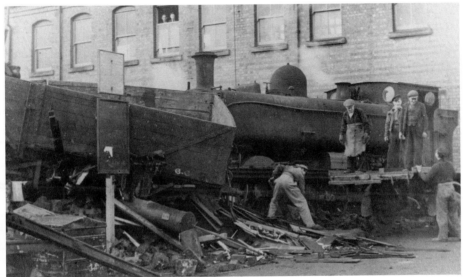

The accident at Amblecote goods on 10th February, 1948.   *Crown Copyright*
Reproduced with the permission of the Contorller of HMSO

Two views of diesel railcar No. W55012 at Stourbridge Town station on 2nd April, 1977 as it overhangs Foster Street East. *(Both) J.W. Gibbs*

Stourbridge Town station after the accident of 21st January, 1989. Note that by the now the Great Western station building has been demolished and replaced with a basic shelter. There is no longer a drop over the road due to redevelopment.   *Newsquest Media Group*

Railcar No. W55034 after the crash at Stourbridge Town station on 1st March, 1990.
                                                                Wolverhampton Express & Star

Railcar No. W55034 lies embedded in the brick wall at Stourbridge Town station on 1st March, 1990.   *Graham Gough/Wolverhampton Express & Star*

power for the line, stood driver 'Tommy' Wyatt and fireman Fisher, whilst at the other end of the train, guard 'Billy' Yardley manned the brake van. At the stop board located in the vicinity of Birmingham Street railway bridge the train drew to a halt allowing the guard to leave his van and pin down the brakes on the wagons. Suddenly, the train began to slip away, even though the train brakes had been applied. The crew made frantic efforts to stop it but to no avail : the fate of the 6.15 was sealed. At the bottom of the incline stood a formidable 15 foot stop block that had been constructed of compacted earth, stone and cement. It was toward this that the freight now headed. When it became clear that nothing could be done to prevent the train running into the block the crew leapt clear, fireman Fisher sustaining injuries to his lower leg and foot. The impact was tremendous, but the stop block did its work bringing the train to a violent halt. The engine remained upright, firmly embedded in the debris, although behind it the first nine wagons, eight full of iron billets the other anthracite nuts, telescoped into one another. Of the remaining wagons, a further nine were derailed, severely damaging seven. Despite the nature of the crash, breakdown gangs from both Stourbridge and Wolverhampton had completely cleared the area by 9.25 pm. It transpires that the accident could have been much worse, for flying debris had damaged a nearby petrol pump. Luckily, sparks from the engine did not ignite the escaping fuel.

On the evening of 1st May, 1900, a freight train bound for the Junction became derailed at the Town station. The engine hit the wooden footbridge supports and brought the bridge down upon track and locomotive. Unusually, the gang of boys that normally played on the bridge were on this occasion absent with the result that the only injuries sustained were those to the crew and these were relatively minor. The line was blocked until midnight by which time the Stourbridge breakdown gang had successfully cleared the line.

The Town station was also to figure in the headlines more than three-quarters of a century later when three accidents occurred in the space of 14 years, two of which were within 14 months of each other. All involved the single car diesel unit which operated the passenger 'shuttle', or 'Dodger' as it was known locally.

The first occurred on 2nd April, 1977, when the unit, No. M55012 driven by 56 years-old Wally Knowles, crashed through the buffers, sand barrier and a bridge parapet before coming to a halt with the front end overhanging Foster Street East some 14 feet below. Had the unit continued for around another six feet it would certainly have overbalanced. As it was, only the leading bogie followed the bricks and rubble into the street. The incident happened at 3.23 pm, coinciding, fortuitously, with the running of the Grand National which undoubtedly explained the lack of pedestrian traffic in what would otherwise have been a very busy area. As a result, injuries were confined to just nine of the 20 passengers aboard the car. A preliminary Inquiry into the accident was held by British Rail on the following Monday 4th April.

On 21st January, 1989 and 1st March, 1990, two further accidents were to occur at the Town station. Both incidents saw the single car diesel unit overrun the tracks to crash through the wall beyond. However, there was no 14 ft drop to await them as the area by this time had been redeveloped to enable the bus station to be enlarged. Amazingly, the buffer stop that had been demolished in the accident in 1989 had not been replaced at the time of the second so there was very little to stop car No. W55034. Luckily, neither accident resulted in a fatality although the guard involved in the 1989 mishap received a suspected fractured neck. Apparently, the first crash may have been caused by trespassers on the track distracting the driver who consequently misjudged his braking. The British Rail investigation into the 1990 incident found the accident to have been caused by brake failure.

Along the Line

On the evening of 22nd January, 1889, the good people of Cradley looked out of their windows to find the railway station occupied by troops of the 1st Worcestershire Volunteer Battalion. Four Companies from Halesowen, Dudley, Oldbury and Stourbridge, comprising 150 officers and men under the command of Major Adams, had been instructed to 'defend' the station against an 'enemy' who was marching upon the town from the direction of Worcester. The exercise commenced at 6.20 pm when the Stourbridge Company 'fell-in' and headed by the military band marched into the town and took up defensive positions alongside their comrades around the station. At about 9.00 pm, with minimum 'casualties', the troops marched out, leaving behind a community very much relieved to know that their town's defence would be in the hands of such a resolute body of men.

Cradley station was again in the news in 1902; this time for less warlike activities. To commemorate the Coronation of Edward VII, the station garden on both platforms had been planted out in labelia and pyrethrum. The larger up platform garden carried the message 'HM Edward VII crowned 26th June, 1902', whilst the smaller garden on the down platform had the motto 'Cradley Heath and Cradley, GWR' with scrolls planted out underneath. Approximately 3,000 plants had been used in the display, many of which had been contributed by passengers using the station. Unfortunately, the Coronation was postponed as the future King was indisposed through illness. However, all was not lost as on 20th December, 1902, station master Mr W. Harris and his staff of four, Messrs F.A. Hingley, J. Grove, G. Humphries and W.H. Tustin, were awarded the £5 first prize for the best kept station garden in the district. The Great Western Directors distributed annually prizes to the value of £250. The local competition had been judged by Mr Murphy (superintendent of the Birmingham District) who for the second time in three years awarded first prize to the station gardeners of Cradley.

One of the major events in the Black Country calendar was the 2/3 week hop picking season in the counties of Worcester and Hereford. Originally seen as an event attended 'by the dregs of humanity', the 1902 exodus received a far better press with families being described in much more charitable terms. There were numerous 'specials' from the Black Country which delivered the throng to the various country sites that, to many, would be the nearest thing to a holiday they would experience in their lives. September 13th saw the first 'hop pickers' special leave the Black Country loaded with 300, the vast majority of whom would be women and children. Each hop picker would be paid 1s. hiring-on fee and given a rail warrant to his or her destination. Altogether, some 30,000 people escaped the industrial dirt for the clean air of the countryside with around 10,000 coming from Cradley, Cradley Heath, Dudley and Lye, the bulk of these (about 4,000) being drawn from the Cradley area. Parties from Old Hill, Rowley and Halesowen, plus groups from all the stations between Wolverhampton, Birmingham and Stourbridge, helped to swell the numbers. However, this mass migration did pose problems for the education system, with the result that some school boards changed the summer holiday arrangements to coincide with the season and so help combat absenteeism. In years gone by, all the family went on the adventure leaving the Black Country cottage industries, such as hand made nails, at a standstill. By 1902 labour was less concentrated and the various trades in the district did not close down simultaneously. The man of the house, even if his work prevented him from enjoying the countryside during the week, would often leave for the hop fields to join his family at the end of the week to return early on Monday morning.

The year 1902 was also notable for a significant political victory for the Labour interest in the area. On 17th May, Mr Oliver Jenkins of Wollescote, a Great Western goods guard by occupation, successfully contested one of nine seats at the Lye and Wollescote Urban Council elections. However, Mr Jenkins was then subsequently dismissed from his post for failing to turn up on his rostered duty, which happened to be on the evening the result was declared! Mr Jenkins excused his absenteeism by referring to the lateness of the hour when the result was announced, plus the fact that on the day in question his wife was taken ill. An active member of the Amalgamated Society of Railway Servants (ASRS), he had been secretary of the local branch for the past 2½ years. Rumour had it, that in addition to not sending word of his impending absence, his local employers had been so incensed that a workman had been elected that a petition was proposed (if not actually sent) requesting that the company dismiss him. The *Railway Review* (journal of the ASRS) spoke of Mr Oliver as someone whose 'restless energy in all working class questions has honoured him with martyrdom for his principles'.

The General Strike 1926

Commencing on 4th May, 1926, the General Strike followed quickly on the heels of the Miners' strike which had begun three days earlier on 1st May. The immediate consequence of this industrial action at Stourbridge was a complete withdrawal of services worked from the depot and no trains from elsewhere on the region were reported as passing through. Apart from the disruption this caused to people using the railways to get to work, major employers in the area were soon forced to close. Messrs John Bradley and Company, the major ironworks in the town, was immediately affected due to a fuel shortage at the furnaces and no rail transport to ship finished products from the goods yard. However, the area seemed to be generally quiet and only a few minor incidents were reported.

On the opening day of the strike, Great Western officials walking the line between Cradley Heath and Old Hill came across 14 fog detonators placed on the line. Initially, strikers were thought to have put them there possibly in an attempt to bring to a halt any train using the line. However, it was later concluded that this was probably the work of children who had broken into a nearby lineside hut. The second day saw a few trains in the area, this being attributed to the Great Western attempting to run at least an emergency service. On the 10th and 11th, a number of volunteers who were attempting to move goods out of the sidings at Lye were subjected to verbal abuse and some mud was thrown. A large crowd, consisting mainly of women, had gathered at the station and was attempting to intimidate those working there. However, the situation did not develop into anything too nasty and the police, although presumably keeping a close eye on developments, did not need to intervene.

Also on 11th May, Great Western officials were able to move a light engine from Stourbridge engine sheds to Halesowen goods station where it was required to move several wagons holding urgently required goods. On the day after there was a feeling in the town that the resolve of the strikers was beginning to crumble and a number of freights were again seen passing through the district. In addition four passenger trains each way were now working the Stourbridge Extension and it was also reported at Brierley Hill that some trains were working through on the ex-OWWR. The General Strike did end on 12th May (although railwaymen generally did not return to work until Friday 14th May) and the Great Western announced its intention to continue working an emergency service over the weekend, but that by Monday up to 50 per cent of the normal services in the district should again be running.

Dean '2021' class 0-6-0ST No. 2108 is seen at Stourbridge Junction on 24th April, 1932.

H.C. Casserley

Also seen at Stourbridge Junction on the same day was No. 2104, the pannier tank version of the same class of locomotive.   *H.C. Casserley*

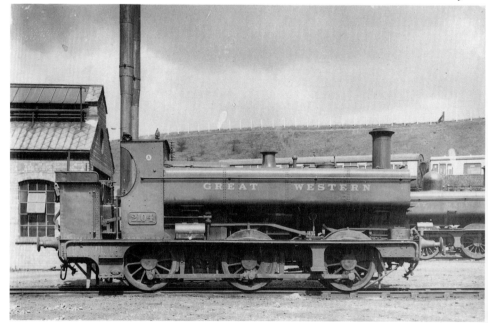

Chapter Nine

Locomotives of Stourbridge
(1901-1966)

Locomotives at Stourbridge

Before leaving 'the Railways of Stourbridge', a look will be taken at the locomotives which were allocated to the depot, or which could be regularly seen at the head of traffic in the area. The depot belonged to the Wolverhampton Division which under BR encompassed the '84' group of sheds headed by Stafford Road (84A). Stourbridge Shed was always renowned for its large locomotive allocation, a position enjoyed until the run down of steam in the 1960s, and although the shed was never seen in quite the same light as its more illustrious near neighbour at Wolverhampton (Stafford Road), the role that the depot played in the provision of locomotives for a wide range of duties should never be underestimated.

Stourbridge Shed - A Locomotive Survey 1901-1947

Stourbridge was principally a freight depot, supplying locomotives and crews for the trip workings to Oxley Sidings and Bordesley Junction, the local Bank Trains, branch line goods trains (Kingswinford, Windmill End and Halesowen branches) and longer distance services to such places as Pontypool Road. However, the shed's range of duties also included providing the motive power for local passenger turns over the main line to Wolverhampton, Worcester and Birmingham, as well as the Stourbridge Town branch, the Dudley-Old Hill-Halesowen line, the Dudley-Birmingham (Snow Hill) services via Great Bridge and the short-lived Wombourn and Oldbury branches. Finally, a less glamorous, but equally important task was ensuring that the required number of shunting engines were available for the numerous yards and sidings to be found on the OWWR between Stourbridge and Dudley (including Tipton Basin and Prince's End) and along the Stourbridge Extension to Old Hill, and during and after World War II, Langley Green sidings and the Oldbury branch. As can be seen below, the allocation tended to be dominated by the tank engine, although in later years diesels took over many of the duties formally associated with these engines.

Table Eleven

Locomotive Allocations - A Summary of Types, 1901 to 1945
(This is only intended to give the reader a guide to typical locomotive allocations to be found at Stourbridge during each of the years shown below.)

Type	1901	1905	1910	1915	1921	1925	1930	1935	1940	1945
0-6-0ST/PT	28	34	36	34	33	33	32	36	31	31
0-4-2T	8	10	5	2	2	3	3		2	2
0-6-0	5	8	11	11	13	10	6	7	2	2
0-6-2T									2	2
2-4-0T				4	5	4				
2-4-2T		3	4	4	5	6				
2-4-0			1	1	1	1	1			
2-6-0						1	4	5	4	4
2-6-2T							21	22	22	22
4-4-0	1				3	3			1	1
Total	42	55	57	56	59	61	70	70	64	64

Class '1016' 0-6-0ST No. 1072 at Stourbridge Junction *c.* 1921.   *Real Photographs*

Great Western outside-framed 0-6-0PT No. 325. This was originally built by Beyer, Peacock in
1864 as a 5 ft goods tender engine.   *Kidderminster Railway Museum*

At the turn of the century, Stourbridge possessed a large number of 0-6-0 saddle tanks. However, the GWR was already planning the conversion of the saddle tanks into panniers and during 1910 this reconstruction programme began in earnest. This process though took a number of years to complete, therefore it was not unusual for both saddle and pannier tanks from the same class to be seen working next to one another. Several of Stourbridge's engines actually left the shed as one type only to return from the Works as another, e.g. '655' class No. 1777 and '2021' No. 2056, both originally saddle tanks, were fitted with pannier tanks in 1923. Eventually, the saddle tank disappeared and although the modified engines lingered on for some considerable time, these too eventually gave way to new designs. However, the pannier tank itself was to outstay all other GWR designs at Stourbridge, with members of the '57XX' class remaining at the shed until the end of steam in July 1966.

On 1st January, 1901, Stourbridge's 0-6-0ST allocation was 28, 16 of which being Dean '645'/'1501' single-framed types built 1872-1881. Additionally there were eight class '655' built 1892-1897 and four class '2021' built 1897-1905. Together, engines from these classes tended to dominate the light tank engine pool at the shed up to the start of World War II, although the writing had begun to appear on the wall for these elderly engines as early as 1931 when modern class '57XX' locomotives began to arrive at the depot. The first to be ousted from Stourbridge were the '645'/'1501' class which had all left by the end of 1936, however, a small number of locomotives from each of the '655' and '2021' classes did manage to soldier on into the British Rail era. The last '655', No. 1749, did not last very long being withdrawn from the shed during October 1948, although the final '2021' at Stourbridge, No. 2107, fared much better remaining until December 1952 before being transferred to Croes Newydd. An interesting locomotive was No. 2105, one of 12 class '2021s' allocated to Stourbridge as early as 1910. During 1939 this engine, along with nine classmates, was provided with increased braking power, a modification that would be especially useful on the severe gradients to be found in the Black Country. No. 2105 subsequently returned to Stourbridge c. 1940/41 after being renumbered into the '2181' class as No. 2189. However, predating its arrival were three other '2181' types; Nos. 2185/86 which arrived on 18th July and 4th August, 1939 respectively, and during April 1940, No. 2187. All four were taken over by BR, the last one at Stourbridge being No. 2187, which was withdrawn from there on 26th February, 1952.

Despite the predominance of the above classes during much of the period in question several other 0-6-0Ts also found a home at the depot, albeit only in limited numbers. For example, by 1905 there were five '850'/'1901' class locomotives, a smaller and lighter design of 0-6-0 Saddle tank that had been built at Wolverhampton between 1874 and 1895. From about 1910 the depot's allocation gradually reduced although one or two could still be seen pottering about as late as 1931, the last one to be found at the depot at this time being No. 2004. The class did make a brief comeback in 1935 in the shape of No. 987. Built in June 1875, this engine spent its last few months at the depot before being sent for scrap during April 1936.

By the beginning of 1910 two of Beyer, Peacock's class '322' Nos. 324 and 326, which were amongst six that had been rebuilt 1878-1885 from 0-6-0 tender locomotives, could be found at the shed. In fact Stourbridge was a regular haunt for this class and possibly with the exception of No. 322, all spent some time there. Unfortunately, for three of them, the shed was also to be their last. Nos. 325 and 327 were condemned there on 15th February, 1930, the pair being withdrawn during March the same year, whilst No. 323 was withdrawn on 2nd July, 1932.

A year into the Great War and Stourbridge had received an ancient double-framed Armstrong class '1016' No. 1027 built at Wolverhampton during September 1867, and a solitary '2721' No. 2778, a relative youngster which had been constructed at Swindon in October 1900. The former was one of several of the class to be employed at Stourbridge between 1915-1925, two other known examples being Nos. 1070/72. Prior to the 1914-18 War engines from the '2721' class had virtually been unknown in the area, in fact No. 2778 had the distinction of being one of only four such machines to have reached the Wolverhampton

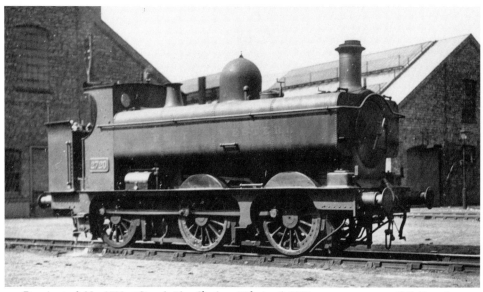

Pannier tank No. 2720 at Stourbridge Shed on 24th April, 1932.　　　*H.C. Casserley*

'655' class 0-6-0PT No. 1777 in the roundhouse at Stourbridge on 24th April, 1932.

H.C. Casserley

Division by the 1920s, the remainder being chiefly used on heavy shunting work in South Wales. This engine probably only stayed for a short time, although from c. 1934 onwards two or three of the class were allocated to Stourbridge including Nos. 2744/2771 and 2777 which were there in July 1943. The class lasted at the depot until the BR era, with No. 2771 (built September 1900) being the last when withdrawn on 2nd June, 1950.

During 1920/21, the variety of 0-6-0T engines at Stourbridge was further enhanced by the addition of two Dean 'Buffalos' or '1076' class engines Nos. 1136/40 built 1874-75, a type that had for many years been employed on longer distance mineral trains between Pontypool Road, Worcester and Wolverhampton. By March 1925 another type had arrived in the shape of '1854' (or '1701') class No. 1712, one of only a very small number to have been allocated to the Wolverhampton Division at this time. The 'Buffalos' only stayed at the depot until 1930, although members of the '1854'/'1701' class had a much longer residence with No. 1766 present during 1930/31 and No. 1863 from 1933/34. By 1945 No. 1863 had been joined by Nos. 1763/93, although all three left Stourbridge shortly afterwards. This diversity of 0-6-0 tank engines persisted at Stourbridge until the early 1950s.

In 1929, the building of heavy shunting tank locomotives was resumed with the construction of the '57XX' class 0-6-0PT and four of these locomotives, Nos. 5790/91/94/95, arrived at Stourbridge during 1930/31. From then on the numbers gradually increased reaching a pre-war maximum of nine, although by July 1943 their number had doubled and by the end of December 1947 Stourbridge could count 21 of these engines on its books.

The influx of up-to-date tank engines after the end of World War II included a number of '74XX' class 0-6-0PTs. However, the GWR register shows that this type may have made an appearance at Stourbridge much earlier. No. 7403, built during August 1936, was apparently at the depot at least during the four weeks leading up to 9th January, 1937 and probably later. It may have even been delivered new to Stourbridge, perhaps for a trial period? Whatever the reason, this engine seems to have been the only example to reach the shed pre-war. During the four month period May-August 1945 it was reported that No. 7402 had been allocated to Stourbridge, followed in 1947 by No. 7428. By 1948, the class had become well established at the depot. The '74XXs' were specifically drafted in to work the Halesowen branch to Longbridge, a move which resulted in the withdrawal or transfer of many of the depot's class '655' and '2021' engines. Finally, during 1947 the shed held one other elderly 0-6-0 tank engine No. 1835. This ancient Dean '1813' single-framed locomotive, which had been built in March 1883, remained at Stourbridge until withdrawn in 1949; more will be said of this engine in the following section.

Whilst the 0-6-0PT tended to dominate the small tank engine allocation at Stourbridge, a number of other types were to be well represented over the years. January 1901 saw eight Armstrong 0-4-2T '517' class engines (built 1868-1885) at the depot, a figure which had increased to 10 by 1905. This was the peak time for the class and by 1910 their numbers at the depot had been halved. The second decade of the century saw the allocation reduce even further and by 1920/21 only two of the class were present. By this time these engines, Nos. 523/25, had probably been equipped with auto-gear, certainly their successors in 1925, Nos. 826 and 1482, were so fitted. By the beginning of 1930 No. 1482 had been joined by classmates Nos. 524 and 839, although by the following year only No. 1482 remained. In the early 1930s the reliability of Stourbridge's steam railmotors may have been causing concern and at times only two of these machines regularly seemed to be in service. This situation possibly explains the appearance c. 1931/32 of the timeworn No. 617 (built August 1871), one of about 40 2-4-0Ts '455' class 'Metro' tanks which had been fitted with auto-gear as a stop-gap measure during 1928-30 pending the arrival of Collett's replacements. 'Metro' tanks, though, were not strangers to Stourbridge with several, including Nos. 6, 460, 617, 1405/19/45/95 amongst others, having spent some time there between 1915-25. The problems for Stourbridge Shed staff were eased when two of the auto-fitted Collett '64XX' class 0-6-0PT, Nos. 6404/05, were delivered new to the depot during April 1932. At about the same time Stourbridge's last '517' class locomotive, No. 1425, left the depot as in all probability did 2-4-0T No. 617,

'57XX' class 0-6-0PT No. 8718 at Stourbridge Shed on 30th October, 1965.   *R.W. Hinton*

'3571' class 0-4-2T No. 3575 stands just outside Stourbridge Junction *c.* 1925. This locomotive was possibly the only member of its class to be actually allocated to Stourbridge.

Real Photographs

consequently, auto-train working was left in the hands of Nos. 6404/05, although by the end of 1934 a third engine, No. 6418, had arrived to share the burden. The delivery of Collett 0-4-2T '48XX' class locomotives during 1935/36, i.e. Nos. 4853/57/58, freed the '64XX' class engines for duties elsewhere and by 1940 only No. 6418 remained. This was transferred to Stafford Road in 1943. During 1946 the '48XX' engines were renumbered into the more familiar '14XX' series and by the end of 1947 three of these, Nos. 1410/14/38, were to be found there. No. 1458, which as No. 4858 was one of the first three engines of the type to be allocated to Stourbridge, renewed its acquaintance with shed staff when it returned c. November 1950. This locomotive was the last of its class at Stourbridge before transfer to Southall on 27th December, 1957, thereby ending an association with the depot that had lasted for over 20 years.

A rarely mentioned class which had a brief affair with Stourbridge was the 0-4-2T '3571' type, a development of the '517' built during 1895. These locomotives were specifically designed for local passenger and branch line work and when No. 3575 arrived c. 1925 it may possibly have been employed on services between Stourbridge Junction and Kidderminster. This engine was not fitted with auto-apparatus, therefore its use to Stourbridge may have been limited.

In addition to the 0-4-2T and the 2-4-0T locomotives, Stourbridge also acquired a number of Dean '36XX' 2-4-2T engines that had been built in the years 1900-1903. By 1905 three of these locomotives, Nos. 3606/29/30, had been transferred to the depot, probably for use on quicker suburban traffic between Kidderminster and Birmingham. The growth in this particular traffic necessitated further engines of this class being drafted in and by March 1925 six engines, Nos. 3608/09/18/21/24/27, were working from the shed. Their reign was subsequently ended by the introduction of the 2-6-2T designs and by 1929/30 all of the 2-4-2Ts had been replaced. The '36XX' was the only significant class utilising this wheel arrangement constructed by the GWR, but the '51XX' made them redundant and all were withdrawn between 1930 and 1934.

The 2-6-2T type probably first arrived at Stourbridge c. 1925; certainly two class '3901' engines, Nos. 3902/03, had taken up their duties there by about 17th May, 1925. These interesting locomotives were actually converted in the Works from 'Dean Goods' Nos. 2498 and 2501 emerging as 2-6-2Ts instead of 0-6-0s in February and May 1907 respectively. However, they did not last too long and like the 2-4-2Ts were replaced by the new 2-6-2Ts around 1929. By 1934 the class was extinct.

Stourbridge's allocation of the new 2-6-2T can basically be described as being comprised of four types; the first were engines numbered in the series 5100 and 5111 to 5149, which were originally '31XX' class locomotives built between 1903 and 1906 and later modified to achieve a better weight distribution. The second was an up-to-date version of the ex-'31XX' class which had been constructed over a 20-year period from 1929, the first batch of these being numbered 5101-5110, the remainder from 5150 to 5199 and then from 4100 to 4179. The third was the smaller '45XX' class introduced 1906 weighing just 57 tons, whilst the fourth type was a 61 ton modified version known as the class '4575', built 1927-29. At the beginning of January 1930 the shed possessed no less than 11 of the larger and 10 of the two smaller types. However, as the 1930s progressed the GWR must have considered that the '45XX'/'4575s' would be more usefully employed elsewhere. Over the years the numbers at the depot dwindled until in January 1935 only No. 4511 remained and this too had departed by the following year. To compensate for the loss of these engines, Stourbridge received a corresponding number of '51XX'/'5101' machines, consequently, by the end of 1939, there were 21 of these allocated to the depot. By 31st December, 1947 Stourbridge's quota had been increased to 25, the type having become firmly established as the backbone of the suburban services worked by Stourbridge crews.

One 2-6-2T class not normally associated with Stourbridge was the '81XX' type. These engines utilised the frames of withdrawn '51XX' types (ex-'31XX') and therefore could probably be classified as 'rebuilds', the work being carried out during 1938/39. Only No.

'51XX' class 2-6-2T No. 4140 at Stourbridge Shed on 15th September, 1963.   *Joe Moss Collection*

'51XX' class 2-6-2T No. 4175 and '57XX' class 0-6-0PT No. 3658 at Stourbridge Shed on 30th October, 1965. To the right of the locomotives is the extended coal stage.   *R.W. Hinton*

8103 has definitely been identified as having operated from Stourbridge, the engine being sent there direct from the Works at the end of 1938. It was subsequently used alongside '51XX'/'5101' engines on local passenger diagrams. The engine was known to have been at Stourbridge during World War II, remaining there until at least July 1943. By 1947 it had been allocated to Oswestry.

The final tank engine design to be found at Stourbridge was the 0-6-2T '56XX' class (built 1924-1928). This design had been a firm favourite with the original South Wales railways and therefore it was not surprising that on their introduction many '56XX' class engines found gainful employment in the Welsh valleys. However, several did arrive in the Wolverhampton Division quite early on, although Stourbridge may not have received a permanent allocation until 1942 when No. 6665 arrived in the area. This locomotive was followed around 1944 by No. 6684 and by 1947 the class had become firmly established at Stourbridge with eight engines, Nos. 6617/46/65/67/74/77/78/84, on the books at the end of December. Classified by BR as '5MT', several examples remained at the depot until withdrawn during 1965.

Last but not least were the tender engines and although as a type they were always in the minority, especially during the GWR period, their presence and contribution cannot be ignored. One of the first known examples known by the author was a Swindon built '131' class 0-6-0 No. 313 which had been allocated to the depot as at 1st January, 1901 remaining there until at least 1902. In general this class tended to be associated with duties over the more northern parts of the GWR system where they were presumably shedded for most of their working lives. However, by 1921 '131' class 0-6-0 No. 132, one of only three to survive the Grouping, had arrived at Stourbridge, remaining until withdrawn during August 1924. No. 132's classmate No. 146 was also there in 1921, although this engine moved on to Shrewsbury where it was to become the last example of its class, being scrapped in April 1925.

From 1901 until about 1920, when the 'Dean Goods' began to arrive in the area, many of the local freight trains, even perhaps some of the passenger diagrams, could be found in the hands of 'Standard Goods'/'388' class locomotives. Built between 1866-1876, Stourbridge had certainly received several of these engines by 1901: i.e. Nos. 407/09/34 and 1103, whilst Nos. 434, 1103 and No. 1105, were there during January 1902. By 1910 the shed's quota had been increased to five, Nos. 428/31/702/95 and 1105. During 1919-21 large numbers of 'Standard Goods' engines were taken out of service, many of their duties being taken over by the newly constructed Mixed Traffic 2-6-0s. At Stourbridge this decimation of the class led to a noticeable reduction in numbers at the depot; by 1921 the allocation had reduced to three and by 1925 two, Nos. 396 and 1087. Over the years Stourbridge gained a reputation for providing a last port of call for many an engine approaching, or in, the twilight of their careers. This was the case for ageing '388' No. 1094 which had arrived c. 1931. Inevitably put to good use, this engine went on to gain a small degree of fame by being the last but one of its class to be withdrawn. This was in March 1934, the last '388', No. 1195, being sent for scrap during October 1934.

A similar type to the 'Standard Goods' was the smaller-wheeled Armstrong '927' class or 'Coal Engines', the name being conferred upon them by the fact of their regular employment on the coal trains between Birkenhead and Pontypool Road. The introduction of newer engines on this work resulted in their transfer to other areas and by 1910 four of these locomotives, Nos. 940/44/45/46, had found their way to Stourbridge where presumably they were engaged upon local mineral workings. This quartet probably continued operating from the depot until at least 1915. Only four of the class were to survive the Grouping and one of these, unsurprisingly, ended its days at Stourbridge. No. 934, built in March 1874 and the only example of the class to be superheated, arrived at the depot c. 1924 where it toiled away until November 1928, finally succumbing after outliving the rest of the class by more than three years. During its lifetime the engine was able to clock up an outstanding 1,144,799 miles.

Another class to be displaced from its original duties was the Gooch '57' outside-framed goods engine, the initial batch having been built at Swindon 1855-56 for use on principal freight workings. The first known example of this class to be allocated to Stourbridge was No. 58 during August 1902. Although this locomotive had moved on by January 1905, four others had arrived, Nos. 63/4/6/8, to be used, in all likelihood, on local freight workings. However, by the beginning of 1910 only No. 68 was present. All of this batch were subsequently withdrawn by 1913, although this was not quite the end of the story. During the early 1920s Stourbridge received No. 316, one of three that were built at Wolverhampton 1890-91, thirty-four years after the original batch had been completed at Swindon! This engine probably stayed at Stourbridge until about 1925 and in so doing became the last member of the class to remain in service. It was later transferred to Tyseley where it was withdrawn during November 1927.

It has already been mentioned that Stourbridge was home to several Beyer, Peacock '322' class tank engines that had been rebuilt from 0-6-0 tender locomotives. However, accompanying these engines were also a number of their un-rebuilt brothers. These efficient double-framed machines had also been originally employed on the Pontypool Road-Birkenhead coal trains before being relegated from the premier freight league to arguably lesser duties on the lines around the Black Country. Consequently, by 1921 Stourbridge had received Nos. 336/38/58 and by March 1925 Nos. 328/30/36/55. The latter group were probably the last of the class to be allocated to Stourbridge, the first three all being withdrawn during 1929. This was another example of Stourbridge providing a home for engines nearing the end of their useful life.

It has been mentioned that Stourbridge was also host to a small number of irregular visitors from lesser known classes. The first of these was No. 582 which had been allocated to Stourbridge by January 1902. This engine was one of 23 that Dean had reconstructed from 'Sir Daniel' class Singles to 0-6-0 goods engines during 1900-02; apparently not such a difficult task as might be supposed. The locomotive did not last too long at the depot, in fact it did not last too long anywhere as it was scrapped in 1904. Following the short-lived 'Sir Daniel' came No. 369, a member of the '360' class built in 1866 which was at the depot during 1905. Subsequent visits by the class were made by No. 367 in 1915 whilst No. 1015 arrived 1924/25. Completing this motley band of wanderers is No. 90, a '79' class engine that was built in its original form way back in February 1858 although it had been 'renewed' during June 1877 ('renewal' was a fairly vague term that tended to hide the fact that often little of the original engine was used in the 'renewed' version. Both class '79' and class '57' engines underwent this process). No. 90 was yet another former Pontypool Road-Birkenhead coal engine that must have been displaced by newer designs and condemned to while away its last remaining years working local freights. The engine arrived at Stourbridge c. 1910 and was later to be the third of its class to be withdrawn, the engine ending as scrap during August 1912.

Ultimately the most numerous 0-6-0 tender engines at Stourbridge were the 'Dean Goods' or '2301' class. The shed had four of these locomotives by 1921 and by 1938 this allocation had increased to seven, Nos. 2320/89, 2413/51, 2513/38/60. However, withdrawals during World War II decimated the class with the result that by July 1943 the depot's allocation of 'Dean Goods' had been reduced to one, No. 2389. This locomotive was subsequently withdrawn from Stourbridge in July 1944. Interestingly, a number of LNER 0-6-0s were drafted in during the War as replacements for those 'Dean Goods' appropriated by the War Department, more on this later. Accompanying the 'Dean Goods' at Stourbridge during 1934 was a single Dean '2361' class No. 2378, one of 20 such locomotives built 1885-1886 for freight duties.

The final class of 0-6-0 to be sent to Stourbridge during the first half of the century was the Collett '2251' built 1930-1948, these machines tending to supersede the 'Dean Goods' on local passenger and freight duties. No. 2275 may have made quite an early appearance at the depot, the GWR Register of Engines recording its presence there during 1934. Apart from this seemingly isolated incident, the class was very much a wartime addition to the shed's complement with Nos. 2279/81 appearing on the books during July 1943. By 31st December, 1947 four of these locomotives, Nos. 2246/70/79/81, had been allocated to the depot.

In addition to the 0-6-0 examples, a number of other types of tender locomotives could also be found in the dark recesses of the shed over the years. Amongst these were a few 2-4-0s, one of the more well known classes being the 'Stellas' which arrived at the depot c. 1920. Certainly by 1921 No. 3503 was there, as was No. 3507 early in 1925. These would probably have been used on local passenger traffic, a far cry from the principal services that the engines would earlier have been employed upon when stationed in the West Country during the 1890s. Strangely, according to the GWR Register of Engines, No. 3517 had been allocated to Stourbridge by January 1902. This seems slightly out of step with the early allocation history of the class, consequently, if any readers can offer any observations on this point the author would be only too happy to hear from them.

Apart from the above, Stourbridge also played host to two other, perhaps lesser known types of 2-4-0 up to and during World War I. By January 1910 the depot had received No. 725, a '717' class locomotive built June 1872, the engine remaining at the depot until at least 1915. In the latter part of the 19th century and the early part of the 20th, six of this class, including No. 725, had been allocated to Bordesley for hauling the Birmingham-Cardiff expresses to and from Hereford. When replaced by 4-4-0s, these engines were redeployed on local passenger services, probably those running between Birmingham, Stourbridge Junction and Worcester. No. 725 was withdrawn from Wolverhampton during August 1917 having clocked up in excess of 1,300,000 miles. The second example was the very interesting '196' class No. 210, which had been sent to the depot by 1915. Originally, this locomotive was West Midland Railway's No. 101, one of six 2-2-2 express engines built by Beyer, Peacock that were taken over by the GWR when the WMR was absorbed. The engine was virtually completely rebuilt during 1883 and emerged from the Works as a 2-4-0 built to George Armstrong's design.

It would appear that the last 2-4-0 to be allocated to Stourbridge was a Dean '3206' or 'Barnum'. This locomotive was No. 3214 which had arrived c. 1929/30, remaining at the depot until withdrawn on 21st March, 1931. No other examples of this class are known to have been allocated to Stourbridge.

During the period in question, the odd 4-4-0 tender locomotive could also be found on Stourbridge's books, examples of this type having been allocated there as early as 1901. However, between 1902 and the early 1920s, when several of the type were again seen at the depot, the 4-4-0 tender engine seemed to be rarely, if ever, allocated to Stourbridge. By 1925 '3300' class ('Bulldog') No. 3317 *Somerset* was part of the shed's allocation although on 11th March the engine was apparently involved in a straight swap with Shrewsbury's No. 3316 *St Columb*. During the same year, Stourbridge also enjoyed the company of two other 'Bulldogs', No. 3325 *Kenilworth* and No. 3450 *Peacock*. From 1925 to 1934, one or two 'Bulldogs' could usually be found at the depot. The 'Bulldogs' had for a number of years been associated with the Birmingham-Cardiff expresses, so their arrival at Stourbridge could imply that these engines had been replaced as the principal motive power on these services, being employed instead on 'semi-fast' passenger trains between Hereford, Worcester, Stourbridge and Birmingham? After 1934, 'Bulldogs' had gone elsewhere, although c. 1947 saw their return in the shape of No. 3450 *Peacock*. This engine remained at Stourbridge until withdrawn on 21st December, 1949.

The third type of 4-4-0 to be associated with Stourbridge was the '3252' class 'Duke'. During World War II at least one 'Duke' arrived at the shed for use on the Severn Valley line; certainly No. 3284 *Isle of Jersey* had been allocated there c. 1943. This locomotive was one of 11 survivors that in 1947 were renumbered into the '90XX' series as No. 9084. The 'Duke' was subsequently transferred to Machynlleth at the end of 1949.

Stourbridge Shed was also the home to two types of 2-6-0 tender engines, with possibly the earliest example being a member of the '26XX' class, known to all as the 'Aberdares'. Built between 1900-07, these locomotives were primarily designed for use on coal traffic so their utilisation on Black Country metals would be far from unexpected. The GWR Register of Engines indicates that No. 2627 may have been sent to Stourbridge sometime in 1904 before being transferred to Pontypool Road on 7th January, 1905. However, such an early allocation

'Aberdare' class 2-6-0 No. 2615 at Stourbridge Shed on 24th April, 1932. The line to the right runs back to the main line.   *H.C. Casserley*

Also at Stourbridge shed on 24th April, 1932 was steam railmotor No. 65.   *H.C. Casserley*

to Stourbridge seems to be a little inconsistent with the history of the class, so it may be advisable to treat this entry with some caution. What is much more likely is that 'Aberdares' had been dispatched to the shed by 1925 or the beginning of 1926,one of the first being No. 2615. Early in 1930 this locomotive had been joined by Nos. 2610/39/70, which were on the depot's books by 18th January, 1930. By 1932 their numbers at Stourbridge had increased to six, although four engines seemed to be the more usual allocation, at least between 1934 and 1940. One of the 1934 locomotives, No. 2655, had quite a lengthy residence, staying at the shed until withdrawn on 8th June, 1949. In fact two of the last four 'Aberdares' to be found on British Railways were at Stourbridge, although it was to be No. 2667 which was to outlive the shed's No. 2620 by about a month to become the final '26XX' to be withdrawn, being sent for scrap during October 1949.

The shed's second group of 2-6-0s was comprised of G.J. Churchward's standard 2-cylinder engines of the '43XX' class built 1911-1932. The versatility and usefulness of these locomotives is well known and by the 1930s the Wolverhampton Division had acquired a large number, although Stourbridge's early experience of this type of engine can be traced back to the 1920s. By the late 1930s, the '43XX' class engines began to be seen more frequently at the depot and Nos. 5346/48 were sent there c. 1935/36. From then on the depot enjoyed the luxury of a regular, if small, allocation including, during 1938, Nos. 5346, 6346/99, and in 1940, Nos. 5370, 6332 and 7310; however, by 1945 only No. 7310 remained. Whilst none of these valuable engines were based at Stourbridge on 31st December, 1947, the class did reappear during June/July 1948 when Nos. 5300 and 6332 arrived together from Oxley.

By the late 1930s the GWR had introduced into Stourbridge's small and ageing fleet of heavy freight locomotives one of the powerful Churchward '28XX' class 2-8-0s. In August 1939 No. 2830, the first of its type to be allocated to the depot, began a short wartime spell that lasted until at least 1940. As far as it is known, this may have been the only example of the class to be assigned to the depot during the War years. By September/October 1946 Stourbridge had acquired Nos. 2852/74/86, although by 31st December, 1947 the allocation had been reduced to one, No. 2852. In view of the traffic passing through the area, enginemen must have wondered when they were going to receive more of these hard working locomotives.

A rare addition to Stourbridge's pool of engines at the end of World War II was 'Grange' class 4-6-0 No. 6812 *Chesford Grange*, the engine taking up its duties during September 1946. No. 6812 remained at the depot for about a year. Although 'Granges' became quite familiar at Stourbridge during the BR era none, apart from No. 6812, are known to have been allocated to the depot previously.

Just after the turn of the century, Stourbridge began to receive GWR steam railmotors for use on local passenger services. The first to arrive at the depot is thought to have been No. 32 which was allocated there on 28th December, 1904. This was soon followed in 1905 by Nos. 25, 35, 36, 37, 53 and 27, although the last mentioned was transferred to Kidderminster on 9th December after about a month. No. 27 would have been employed on the Bewdley-Kidderminster service. Altogether, 99 of these machines were built between 1903-08 for use throughout the GWR system and many did spend some time at Stourbridge. During both 1910 and 1915 as many as eight railmotors were on the depot's books, including Nos. 15, 16, 18, 21, 25, 28, 64, 67, 68, 69, 70, 79, 93 and 95. By 1925 there seemed to be major mechanical problems plaguing the depot's allocation and only No. 37 appeared to spend any length of time in service, with Nos 38, 68, 89 and 95 languishing in Swindon Works for months at a time. Reliability may have been a persistent problem with the fleet as a whole, for by the end of 1920 thirty-four machines had been withdrawn and by 1st January, 1931 only 30 were actually in revenue earning service. Possibly the last railmotors sent to Stourbridge were Nos. 64, 66 and 93 which were there at the beginning of 1934. By October 1935 the GWR had withdrawn all remaining machines, although it is thought that Stourbridge's railmotors had departed by the end of the previous year. The successor to the steam railmotor was the GWR diesel railcar which first arrived at Stourbridge c. 1940, Nos. 3 and 4 being there in January of that year. At the beginning of 1945 these had been joined by Nos. 25, 26 and 29.

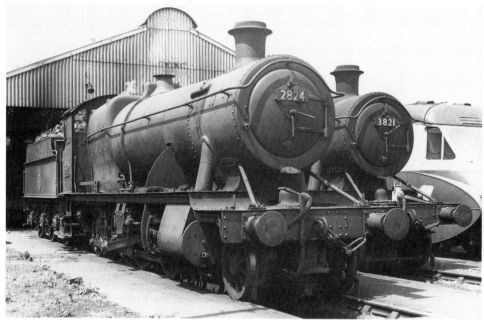

'28XX' class 2-8-0s Nos. 2824 and 3821 at Stourbridge Shed on 14th June, 1953, with an ex-GWR railcar in the background.   *Norman Preedy*

'Grange' class 4-6-0 No. 6867 *Peterson Grange* is seen at Stourbridge on the same day.
                    Norman Preedy

Locomotives and Workings in and around the Stourbridge Area

One of the most well known workings is of course the intensively operated Stourbridge Junction to Stourbridge Town shuttle service, known in steam days as the 'Dodger'. This service was worked at various times by a range of motive power including the steam railmotor from January 1905 to *c.* 1934, the GWR diesel railcar and two generations of BR diesel railcars. However, the service was operated for many years by an auto-train which utilised a single auto-trailer, one of which had been named *Wren*, attached to an 0-4-2T 'push and pull' equipped class '48XX'/'14XX' tank engine. *Wren* was one of a batch of additional trailers that had been built by British Railways during 1952. Apparently, BR's original intention was to name all of these trailers after British birds, although only two, *Thrush* and *Wren*, were so treated. Due to the nature of this service, there were often difficulties with coaling the locomotive. However, this was overcome in a fairly novel manner. At approximately 11.30 am, a tender locomotive would leave the shed fully coaled and would draw up alongside the Town engine using the down goods line. From this position coal would be shovelled from the tender into the bunker of the 0-4-2T. By about the beginning of 1957, the regular steam-hauled service had been replaced by a single diesel unit, the duty initially being worked by an ex-GWR railcar. However, the auto-trains were not totally banished from the line as occasionally an 0-4-2T, or later, an 0-6-0PT, could be seen working the service, presumably deputising for a failed diesel unit. When this steeply inclined branch was steam worked, the locomotive would have to be positioned so that it faced the Town station. Consequently, the auto-coach would always be propelled towards the Junction.

By far the most numerous locomotive allocated to Stourbridge Shed was the ubiquitous 0-6-0 pannier tank. These little locomotives were regularly employed on shunting, banking and operating the numerous trip workings. Prior to World War II, pannier tanks at the depot were largely those in Power Group 'A': class '1501', '2021' etc., but as older engines were withdrawn, more modern panniers in Power Class 'C' began to appear in increasing numbers. These newer engines were in the main '57XX' class panniers, although a small number of Hawksworth's heavy shunting '94XX' class 0-6-0PT were also allocated to the depot in the early 1950s. Of the latter Nos. 8418/19 were dispatched new to Stourbridge during April 1950. No. 8419, together with Nos. 8437/38 and 9477, left the depot at various times between August and November 1955, the former being transferred to Treherbert, the remaining three to Cardiff East Dock.

Probably the most arduous duty asked of the small tank engine was to work out of Stourbridge Goods. Originally, working of the Goods branch was limited to engines in Group 'A', however, either during or just after World War II, the line was upgraded to give access to locomotives in the Group 'C' power band. The notorious incline out of Stourbridge Goods meant that Group 'A' locomotives working up the slope were usually confined to trains consisting of the equivalent of seven Class 1 wagon loads (112 tons). But by 1947 class '57XX' engines were allowed a maximum train weight of 160 tons, although by 1951 the limit for all Group 'C' locomotives working out of the Goods yard had been reduced to 144 tons. When it came to the test though, it was the elderly Group 'A' No. 1863, a class '1854' engine, which would lift its train out of the yard with ease, putting to shame its newer and more powerful brothers who sometimes required two attempts to scale the daunting gradient. It was probably a sad day at the shed when this spirited little performer was transferred to Stafford Road Shed in Wolverhampton.

Stourbridge also supplied motive power for workings over the Netherton and Halesowen branch (N&H) which included both freight and local passenger services operating between Dudley, Old Hill and Halesowen, including the 'Workmen's Specials' which ran from Old Hill over the southern section of the N&H to Halesowen before continuing to Longbridge over the Halesowen Railway. In 1905, many of the loco-hauled passenger services between Halesowen, Old Hill and Dudley were taken over by Stourbridge based steam railmotors. In fact these machines were also used on the short Oldbury branch from Langley Green and

'14XX' class 0-4-2T No. 1458 propels the auto-coach towards Stourbridge Junction from the Town and is seen passing St John's Parish Church on 19th April, 1954. The line on the right is the independent goods line to Amblecote yard.   *W.F. Deebank*

'14XX' class 0-4-2T No. 1414 stands at Stourbridge Town station on 8th March, 1956.
                                                                    R.M. Casserley

'31XX' class 2-6-2T No. 3101 approaches Old Hill with the 1.15 pm Stourbridge Junction to Birmingham (Snow Hill) train on 13th August, 1955. *R.M. Casserley*

'43XX' class 2-6-0 No. 7301 arrives at Old Hill on the 1.15 pm Birmingham (Snow Hill) to Kidderminster on 13th August, 1955. *R.M. Casserley*

Table Twelve

Steam Locomotive Allocations to Stourbridge

Date*	0-4-2T	0-6-0T	0-6-2T	2-6-2T	0-6-0	4-4-0	2-6-0	2-8-0	4-6-0	Total
January 1948	14XX (3)	1501 (2), 1813 (1), 2021 (3), 2181 (4), 655/2700 (3), 57XX (21), 74XX (2)	56XX (8)	51XX (27)	2251 (4)	Bulldog (1) Duke (1)	Aberdare (2)	28XX (1)		83
January 1951	14XX (3)	16XX (1), 2021 (2), 2181 (3), 57XX (22), 74XX (8), 94XX (3)	56XX (9)	51XX (24)	2251 (3)		43XX (6)	28XX (6)	Grange (2)	92
January 1954	14XX (3)	16XX (2), 57XX (24), 74XX (8), 94XX (4)	56XX (13)	51XX (12)	2251 (4)†		43XX (7)	28XX (4)	Grange (4)	85
January 1957	14XX (4)	16XX (2), 57XX (24), 74XX (10)	56XX (13)	51XX (12)			43XX (5)	28XX (6)	Grange (2)	78
January 1960		16XX (3), 57XX (22), 74XX (7), 64XX (1)	56XX (8)	51XX (8)			43XX (5)	28XX (9)	Grange (3)	65
January 1963		57XX (12), 64XX (2), 74XX (5)	56XX (5)	51XX (3)			Ivatt 2MT (4)	Stanier 8F (14)	Grange (3)	48
January 1966		57XX (9)					BR 4MT (2)	Stanier 8F (13)		24

* Includes all locomotives allocated to the depot during that month. *(Derived from data supplied by Richard Strange of Steam Archive Services.)*

† These engines had all been transferred by February.

Left: '51XX' class 2-6-2T No. 5109 passes Stourbridge North Junction on its way towards Dudley with a two-coach local service *c.* 1957.

E.J. Dew

Table Thirteen

Ex-GWR Named Locomotives Allocated to Stourbridge 1948-1966

Class	No.	Name	Arrived on (or thereabouts)	Left on (or thereabouts)	From	To	Withdrawn
Bulldog	3450	*Peacock*	Pre-1948	21st December, 1949			Withdrawn
Hall	4974	*Talgarth Hall*	4th April, 1960	7th October, 1961 (iii)	Tyseley	Gloucester	
	4986	*Aston Hall*	13th June, 1959 (i)	26th December, 1959 (iii)	Stafford Road	Stafford Road	
	5912	*Queen's Hall*	4th April, 1960	11th September, 1961	Landore	Machynlleth	
	5930	*Hannington Hall*	4th April, 1960	11th September, 1961	Tyseley	Worcester	
	5944	*Ickenham Hall*	5th November, 1960 (i)	11th September, 1961	Oxley	Worcester	
	5988	*Bostock Hall*	3rd August, 1962	22nd October, 1962	Banbury	Old Oak Common	
	6904	*Charfield Hall*	13th September, 1960	11th September, 1961	Shrewsbury	Banbury	
	6930	*Aldersey Hall*	26th September, 1958	26th December, 1959 (iii)	Worcester	Stafford Road	
	6956	*Mottram Hall*	13th June, 1961	11th September, 1961	Oxford	Gloucester	
Grange	6803	*Bucklebury Grange*	14th July, 1951 (i)	4th April, 1960	Banbury	Tyseley	
	6811	*Cranbourne Grange*	7th September, 1962	11th April, 1964 (ii)	Bristol StPM	Oxley	
	6823	*Oakley Grange*	16th May, 1953 (i)	8th October, 1955 (iii)	Swindon	Chester West	
	6827	*Llanfrechfa Grange*	7th September, 1962	11th April, 1964 (ii)	Bristol StPM	Oxley	
	6828	*Trellech Grange*	12th June, 1948 (i)	13th July, 1957 (iii)	Landore	Llanelly	
	6834	*Dummer Grange*	29th April, 1963	11th April, 1964 (ii)	Reading	Tyseley	
	6842	*Nunhold Grange*	7th September, 1962	11th April, 1964 (ii)	Bristol StPM	Tyseley	
	6855	*Saighton Grange*	4th November, 1959	4th April, 1960	Penzance	Tyseley	
	6857	*Tudor Grange*	12th June, 1948 (i)	8th October, 1955 (iii)	Landore	Chester West	
	6879	*Overton Grange*	4th November, 1959	4th April, 1960	St Blazey	Tyseley	
Modified Hall	6986	*Rydal Hall*	13th August, 1962	3rd December, 1962	Swindon	Southall	
	6987	*Shervington Hall*	26th September, 1958	26th December, 1959 (iii)	Worcester	Stafford Road	
	7922	*Salford Hall*	8th September, 1962 (i)	3rd December, 1962	Shrewsbury	Southall	
Manor	7806	*Cockington Manor*	18th January, 1961	8th September, 1962 (iii)	Tyseley	Oxley	
	7816	*Frilsham Manor*	11th September, 1961	7th September, 1962	Tyseley	Reading	
	7817	*Garsington Manor*	25th January, 1961	7th September, 1962	Croes Newydd	Reading	
	7824	*Ilford Manor*	18th January, 1961	11th August, 1962 (iii)	Tyseley	Oxley	
Duke	9084	*Isle of Jersey*	pre-1948	31st December, 1949 (iii)		Machynlleth	

Notes: (i) Locomotive arrived during four weeks ending on the Saturday given; (ii) Locomotive left during one week ending on the Saturday given; (iii) Locomotive left during four weeks ending of the Saturday given. (*Derived from data supplied by Richard Strange of Steam Archive Services.*)

'57XX' class 0-6-0PT No. 3677 arrives at Brierley Hill with the 5.27 pm Stourbridge Junction to Wolverhampton on 28th April, 1962.   *E.J. Dew*

'Grange' class 4-6-0 No. 6842 *Nunhold Grange* passes Oldbury & Langley Green on the Stourbridge Extension. The engine displays its '2C' shed plate on the smokebox door. This was Stourbridge's shedcode in 1963.   *R.J. Buckley*

later, on the short-lived Stourbridge Junction to Wolverhampton (Low Level) service which ran via the Wombourn branch. These railmotors, which were steam engine and passenger carriage combined into a single unit, continued to work over the southern section of the N&H branch until the Old Hill to Halesowen public passenger services, and later the workmen's specials which had been provided to connect with those Longbridge trains terminating at Halesowen, were discontinued on 5th December, 1927 and 31st March, 1928 respectively. However, railmotors continued to work over the northern section of the branch between Dudley and Old Hill until the machines themselves were withdrawn in the 1930s. The demands of the Austin car factory at Longbridge did ensure that at least the unadvertised locomotive-hauled workmen's specials, which had been introduced on 18th April, 1917, would remain, working over the whole length of the line between Old Hill and Longbridge until withdrawn on 1st September, 1958. During the 1930s and 1940s these workmen's specials were normally in the hands of such locomotives as the ageing class '655' pannier tanks, for example Nos. 2706/12/16/18 as well as class '1813' No. 1835. The introduction of the more modern class '74XX' panniers, which by 1948 had become well established on Stourbridge Depot's books, meant that several of these elderly locomotives were transferred to duties elsewhere (*see below*).

Although the Longbridge passenger services had been withdrawn, class '74XX' engines continued to work freight over the branch, the most interesting of which being the Swindon to Longbridge car parts train. This class 'C' fitted freight (informally known as the 'Panic') would usually arrive at Stourbridge Junction in the hands of an ex-GWR 'Hall'. Here, the engine would be replaced by two pannier tanks, one at each end of the train. At Old Hill, engine duties would be reversed with the banker taking over as train engine for the journey over the Halesowen branch. Old Hill to Longbridge freight trains were confined to class '74XX' engines as the '57XX' pannier tanks were prohibited from crossing the rather insubstantial looking Dowery Dell viaduct. The latter could still work between Old Hill and Halesowen itself, often being employed on Stourbridge Bank Train duties clearing Halesowen Goods and Canal Junction sidings and carrying out trips to and from the Canal Basin. Halesowen Goods closed on 9th September, 1968, although the Canal Basin line continued for another year, services being withdrawn on 1st October, 1969, the same day as the closure of the branch from Halesowen to Old Hill.

To the north of Old Hill lay the Old Hill to Dudley section (or Windmill End branch as the line became known) of the N&H branch which joined the former OWWR main line at Blower's Green on the south side of the Dudley tunnel. Local freight traffic over this line, including Trips to and from the goods depot located at the far end of the Withymoor Basin (later Netherton Goods) branch which terminated at Bishton's Bridge on the Dudley canal, would normally be found in the hands of class '57XX' pannier tanks. However, traffic between Round Oak and Bordesley Junction or Dudley and Oldbury & Langley Green, for example, would usually be hauled by the larger 0-6-2T or 2-6-2T engines. Long distance freight services using the branch utilised more powerful locomotives, especially ex-Great Western 4-6-0 'Grange' or 'Hall' mixed traffic engines, '28XX' 2-8-0 heavy freight engines or 2-6-0 Moguls, whilst in BR days the class '9F' 2-10-0s could be seen on oil tank trains. Some of the heavier freight trains required banking assistance, in either direction, away from Cox's Lane sidings, the task falling to one of Stourbridge Depot's 0-6-2T or 2-6-2T engines. On 15th September, 1963 engineering work on the main line between Birmingham (Snow Hill) and Wolverhampton (Low Level) resulted in traffic being diverted over the branch. Amongst the trains affected were the Paddington to Wolverhampton/Birkenhead expresses hauled by 'Western' class 2700 hp diesel-hydraulic locomotives which, despite being heavily loaded, were able to tackle the climb out of Cox's Lane unassisted.

Post-war auto-train workings over the Dudley-Old Hill and the Dudley-Great Bridge-Birmingham (Snow Hill) routes were normally to be found in the hands of Stourbridge based 'push and pull' fitted 0-4-2T engines, although the Old Hill auto-train was also worked by similarly equipped class '64XX' pannier tanks based at Wolverhampton, Stafford Road.After

'74XX' class 0-6-0PT No. 7432 approaches Old Hill on the Halesowen branch on 8th April, 1957.
H.C. Casserley

'64XX' class 0-6-0PT No. 6424 is seen at Kidderminster on the Bewdley auto-train service on 26th August, 1963.   *B.W.L. Brooksbank*

1957 all 0-4-2T engines had left Stourbridge, auto-fitted panniers taking their place on the Old Hill services. During the summer of 1962, responsibility for providing all motive power for the Dudley/Old Hill services was vested in Stourbridge and as a result Stafford Road's No. 6418 was transferred there at the end of July. A further two class '64XX' engines were moved to Stourbridge during 1962, No. 6403 arriving on 14th September from Banbury and from Gloucester, No. 6424 on 11th December, the latter succeeding No. 6418 which was withdrawn on 26th November. In 1963 No. 6434 was transferred from Tondu, taking up residence at Stourbridge on 7th October, presumably as a replacement for No. 6403 which was subsequently withdrawn around the beginning of December. Although class '74XX' engines were not fitted with 'push and pull' equipment, they too could be seen working the Old Hill auto-train. In fact, it was class '74XX' No. 7418 that had the dubious honour of hauling the last passenger train on the branch on Saturday 13th June, 1964 when neither No. 6424 nor No. 6434 were available. The following year saw the closure of the Netherton Goods branch on 5th July, although the Windmill End branch itself continued to be used as a freight-only line until 1st January, 1968.

An unusual working for one of Stourbridge's '64XX' class engines was recorded during 1962/63 when an auto-train left Stourbridge empty at 3.00 pm arriving at Kidderminster ten minutes later. It then returned as the 4.10 pm departure calling at all stations, terminating at Stourbridge Junction at 4.26 pm. It is believed that this auto-train then formed the 5.45 pm to Old Hill (arriving 5.58 pm), where it reversed to continue over the Windmill End branch as the 6.15 pm from Old Hill to Dudley (arriving 6.29 pm). It then completed one more round trip between Dudley and Old Hill, before terminating at 7.15 pm. The train then returned to Stourbridge Junction as empty stock. Also in the early 1960s, Stourbridge supplied class '64XX' locomotives for the auto-train between Kidderminster and Bewdley.

Stourbridge Shed had a policy of allocating locomotives to specific drivers with the result that some crews would treat their engine like one of their own. One incident has been recalled which highlights this relationship. On arriving at the shed at the beginning of the shift a certain driver noticed that the steps on 'his' locomotive had been bent in a minor collision. Incensed by this sacrilege, he demanded that the damage be repaired immediately. However, as the damage clearly did not prevent the engine from carrying out its duties it was decided that the repairs could wait, a reply that did not impress the irate driver. Having repeated his request on several occasions and having received the same reply each time, the driver decided on another course of action. A local blacksmith was contacted who carried out the job for him. It is not known what the reaction was when the bill for the work arrived at the depot!

It has been said that Stourbridge depot was one of the last refuges for some of the more antiquated designs of Great Western locomotive. Certainly several of these did end up spending the twilight of their careers eking out an existence at some of the more remote outposts within the shed's operational area and as a result came to be associated with particular tasks and duties. For example, No. 1835, the last of the '1813' class and the only one to pass into British Railways ownership, was, during the 1940s, seen regularly on the Town Goods duty along with that ever popular locomotive No. 1863. Other 'old soldiers' working regular turns at about the same time would be the shed's class '2021' locomotives Nos. 2090/92 and 2107. Working Lye Goods yard would be No. 2107, whilst No. 2092 could be found pottering around at Cradley; No. 2090 would presumably cover where and when necessary. Stourbridge also had four '2181' class panniers, which were '2021' class engines fitted with improved braking systems for working heavy gradients, Nos. 2185/86/87/89. Two of these engines were always associated with the Brierley Hill area, with No. 2186 fussing away around Brettell Lane sidings and No. 2189 being kept busy at Round Oak. Of the three remaining '655' class tank engines, Nos. 2706 and 2712 worked the Cradley 'pick-up' freights and sometimes the Town Goods yard. These two locomotives were withdrawn in October 1948 and March 1950 respectively, although the third, No. 2771, lasted until June 1950.

'51XX' class 2-6-2T No. 4173 arrives at Lye with the 5.45 pm Birmingham (Snow Hill) to Stourbridge Junction on 22nd May, 1957.   *E.J. Dew*

'51XX' class 2-6-2T No. 5199 passes Brettell Lane with the 12.25 pm Wolverhampton to Stourbridge Junction train on 28th April, 1962.   *E.J. Dew*

In addition to Stourbridge's ex-GWR pannier tanks were the BR '16XX' class. Built 1949-1955, these lightweight engines were designed for use in yards where space was tight and the curves sharp. The locomotives were in fact updated versions of the '2021' class and would probably have been used on similar duties when the latter were finally withdrawn from Stourbridge between 1950 and 1952. The first '16XX' at the shed was No. 1621 which arrived during the summer of 1950, probably straight from the Works, remaining at Stourbridge for 10 years. No. 1619 arrived early in 1953 and remaining until the end of October 1960. Stourbridge's last '16XX' was No. 1663 which departed for Abercynon around April 1961 having been at the depot since January 1960.

Collett's class '51XX' 2-6-2T locomotives first arrived at Stourbridge c. 1929, taking over the busy Birmingham (Snow Hill) commuter services that ran over the Stourbridge Extension. These capable locomotives could be found working on local passenger duties throughout the Black Country and were often employed on stopping trains between Wolverhampton (Low Level) and Stourbridge Junction/Worcester (Shrub Hill). In fact these engines worked the Wolverhampton line right up to closure on 30th July, 1962 when No. 4173 had the dubious distinction of hauling the last 'local' between Wolverhampton (Low Level) and Stourbridge Junction. Just prior to its withdrawal, this service was used to provide crew training on the first 'Western' diesel-hydraulic locomotive to arrive in the West Midlands, No. 1004 *Western Crusader*. This locomotive was seen on the 6.50 am and 10.15 am to Stourbridge, returning on the 7.15 am and 11.50 am. Going back 10 years to the middle of 1952, there was a rumour that Stourbridge was to receive four of the new Riddles '3MT' '82000' Standard 2-6-2Ts. In the event all of the Western Region's first batch (Nos. 82000-9) were allocated to Tyseley.

A rather surprising addition to Stourbridge's complement of 2-6-2 tank engines were two unexpected strangers that were to be found amongst their ranks during 1963-65. Class '61XX' engines had been built specifically for the London suburban services and it was in the London Division where these spent most of their working lives. Widespread dieselisation during 1960 changed things dramatically and many of these locomotives found themselves redundant. As a result some moved north and two, Nos. 6129/37, found their way to Stourbridge via Banbury and Tyseley respectively. However, by this time their innings were almost over, No. 6137 being the first to fall, withdrawn from the shed during November 1964 having almost completed a full year there. No. 6129 did not last that long; having arrived at Stourbridge in January 1965 it was consigned to the scrap heap just eight months later.

Another mainstay of the Stourbridge stable was the class '56XX' 0-6-2T tank locomotives, in particular those from the 1927 batch numbered 6600 to 6699 (the shed did acquire Nos. 5606, 5642, 5651 and 5658 for various periods between 1948 and 1958). As previously mentioned, the first of these engines to arrive on a permanent basis did so during World War II. By this time freight workings had become much heavier and perhaps some banking turns over the steeply graded lines around Stourbridge had become too much for the lighter 0-6-0Ts. In the 1950s class '56XX' engines were also found at the head of local coal or mineral workings from the Junction to Oxley Sidings, or Bank Train trips to Dudley and Blower's Green sidings. Coal empties for Dudley Exchange Sidings and freight to or from Cannock Road Junction or Five Ways, Tipton, were amongst duties sometimes shared with class '51XX' engines. Through freights from Great Bridge to Hartlebury or from Blower's Green to Worcester Goods were also the province of the 0-6-2T, an example of the latter being in 1951 the 6.18 pm departure, arriving Worcester at 10.48 pm. Here it would combine to form a London-bound freight, possibly the 11.35 pm departure arriving Paddington at 5.40 am.

By the end of World War II, all of Stourbridge's 'Dean Goods' had been withdrawn or reallocated, although two 'Aberdares' still remained, one of which was to be involved in an unusual fuel experiment. Instead of normal steam coal, which was at this time both in short supply and expensive, the tender was one day filled with coke. The trial proved to be a rather embarrassing failure when all the coke was consumed on the return leg of a Bordesley Junction 'pick-up' freight just outside Langley Green. The successor to the 'Dean Goods' was the more modern Collett '2251' class 0-6-0 tender locomotive. Although occasionally found on banking

'56XX' class 0-6-2T No. 6667 at the north end of Stourbridge Junction on 10th September, 1949.

H.C. Casserley

One of Stourbridge's '56XX' class 0-6-2Ts No. 6681 enters Soho & Winson Green *c.* 1955.

D.K. Jones Collection

duties and on No. 7 Bank Pilot Trip between Dudley and Elmley Lovett sidings, these locomotives proved to be particularly useful when working cattle trains off the Severn Valley line and from the Tenbury Wells area. Apparently, the popularity of these engines on this work derived from their use over the Tenbury and Bewdley line where the fairly generous water capacity of their tenders proved invaluable in helping to offset the paucity of available watering facilities on the line. Some of this class were fitted with larger tenders acquired from withdrawn '3000' class ROD 2-8-0 locomotives, although it is not known whether engines so fitted were actually part of the Stourbridge allocation.

The transfer of 2-8-0s Nos. 2874 and 2886 away from Stourbridge early in 1947 left the shed with only one heavy goods locomotive, No. 2852, that was capable of adequately dealing with the weight of traffic now flowing through the area. The 'Aberdares' could not really cope therefore creating a problem that would only be resolved by the introduction of additional '28XX' 2-8-0s. During 1948, No. 2852 was joined by Nos. 2885, 3821 and 3827 and between 1950 and 1958, the depot rarely saw its allocation of this type of locomotive fall below six. In addition, for two years between October 1951 and October 1953, the allocation was even supplemented by the arrival of ROD No. 3028. As the 1950s drew to a close, further examples of the '28XX' class were drafted in with the result that by 1960 the shed had acquired nine of these powerful engines. However, early in 1961 the wind of change began to blow in Stourbridge's direction and between March and May six of the class, Nos. 2856/88/97, 3816/31/39; had been reallocated, the gap being filled by the arrival of a similar number of ex-LMS '8F' 2-8-0s. This influx of 'foreign' locomotives was followed by a Regional reorganisation which saw responsibility for Stourbridge transfer to the London Midland Region in September 1963. Following the formal transfer to the LMR further '8Fs' were allocated there and by the closure of the shed to steam in July 1966, 13 of the class were on the depot's books. The ex-LMS '8F' though was not a new engine to Stourbridge men, examples turning up in the area during World War II before becoming fairly regular visitors to the Wolverhampton, Stourbridge Junction and Worcester section by the late 1940s/early 1950s. However, the Stanier '8F' may not have been too popular with some Stourbridge crews who had been brought up on locomotives designed to burn soft Welsh steam coal, '8Fs' being built for hard coal such as Yorkshire 'bright'.

Some longer distance coal trains would occasionally bring to the area both Collett '72XX' class 2-8-2 tank engines or the slightly smaller Churchward '42XX' class 2-8-0Ts. Although both classes are normally associated with duties in South Wales, a few of the former were allocated to Oxley at various times between 1939 and 1963, whilst in the early 1960s Worcester Shed enjoyed the company of a small number of 2-8-0Ts and at about the same time a single 2-8-2T. Another visitor to the Stourbridge area would have been the ex-LNWR 'Super D' 0-8-0 freight locomotives which often could be seen hauling heavy inter-Regional mineral workings to or from such places as Essington colliery or Wichnor Junction. Finally, oil traffic also required the use of heavy freight locomotives and both GWR class '28XX' and the WD 'Austerity' worked traffic between Stanlow/Ellesmere Port and Rowley Regis.

By the early 1920s, 'Bulldog' 4-4-0 locomotives had become regular visitors to Stourbridge Junction taking over passenger services on the Birmingham (Snow Hill), Worcester (Foregate Street), Hereford and Cardiff route from the 4-4-0 '41s', i.e. 'Badmintons', 'Atbaras' and 'Flowers'. Additionally, outside cylinder 4-4-0 'Counties' or '43XX' Moguls were also occasionally employed on these workings. However, in the years leading up to the outbreak of World War II, these trains, in particular the South Wales expresses, became increasingly associated with Tyseley or Hereford based 'Saints' or 'Halls'. In fact, hauling expresses over the route between Birmingham and Cardiff was one of the last duties for 'Saint' No. 2920 *Saint David* before its withdrawal from service. 'Halls' continued as the principal motive power for these trains until the replacement of steam by dmus in the late 1950s. The daily working arrangements for steam engines on services between Birmingham and Cardiff north of Hereford during 1956/57 for example (and probably up to June 1958) are shown below (locomotives employed on these services were changed at Hereford):

Table Fourteen

Extracts from the working Log of Charles Lawrence - Stourbridge (1918-1963)

22nd October, 1962
No. 6403 (84F)
Fireman G. Evans

Location	am	am
Stourbridge Loco	5.25	
Stourbridge Jn	5.35	6.20
Dudley	6.40	6.52
Old Hill	7.05	7.20
Dudley	7.33	7.45
Stourbridge Jn	8.05	8.15
Stourbridge Loco	8.25	11.25
Stourbridge Jn	11.35	1.35
Stourbridge Loco	1.45	

27th December, 1962
No. 6424 (84F)
Fireman S.R. Hudson

Location	pm	pm
Stourbridge Loco	2.40	
Stourbridge Jn	2.50	3.00
Kidderminster	3.15	4.10
Stourbridge Jn	4.26	5.45
Old Hill	5.58	6.15
Dudley	6.29	6.36
Old Hill	6.50	7.00
Dudley	7.15	
Stourbridge Jn	nk	
Stourbridge Loco	nk	

21st January, 1963
No. 48424 (84F)
Fireman G. Evans

Location	am	am
Stourbridge Loco	5.45	
Cradley	6.10	7.25
Langley Green	7.45	10.30
Rowley Regis	10.35	11.25
Cox's Lane (Wait	11.35	
Banker	12.55	
Dudley (Water)	2.10	2.25
Oxley (Relief)	3.15	

8th January, 1963
No. 6384 (86E)
Fireman G. Evans

Location	am	am
Log from Worcs		
Worcester	6.35	6.50
Shelwick Jn	6.55	8.10
Hereford (Relief	8.15	
by Cardiff crew)		
Hereford (Return	9.55	
with No. 48402)		
Shelwick Jn	10.25	10.35
Stoke Edith	10.55	11.30
Stourbridge Loco	2.00	

23rd January, 1963
No. 48691 (6C)
Fireman G. Evans

Location	am	am
Stourbridge Loco	7.15	
Langley Green	7.50	9.35
Rowley Regis	9.40	10.15
Cox's Lane	10.25	10.45
Stow Heath	11.30	11.55
Oxley Sidings	12.30	12.35
Oxley Loco	12.40	

31st January, 1963
No. 6667 (84F)
Fireman G. Evans

Location	am	am
Stourbridge Loco	5.15	
Dudley	5.50	6.59
Birmingham	7.32	7.38
Spring Road	7.52	7.55
Shirley	8.00	8.35
Moor Street	8.55	9.25
Tyseley Shed	9.45	10.00
Bordesley Jn	10.10	11.25
Cradley	12.10	12.20
Lye	12.25	12.35
Stourbridge Loco	12.50	

14th January, 1963
No. 6832 (87F)
Fireman G. Evans

Location	am	am
Stourbridge Loco		6.15
Stourbridge Jn	6.25	7.30
Birmingham SH	8.10	8.25
Carriage Sidings	8.45	9.00
Tyseley Shed	9.05	9.45
Bordesley Jn	10.00	10.25
Rowley Regis	11.10	11.15
Blower's Green	11.45	12.00
Round Oak	12.10	12.35
Stourbridge Loco	12.55	

16th February, 1963
No. 6827 (84F)
Fireman B. Shillingford

Location	am	am
Stourbridge Loco		8.55
Stourbridge Jn	9.00	9.04
Worcester SH	9.54	
Worcester Shed	11.25	
(Return with		11.30
No. 7026 - 84A)		
Stourbridge Loco	12.45	1.00

nk   Not known.

(Reproduced by kind permission of Trevor Lawrence.)

4.00 pm Snow Hill-Hereford (Sunday): 84E Tyseley 'Hall'
 - returns to Birmingham on 9.50 am Cardiff-Snow Hill (Monday)
7.13 pm Hereford-Snow Hill (Sunday): 85C Hereford 'Hall'
 - returns to Hereford on 7.45 am Snow Hill-Cardiff(Monday)
7.45 am Snow Hill-Cardiff: 84E Tyseley 'Hall' (Tuesday to Saturday)
 - returns to Birmingham on 9.50 am Cardiff-Snow Hill
9.45 am Snow Hill-Cardiff: 84E Tyseley 'Hall' (Monday to Saturday)
 - returns to Birmingham on 1.30 pm Cardiff-Snow Hill
7.55 am Hereford-Snow Hill: 85C Hereford 'Hall' (Monday to Saturday)
 - returns to Hereford on 12.45pm Snow Hill-Cardiff
8.35 am Cardiff-Snow Hill: 85C Hereford 'Hall' (Monday to Saturday)
 - returns to Hereford on 5.00pm Snow Hill-Cardiff

The introduction of dmus on the Cardiff-Birmingham services did not totally result in the demise of steam-hauled trains on the route. From *circa* 1958/59 the Summer timetable included a 'Saturdays Only' service departing Cardiff at 7.05 am, returning from Birmingham (Snow Hill) at 11.40 am. This service continued to be steam hauled up to and including 9th September, 1961 when No. 6366 (86G) worked the eastbound service throughout, as did No. 4986 *Aston Hall* (81C) on the return.

Whilst mixed traffic 4-6-0 locomotives regularly passed through Stourbridge Junction at the head of both express freights to or from South Wales, Oxley and the North West, and passenger workings between Birmingham-Cardiff/Wolverhampton-London, the shed itself did not receive any examples of this type of engine until after World War II when a 'Grange' arrived in 1946. From 1948 onwards, 'Granges' became very familiar at the depot. Later, Stourbridge also received an allocation of 'Halls', although the first of these did not appear until around September 1958. Perhaps local railwaymen were reflecting upon the absence of powerful four-cylinder locomotives, which could be found in abundance a few miles away at Stafford Road Shed, when they nicknamed the former, 'Stourbridge Castles' and the latter, 'Stourbridge Kings'?

By June 1948 two 'Granges', No. 6828 *Trellech Grange* and No. 6857 *Tudor Grange*, had begun a lengthy residence which lasted until about July 1957 and October 1955 respectively. During 1951 No. 6803 *Bucklebury Grange* also arrived, remaining at Stourbridge until April 1960. The number of 'Granges' allocated to the depot was increased to four between May 1953 and October 1955 with the arrival of No. 6823, *Oakley Grange*. However, following the departure of Nos. 6803 and 6879 in April 1960, the class did not again feature on Stourbridge's books until the transfer of No. 6811 *Cranbourne Grange*, No. 6827 *Llanfrechfa Grange* and No. 6842 *Nunhold Grange* during September 1962. At about the same time, one 'Hall' and two 'Modified Halls', No. 5988 *Bostock Hall*, No. 6986 *Rydal Hall* and No. 7922 *Salford Hall*, were also drafted in. However, by the end of 1962, all the 'Halls' had gone, although the 'Granges', including No. 6834 *Dummer Grange*, which had arrived from Reading around May 1963, remained at Stourbridge until April 1964. Incidentally, none of the 12 'Halls' and 'Modified Halls' that saw service at Stourbridge during 1958-62, appeared to have stayed at the depot for much longer than 18 months.

Although 'Castles' were never allocated to Stourbridge, these locomotives were certainly not strangers to the area and could be seen on through passenger services operating between Wolverhampton, Stourbridge, Worcester, Oxford and Paddington, a duty which would also have brought over the years 'Bulldogs', 'Saints' and 'Stars' to the Junction. In fact the occasional 'Star' could still be seen working through Stourbridge Junction as late as the mid-1950s, one example, No. 4056 *Princess Margaret*, heading the 12.25 pm Wolverhampton-Paddington service on 19th January, 1955. Later, as main line steam began to be displaced by diesel traction, it was not uncommon to witness 'Castles' at the head of stopping trains between Birmingham (Snow Hill), Stourbridge Junction and Worcester, sharing duties with 'Halls' and 'Granges'. In fact, these services continued to provide passengers with a wide variety of steam haulage until well into the 1960s. Another working which brought a 'Castle'

'Star' class No. 4044 *Prince George* approaches Stourbridge North signal box with a train for Wolverhampton (Low Level) on 2nd October, 1949.   *W.F. Deebank*

'Grange' class 4-6-0 No. 6857 *Tudor Grange* at Stourbridge Shed on 14th June, 1953.
Norman Preedy

to Stourbridge during the early 1960s, was the 2.10 pm local service from Wolverhampton (Low Level). At this time Shrewsbury's No. 5070 *Sir Daniel Gooch* was a regular performer on the Shrewsbury to Wolverhampton leg of the 'Cambrian Coast Express'. Having been detached at Wolverhampton the engine continued to Stourbridge on the 2.10 pm service. From Stourbridge Junction the 'Castle' would often be employed on the 4.45 pm local to Kidderminster and after being turned on the Kidderminster-Bewdley-Hartlebury triangle, the engine returned to Stourbridge taking over the 5.15 pm Evesham to Crewe parcels running via the Wombourn branch, Wellington and Market Drayton.

Finally, just a mention of three other interesting workings involving 'Castles'. Firstly, the Sundays Only 1.40 am Crewe to Plymouth express. Quite often this would be hauled from Wolverhampton by a Stafford Road 'Castle' (or an Oxley one after Stafford Road's closure), the train passing through Stourbridge Junction at around 3.25 am. On 18th January, 1965 this service was hauled by an Oxley (LMR) based 'Castle' for the last time when No. 7019 *Fowey Castle* took over the train at Wolverhampton, although the service itself remained steam hauled using 'Halls' or 'Granges' until at least 31st October, 1965. (It will be noted that this service was still running over the Wolverhampton-Stourbridge line well after its official closure to passenger traffic in July 1962.) The second involved a visit by the Royal Train on 27th June, 1957. The train was hauled by two immaculately turned out 'Castles', one of which was No. 7001 *Sir James Milne*. Lastly, 'Castles' employed on unfitted freights were something of a rarity, however, No. 7013 *Bristol Castle* did find itself on such a working on 22nd January, 1955, being employed upon what was probably the 12 noon Crewe to Moreton Cutting goods.

Despite the fact that men in the Stourbridge passenger links were usually confined to local services to and from Birmingham, Leamington Spa, Wolverhampton, Stratford-upon-Avon and Worcester, on occasion they were required to take a train to destinations far beyond their regular operational boundaries. These trains were often holiday excursions bound for resorts in South Wales, the South and South West of England, although probably the longest working involving a Stourbridge engine and crew was to the Southern Region with the Lenches Nut and Bolt Company's annual excursion to Portsmouth. This being a round trip of some 396 miles was something of an event. The crew signed on at Stourbridge at 6.30 am on Sunday morning and would book off at 3.30 am Monday with seven hours free time in the seaport itself: a very long but lucrative day out! During July and August Stourbridge men would work the Saturdays-Only Bournemouth train as far as Basingstoke, usually with a 'Grange' or 'Hall'. The engine would leave Stourbridge Junction at the head of an early morning local service to Birmingham (Snow Hill), where it would then be attached to a train of 10 coaches of Southern Region green stock. During the late 1950s this train departed Snow Hill at 6.05 am and was timed to reach Bournemouth (Central) at 11.16 am. At Basingstoke the Western Region locomotive would be detached, driver and fireman then preparing it for the return trip, possibly the 9.30 am departure from Bournemouth to Wolverhampton (Low Level) arriving Basingstoke at 11.30 am. On arrival at Birmingham the crew would usually be relieved, the train continuing with Wolverhampton men on the footplate.

Men in the freight link found themselves less confined to local traffic and would often have to take their trains to one of the many distant corners of the GWR empire. Normally though, a crew on a South Wales freight for example, would expect to be relieved at Hereford by Cardiff men, whilst those on say a North West-bound goods running via the Wombourn branch might leave the footplate at Oxley Branch Junction. In the years before World War II, Stourbridge also had their own 'double home' workings which required a crew to spend the night in lodgings before returning home the following day. Known 'double home' workings were Pontypool Road, Cardiff, London and Crewe. During May 1954, unofficial strike action was taken by some branches of ASLEF in response to a proposed new agreement relating to the 'lodging' minimum mileage from the home depot. However, on 23rd May the Stourbridge branch of ASLEF voted against joining the strike, passing instead a resolution stating 'that this branch does not accept the contention of the Railway Executive Committee that the 'double home' turns in dispute are essential to the efficient working of the railways'. (Source: *County Express*, 29th May, 1954.)

'Modified Hall' class 4-6-0 No. 7918 *Rhose Wood Hall* approaches Lye with the 3.50 pm Birmingham (Snow Hill) to Hereford train. The Hayes Lane branch runs alongside the main line.   *W.F. Deebank*

'Hall' class 4-6-0 No. 5900 *Hinderton Hall* waits on an up class 'H' (8) freight near Oxley Branch Junction on 4th September, 1962.   *B.W.L. Brooksbank*

Discontentment and unrest on the railways had been brewing for some time. Late in 1953 both ASLEF and the NUR had submitted a claim for a wage increase of 15 per cent on the flat rate. However, failure to resolve the claim led, in November 1954, to the negotiations being turned over to the independent Railway Staff National Tribunal which was the final arbiter in the laid down negotiating process. Consequently, awards were made to both locomotive men and other operating staff in the 'conciliation' grades, e.g. shunters, signalmen, guards etc., which raised the differential in favour of the former by comparison with existing 1953 wage levels (there was a tradition in the railway wage structure that there should be a differential between the pay of locomotive grades and that of the other 'conciliation' grades by virtue of the special skill and responsibility a footplate job demanded). The NUR, dissatisfied with these proposals threatened a nationwide strike which was only averted after a special Court of Enquiry was convened in December and its findings accepted by both the Government and the British Transport Commission. As a result, 'conciliation' grades were offered a new wage deal which was accepted by the NUR. Unfortunately, this settlement was seen by ASLEF as eroding the higher differential awarded to its members in the November agreement and accordingly submitted a fresh pay claim to the Tribunal which would in effect increase the maximum driver's and fireman's wage to £10 0s. 6d. and £8 6s. 6d. respectively as against the £9 15s. and £8 4s. offered by the British Transport Commission. This the Tribunal rejected. Not unexpectedly, ASLEF saw this decision as a direct reversal of accepted policy on 'differentials' which was wholly unacceptable. In defence of the offer, BTC argued that whilst the final rates proposed for 'conciliation' grades amounted to a flat rate increase of 15 per cent on existing pay, those offered to locomotive grades did on average raise, not lower, the differential. However, dissatisfied by the outcome, ASLEF gave notice of strike action to take place on 1st May, 1955, a threat that was only narrowly averted by an agreement to put the BTC wage offer into effect and for BTC to begin discussions immediately with the major railway unions, a move initially condemned by ASLEF who had insisted that the NUR be excluded (the NUR had condemned the May strike threat). Unfortunately, following a breakdown in talks ASLEF called a national strike which began on Sunday 29th May, 1955 (Whit Sunday) and lasted for 17 days at a cost to British Railways of at least £10 million.

The consequences of the action were felt immediately at Stourbridge with the first casualties being the popular holiday excursions to such places as Weston-Super-Mare, Bridgnorth, Llangollen and Chepstow races. By the end of the first week of the strike less than 20 per cent of the normal passenger service was running and virtually all freight was at a standstill. Although many local firms relied on the railways, in particular to deliver fuel and raw materials, most reported sufficient stocks to enable production to continue for between two and three weeks. There were, though, serious implications for the railways in the steps being taken by industry to minimise the effects of the strike, not least the increase in applications for 'C' licenses by firms looking to carry out their own deliveries and the use of road vehicles in general. The local consensus was that intermittent problems on the railways in recent times had led to a large measure of confidence being lost, which together with increases in freight charges had forced industry to look for cheaper and more reliable forms of transport.

On Tuesday 14th June, 1955 the national rail strike was called off; unfortunately, the return to work of the 374 branch members at Stourbridge depot was far less smooth than elsewhere. The 71 drivers and 62 firemen forming the first shift commencing at midnight had, with one exception, assembled at the local Labour Club at 10.00 pm to receive official notification from the Union's Secretary Mr Jim Baty of the return to work. However, the telegram dispatched from London at 6.55 pm on the Tuesday evening did not arrive and the return to work was postponed until the men could be officially notified, although one fireman, who had not attended the meeting and had heard the announcement on the radio, did report for work at midnight. A copy of the telegram was eventually delivered at 12.25 on Wednesday morning, whilst the original turned up at the Labour Club at 8.10 am in time to be displayed to drivers and firemen who were to meet again at 10.00 am.

Most footplatemen will agree that 'dropping' a plug is one of the worst things that can happen to an engine crew and often the stigma associated with such an event will remain with those concerned for the rest of their careers on the railway. One former Stourbridge fireman clearly recalls narrowly avoiding one such embarrassing incident. The train concerned was the 9.40 pm Victoria Basin to Cardiff. On arrival at Stourbridge yards the Oxley crew prepared the engine, No. 6980 *Llanrumney Hall* (an Oxley locomotive from 1959 to 1964), prior to it being taken over by Stourbridge men who would then take the train on to Hereford. Having passed Ashperton, the crew began to suspect that something was wrong. By now a roaring fire had been built-up in the firebox and the engine began 'blowing off' furiously and although the fireman put on the injectors it was to no avail. The tender water gauge showed that the tank was still half full, however, a quick visual inspection of the contents confirmed the crew's worst fears: the tank was empty and the gauge was showing a false reading. On arrival at Stoke Edith there was no alternative but to detach the engine and run it into the adjacent refuge siding. Here, the fireman, closely supervised by his driver, began to bale the fire out onto the ballast below. During the course of this operation, the long handled shovel became so hot that it had to be cooled down with buckets of water brought to the scene by the signalman. Luckily, the efforts of the fireman were not in vain and the fire was dropped in time to prevent the water level in the boiler from falling below the top of the firebox crown and causing the fusible plugs to melt or 'drop'.

During 1961/62 the Junction also played host to four 'Manor' class mixed traffic locomotives, Nos. 7806 *Cockington Manor*, 7816 *Frilsham Manor*, 7817 *Garsington Manor* and 7824 *Ilford Manor*. These engines were often used on Wolverhampton 'locals', although they could also be found working services to and from Leamington Spa.

Two interesting locomotives that could be found at Stourbridge Junction at the end of World War II were an ancient 'Duke' class No. 3284 (9084) *Isle of Jersey* (built 1899) and 'Bulldog' class '3300' No. 3450 *Peacock* which had been constructed during 1909; both engines were inside-cylinder 4-4-0s. 'Bulldogs' had once been familiar on Hereford and/or Worcester to Birmingham trains during the 1920s and 30s, although by this time both types would only be utilised on local or not too exacting freight duties and light passenger workings. Unfortunately, it was on the former that the 'Duke' was involved in a 'runaway' incident. The engine was booked to work a freight to the Halesowen branch banked by an 0-6-0PT which would act as the train engine after the freight had reversed onto the branch. On completion of this duty the 'Duke' was booked to work engine and brake van back to Stourbridge. However, before it could return, the engine would first have to run round its brake van. So, just outside Old Hill station the engine was uncoupled and the lamps changed in readiness for the journey back down the Extension. Suddenly, before the engine had run round, the van began to roll down the gradient towards Old Hill station: the hand brake had not been screwed down! With no one on board to stop it, the van rumbled past Old Hill and on through Cradley and Lye before eventually coming to a halt at Stourbridge North Junction!

This Old Hill working was a regular turn for No. 3284, being part of an interesting diagram which eventually took the engine to Shrewsbury. During World War II, No. 3284, together with Shrewsbury's No. 3276, would be employed on the Severn Valley line working alternate morning and afternoon passenger trains. The engine used on the 8.15 am Shrewsbury to Birmingham (Snow Hill), which ran via Bewdley and Kidderminster, would be detached at Stourbridge Junction, spending the rest of the day banking freight trains operating over the Stourbridge Extension. The second 4-4-0, which had been the morning assisting engine on the Extension, would take over the 2.20 pm ex-Birmingham (Snow Hill) at Stourbridge Junction and work tender first to Hartlebury, next working the 4.00 pm to Bewdley and return. To complete the diagram, the 4-4-0 would take the 6.15 pm from Hartlebury to Shrewsbury. This locomotive would then return to Stourbridge the following day via the aforementioned 8.15 am from Shrewsbury. These working arrangements probably remained in operation throughout the 1940s until the introduction of the 11.10 pm class 'D' freight from Welshpool to Cradley which conveyed empty wagons to the Black Country. It is believed that this train was used to return the locomotive that had been employed on the afternoon Severn Valley passenger workings to Stourbridge Junction, thereby doing away with the need for this engine to remain at Shrewsbury for three nights out of six.

By the early 1960s, ex-LMS classes were regularly to be seen working inter-Regional freight trains through Stourbridge Junction, for example, on 30th December, 1961 'Royal Scot' No. 46145 *The Duke of Wellington's Regiment* (West Riding); on 12th March, 1962, 'Royal Scot', No. 46132 *The King's Regiment*; and on 29th November, 1961, 'Black Five' No. 45417. Late in 1962, the Junction received four ex-LMS Ivatt class '2' mixed traffic locomotives Nos. 46506/17/26/27. Originally intended for banking and light freight duties, these engines were occasionally employed on the Old Hill to Dudley service. A visit to Stourbridge Shed on Saturday 29th January, 1966 found three of this class present, Nos. 46427/442/492, the former being the only member of the class to be allocated there during 1966, together with four 'Black Fives' Nos. 44766, 44875, 45064 and 45300. Alongside these were four representatives of the new age in the form of diesel-electric locomotives: English Electric type '4' No. D236 and three Brush type '4' Nos. D1708/1921/1966. By the mid-1960s some freights, in particular oil trains, were turning up at the Junction in the hands of type '3', diesel-hydraulic 'Hymeks'.

Diesels had been seen at the Junction for a number of years, the earliest being the GWR railcars which had first visited Stourbridge at the end of the 1930s. During the Summer of 1939, the 11.40 am Birmingham to Worcester (Foregate Street) was a diesel railcar working whilst one of Worcester's cars was employed on the last service from Henwick to Droitwich. This working was extended to Stourbridge Junction on Thursdays and Saturdays only, arriving at 11.32 pm. The railcar returned to Worcester (or Henwick if required) at midnight. During the 1940s Stourbridge Depot received its own allocation of railcars, in particular, Nos. W3, W4, W8, W14 and W22, although Nos. W25, W26, W29 and W33 also paid visits to the area. These cars were employed on the Dudley-Old Hill route alongside steam-hauled services; one even had a spell on the Stourbridge Town route, however, their principal use was on the Dudley to Birmingham (Snow Hill) services. An unusual departure from scheduled workings led to No. W14 appearing at Welshpool and Moat Lane Junction on 10th and 12th February, 1953. Apparently the machine had been employed on clearance trials in the area. Ex-GWR railcars continued to work from the depot until the very late 1950s when they were replaced by examples of the newly-built British Railways diesel units.

In line with the 1955 Modernisation Plan, diesel multiple units were to be introduced into the Birmingham Area (Western Region) as from 17th June, 1957. Local routes effected by these changes included the Birmingham (Snow Hill) to Stourbridge Junction and Bewdley, and Stourbridge Junction to Wolverhampton (Low Level). From May 1958, first generation British Railways diesel railcars were employed on the Stourbridge Town branch in the shape of Gloucester RC&W Co. Motor Brake Second single units in the number series W55000-19, and began to appear on the Dudley-Great Bridge-Birmingham (Snow Hill) route, displacing the ageing ex-GWR machines. When working over both these lines, the new railcars would sometimes be coupled to a single Driving Trailer Second presumably to provide greater passenger carrying capacity at peak times. These new single units were also employed on the Dudley-Old Hill branch. Following the closure of Stourbridge depot these units were maintained at Tyseley. Today, the Town service is in the hands of one of BR's second generation class '153' railcars.

The depot was allocated a number of 0-6-0 diesel shunters, the first three of these being Nos. 13112/13/15 which arrived between April and July 1955. However, a visit to the shed on 9th June, 1963 revealed the presence of thirteen!

An unexpected visitor to Stourbridge Junction on 25th November, 1961 was a Western Region Pullman diesel-electric set. Reports indicate that the unit had been sent from Tyseley to Swindon via Stourbridge, Worcester and Cheltenham for attention at the Works. This was probably the first time that a 'Blue' Pullman had been seen on the Birmingham-Stourbridge route or the former OWWR between Stourbridge and Worcester. This train actually entered revenue earning service between Wolverhampton (Low Level), Birmingham (Snow Hill) and London (Paddington) on 12th September, 1960.

During the last few years of steam working at Stourbridge, a variety of British Railways Standard locomotives could be seen in the area, including some rare sightings of 'Britannia' 4-6-2s. One such visit was brought about by a derailment on the 'North to West' route at Ludlow on 24th March, 1960 which resulted in several trains being re-routed to run to or from Hereford via Wolverhampton (Low Level), Stourbridge Junction, Worcester (Foregate Street) and Great Malvern. One of these trains was the 12.10 pm Manchester to Plymouth express, headed by No. 70022 *Tornado*, which was diverted at Shrewsbury to run to Hereford over this route. In fact No. 70022 may have been the first of its type to be seen at Stourbridge Junction when it was hauled 'dead' through the station on 11th August, 1954 by 'Hall' No. 5914 *Ripon Hall*. The engine was on its way to Crewe Works for repairs. Another 'Britannia' to arrive at Stourbridge in 1960 was Trafford Park's No. 70017 *Arrow* which had been used, on 13th September, to take the 8.42 am Shrewsbury to Paddington parcels train as far as Wolverhampton (Low Level). After being relieved of its front line duties the engine headed the 2.15 pm local service from Wolverhampton to Stourbridge Junction; its return journey is unknown. Easter Saturday 1961 once again brought Pacific steam to Stourbridge when Cardiff Canton's 'Britannia' No. 70026 *Polar Star* was employed on an extra service between Birmingham (Snow Hill) and Cardiff. Finally, one of the last trains to travel over the Wombourn branch was hauled by 'Britannia' No. 70015 *Apollo* on a freight to Crewe.

Probably one of the most unusual arrivals at Stourbridge Junction was that of class '8P' 4-6-2 No. 71000 *Duke of Gloucester* on 19th December, 1961. Once again it was the Shrewsbury to Wolverhampton leg of the up 'Cambrian Coast Express' that initially brought the locomotive to the Black Country where it was employed on (presumably) the same diagram that took 'Castle' No. 5070 on to Kidderminster. However, after being detached at Kidderminster the 'Duke' must have continued to Worcester as it later returned to the LMR hauling the 7.50 pm Worcester to Burton Parcels via Droitwich, Kidderminster, Stourbridge Junction and Dudley, and then onto the LMR via Walsall and Lichfield (High Level). The appearance of the engine at Stourbridge was made even more remarkable by the fact that No. 71000 should adhere to the same route restrictions as ex-GWR 'Kings', a class of locomotive that is specifically prohibited from normal working on the former Oxford, Worcester and Wolverhampton Railway! On the subject of 'Kings', the nearest Stourbridge ever came to acquiring one of these express passenger engines was in 1952 when No. 6020 *King Henry IV* was released from Swindon Works complete with an 84F shedplate. Whether this was simply a mistake or someone's idea of a joke remains a mystery.

It was reported that the first British Railways class '9F' 2-10-0 to visit the Stourbridge Junction-Wolverhampton line had been seen passing through Blower's Green in the direction of Dudley on 4th May, 1960. The locomotive, Banbury's No. 92226, was travelling 'light' coupled to 'Hall' No. 7923 *Speke Hall*. By 1962, 2-10-0 '9F' freight engines had become frequent visitors to the area, often working through the Junction on heavy mineral trains or being noted 'on shed'. A regular working for a '9F' would be hauling the Cardiff to Soho Pool tanker trains and it was on one of these that a Stourbridge crew had a quite unforgettable experience. The engine involved was No. 92220 *Evening Star*, a celebrity in today's preserved ranks, but not too popular with Stourbridge drivers and firemen. The train was approaching Ledbury tunnel when the crew began to experience difficulties. First, the fire-hole doors jammed shut followed by priming which prevented the regulator from being closed. Then, as the train entered the tunnel the engine began 'blowing-off' with such force as to bring down a torrent of slime and dirt off the tunnel roof onto the helpless crew below.

A '9F' also got into trouble outside Stafford Road Works, although on this occasion the problem arose from a misjudgement on the footplate. The locomotive was at the head of a heavy train of sugar beet pulp when it was brought to a halt at Stafford Road Junction home signal in the dip outside Dunstall Park station. Here, a lengthy wait made it necessary to top up the boiler using the injectors to keep the engine quiet. Then, as the signal came off the driver opened the regulator; unfortunately, instead of moving forward the engine developed a ferocious wheel slip. Frantically, the crew tried to bring it under control but with the boiler over full, the combination of water pressure and priming prevented the regulator from being closed. Eventually, with cylinder drain cocks fully open, pressure was reduced sufficiently to enable the regulator to be closed, however, by now the whole fire had been drawn through the tubes and dispersed by the blast over the nearby Works. Later two diesel locomotives were dispatched from Oxley to remove the stricken train to the sidings. Needless to say it was not praise that was heaped upon the shoulders of the crew that day!

WD class 2-8-0 freight locomotives were also to be seen in the area, and one unusual working involving one of these engines was on 28th January, 1953 when Bolton's No. 90271 passed through Stourbridge Junction on its way to Oxley via the Wombourn branch, hauling a rake of newly-built carriages earmarked for use on the Rhodesian Railway. Between February and July 1962 three of these engines, Nos. 90148/261/268, were allocated to the depot.

The closure of Wellington Shed (2M) on 8th August, 1964 resulted in those diagrams formerly covered by the depot, Wellington-Madeley Junction and the Buildwas line, being assigned to Crewe South, Oxley and Stourbridge. Although it is not known which of Stourbridge's engines were actually employed on these turns, Crewe South did normally provide Ivatt class '4' 2-6-0s. It is possible, therefore, that the depot allocated its only BR class '4MT' 2-6-0 available at the time, No. 76022. Alternatively, engines from its pool of six remaining ex-GWR 0-6-2Ts might also have been used. Further information regarding these workings would be welcome.

In the last months of steam at Stourbridge both BR class '4' and '5' tender engines had become regular visitors to the area with three of the former, Nos. 76036/042/087, being among some of the last steam locomotives to be assigned to the depot. Often to be found on freight workings, these locomotives would also be put to work on longer distance passenger trains such as the service to and from Leamington Spa. BR class '5' 4-6-0s were sometimes to be seen on local services between Birmingham (Snow Hill), Stourbridge Junction, Kidderminster and Worcester, duties which incidentally saw the use of a wide range of motive power including ex-GWR '56XX' class 0-6-2Ts and on at least one occasion an ex-LMS 'Jubilee'.

As a matter of interest there has been included below a list of those locomotives that were allocated to Stourbridge during the last month of steam operation at the shed, July 1966:

'5700' 0-6-0PT									Ivatt '2MT' 2-6-0
3607	3619	4646	4696	8718	8767	9608	9614	9641	46427

Stanier '8F' 2-8-0									
48121	48410	48412	48417	48424	48450	48459	48460	48468	48526
48531	48550	48757							

To complete this chapter, the story turns to some of the more unusual locomotives to visit the Stourbridge area.

On Saturday, 27th April, 1963 Villa Park hosted the FA Cup Semi-Final between Manchester United and Southampton. As a result the city of Birmingham was inundated with football supporters many of whom had arrived on excursions specially laid on for the event. Twelve trains were provided to transport Southampton supporters to the match, all of these being hauled by Bulleid 'West Country' or 'Battle of Britain' class Pacifics. Both routes from Oxford to the West Midlands were utilised, although it was the Oxford, Banbury and Leamington Spa line which saw most of the action with the majority of the Light Pacifics reaching Birmingham (Snow Hill) by this route. However, three 'West Country'-hauled excursions did arrive in the West Midlands by way of the former OWWR route to Worcester (Shrub Hill) and Stourbridge Junction and then over the Stourbridge Extension Railway to Birmingham. Consequently, these lengthy and heavily laden specials gave local enthusiasts the opportunity to enjoy the very rare, if not unprecedented sight of Southern Region 4-6-2s (No. 34009 *Lyme Regis*, No. 34046 *Braunton* and the now preserved No. 34039 *Boscastle*), hard

SR 'West Country' 4-6-2 No. 34039 *Boscastle* with a return football special for the Southampton area approaches Stourbridge Junction on 27th April, 1963.   *E.J. Dew*

SR 'Battle of Britain' class 4-6-2 No. 34088 *213 Squadron* receives a helping hand from Stourbridge '8F' class 2-8-0 No. 48478 on empty coaching stock at Lye on 27th April, 1963. The stock was for a football special from Birmingham (the semi-final of the FA Cup).   *E.J. Dew*

at work in the Black Country. In addition, Stourbridge Junction played host to two empty stock trains, the locomotives which brought them down from Snow Hill, No. 34045 *Ottery St Mary* and No. 34088 *213 Squadron*, being subsequently serviced at the depot. To cope with the severe gradient between Cradley Heath and Rowley Regis, the excursions were piloted by Stanier '8F' 2-8-0s provided by Stourbridge Shed. It appears that Nos. 48417/430/478 were on duty that day, all three being resident at 84F at the time. As a matter of interest, the other Light Pacifics employed on the 'football excursions' were: 34028 *Eddystone*; 34040 *Crewkerne*; 34042 *Dorchester*; 34050 *Royal Observer Corps*; 34052 *Lord Dowding*; 34094 *Mortehoe* and 34098 *Templecombe*.

A football excursion from Burton-on-Trent to Brierley Hill also brought an unusual, if less spectacular visitor to Stourbridge on 22nd April, 1953. Class '2P' 4-4-0 No. 40364 (17B) was serviced at the depot during the game whilst the stock was stabled at the Junction.

During World War II several unfamiliar engines were to be seen in the district. In 1939 the War Department requisitioned a number of 'Dean Goods' from the GWR which were replaced by 40 'J25' 0-6-0 tender engines borrowed from the LNER. The 'J25s' became quite familiar on the Worcester and Wolverhampton Divisions and six were actually allocated to Stourbridge Shed on or just after arrival in the area. These were No. 29 (November 1939); followed by No. 2000 (December 1939); No. 1973 (January 1940); Nos. 1970 and 2043 (both in February 1940) and finally, No. 2126 in March 1940. Of these, Nos. 1973 and 2000 returned to the LNER during March 1943, although the others, with the exception of No. 2126 which went north during August 1946, left Stourbridge for Darlington during January 1946. Unfortunately, like other non-Great Western engines to visit the depot, they were not too popular and few tears were shed when these 'Spitfires' (the origins of this nickname have been lost in the mists of time) made the long journey home.

Most unusual, perhaps, was the arrival during the War of the American-built 'S160' 2-8-0 freight locomotive. Late in 1942 the first of 400 such engines was landed at a port in Britain. A number of these engines were employed on the GWR with several being noted on the West Midland Section between Worcester, Stourbridge and Wolverhampton. During 1943 Nos. 1614/44/65 were sent to Worcester and Nos. 1648, 1841 and 2314 to Oxley, whilst No. 1607 (on 20th June, 1943) and Nos. 1611 and 1803 were noted working in the Stourbridge area. A very functional looking locomotive, the design reminded railwaymen of the WD 'Austerity' which had also been constructed under wartime conditions. One unusual feature was the positioning of the sandboxes on top of the boiler. Although this had the advantage of keeping the sand dry, filling them using the conventional method was both time consuming and laborious. However, the problem was solved when one enterprising individual decided it would be easier to fill a sack with sand and empty it into the sandbox as the locomotive stood at the coaling stage. The departure of all US 2-8-0s from Great Western metals during 1944 left a void which was to be filled by the transfer of a large number of War Department 'Austerity' 2-8-0s from other areas. By 28th October, 1944 Stourbridge Shed had received four of these locomotives, Nos. (7)7140/150/366/419. No. A77234 also spent some time at the shed having been allocated there by May 1947.

Through the British Railways era, visits by ex-LNER locomotives to the area, although rare, were certainly not unknown. For example in 1951 a complicated inter-Regional freight locomotive exchange programme led to the transfer of nine North Eastern Region '04' class 2-8-0s from Hull to the Western Region. Two of these found their way to Oxley whilst at least one, No. 63816, would have been seen at Stourbridge Junction when it headed a freight from Worcester to Market Drayton on 7th September, 1951. Early in 1964 '04' class locomotives were again seen in the Black Country, a number having been dispatched to Round Oak, destined to be broken up for scrap at the steelworks. Locomotives disposed of at the works included Nos. 63574/85; 63657/72/93, 63832/59/80 and 63900. A very unusual visitor to the area on 26th January, 1963 was 'B1' class 4-6-0 No. 61018 *Gnu* which was observed passing light engine through Blower's Green towards Dudley.

Class '56' No. 56 053 is seen at Stourbridge Junction on the 6V69 Brierley Hill to Cardiff Tidal
service on 21st September, 1995.   *Author*

Two class '37s' Nos. 37 670 and 37 671 double-head the 6V70 Bescot to St Blazey china clay
empties through Stourbridge Junction on 28th October, 1995.   *Author*

Chapter Ten

Locomotives Today

Locomotive Hauled Passenger Trains

Today, there are not normally any locomotive-hauled passenger trains through Stourbridge Junction, all main line services being operated by two-, three- or four-car 'Sprinters'. Occasionally, a Saturday railtour will call and these are usually, but not always, headed by class '47' diesel-electrics. In 1990, engineering work south of Birmingham did lead to a number of loco-hauled passenger trains and HSTs running to and from the South West to be diverted over the Stourbridge loop on Sundays.

Freight Workings

There are still a few freight workings which pass through the area and these at least have ensured that rail activity at the Junction has not totally deteriorated into a continuous procession of diesel units plying their trade to and from Snow Hill or New Street stations. During 1995 there was a particularly interesting working consisting of china clay empties hauled by two class '37s'. A regular Saturday morning service running between Bescot and St Blazey, the roar of these engines as they accelerated out of the station was guaranteed to catch the attention of early morning Birmingham-bound passengers waiting on the opposite platform. Class '37s' had also found employment on steel workings to and from the Brierley Hill area and notable amongst these visitors have been the powerful class '37/9s'. However, today, steel trains working into and out of Moor Street and Round Oak are now in the hands of Cardiff-based class '56' or '60' locomotives, although class '47s' can also be seen in the area. In 1995, workings to and from the Brierley Hill terminals were as follows:

6M11	SX	00.05	Margam-Round Oak (Class '60')	arrival 05.45 (approx.)
6M13	MWFO	02.52	Cardiff Tidal-Brierley Hill (Class '56')	arrival 06.30 (approx.)
6V05	SX	10.15	Round Oak-Margam (Class '60')	
6V69	MWFO	13.19	Brierley Hill-Cardiff Tidal (Class '56')	
6G21	SX	08.25	Washwood Heath-Brierley Hill (Class '47')	arrival 09.45 (approx)
6G22	SX	12.33	Brierley Hill-Washwood Heath (Class '47')	

Interestingly, 6G21/22 were Railfreight Distribution 'Connectrail' services which although intended to carry traffic for the continent, also provided a wagonload service for domestic customers. In addition to calling at Transrail's depot in Moor Street, this train also visited Round Oak Rail. 'Connectrail' services were routed via Bescot, Perry Barr, Soho and Stourbridge Junction, the locomotive running round its train at the latter. Stourbridge Junction also saw an 'Enterprise' working in the form of the 6M24 SX 12.45 Newport ADJ-Bescot Yard which was usually in the hands of a Wigan-based class '56' locomotive. This service was routed through the Junction to avoid the Lickey Incline.

An addition to the Working Timetable during the summer of 1995 was an early evening southbound 'Rail Express Parcels' service operating between Low Fell and Plymouth. Reporting as 1V64 and timed to pass through Stourbridge Junction at 8.05 pm, this train was headed by a red liveried 'Res' (Rail Express Systems) class '47'.

By Spring 1996, the last service booked for class '37' haulage, the Bescot-St Blazey china clay empties, had been withdrawn. In its place was a Monday to Saturday St Blazey-Bescot 'Enterprise' service hauled by a class '60', timed to pass through Stourbridge Junction at about 05.30 (Monday-Friday) and 06.00 Saturdays. However, in spite of this, class '37s' were still to

Class '47' No. 47 767 prepares to leave Stourbridge Junction with a railtour to Carlisle on 28th October, 1995. The shuttle service to Stourbridge Town can also be seen leaving in the background. *Author*

Class '37' No. 37 411 races into Stourbridge Junction from the south with the 'Pathfinder Regional Rambler' on 28th October, 1995. *Author*

Class '56' No. 56 038 hauls its train of wire coil past Withymoor towards Brierley Hill on 15th
November, 1995. *Author*

Class '60' No. 60 089 is seen with the 6V05 Round Oak to Margam train passing Withymoor
village on 15th November, 1995. *Author*

Class '60' No. 60 063 passes Kingswinford Junction signal box with the 6V05 service on 18th January, 1996.   *Author*

Class '150' No. 150 018 arrives at Lye with a Birmingham-bound train on 28th October, 1995.
                                                                            Author

Class '47' No. 47 313 is seen on 11th April, 1996 with a Connectrail service passing Dudley Football Club, Brierley Hill having just left Round Oak. *Author*

Class '47' No. 47 285 reverses past Stourbridge Junction Middle signal box with a Connectrail service in May 1997. *Author*

Class '56' No. 56 117 heads towards Round Oak on 19th September, 1997.   The former Kingswinford Sidings can be seen in the distance.   *Author*

Class '37' No. 37 680 heads the return trip working to Bescot past Stourbridge North Junction and onto the Stourbridge Extension on 27th February, 1998.   *Author*

be seen at Stourbridge on a regular basis, usually at the head of trip workings between Bescot and Moor Street steel terminal, a duty shared with both class '31' and class '47' locomotives. By early 1998 train 6E21, the Baglan Bay to Humber service conveying empty polypropylene tanks, had for its booked motive power a single class '37'. This working would pass Stourbridge Junction at 12.45 pm on Tuesdays and Fridays, before making its way eastwards over the Stourbridge Extension.

As at 7th September, 1998, freight (including Mail) trains working through Stourbridge Junction were as follows (derived from information supplied by Mark Rawlinson, Freightmaster):

Northbound			*Pass Stourbridge*
5M02	Bristol-Warrington RMT (Class '47')	Empty mail vans	09.45
6M81	Margam-Round Oak (Class '60')	Loaded steel	11.00 (RR)
6M46	Cardiff Tidal-Ironbridge (2 Class '37s')	Loaded tanks	12.15 (RR)
6E21	Baglan Bay-Humber (Class '37')	Pressure tanks	12.45 (TFO)
6E20	Margam-Lackenby (Class '37')	Empty steel	22.45
6M11	Margam-Round Oak (Class '60')	Loaded steel	05.30
6M98	Cardiff Tidal-Handsworth (Class '60')	Empty scrap wagons	05.45 (WO)

Southbound			*Pass Stourbridge*
6V05	Round Oak-Margam (Class '60')	Empty steel	10.15
6V07	Round Oak-Margam (Class '60')	Empty steel	15.45 (RR)
6V06	Handsworth-Cardiff Tidal (Class '60')	Scrap metal	18.30 (WO)
6V52	Ironbridge-Cardiff Tidal (2 Class '37s')	Empty tanks	20.00 (RR)
6V05	Round Oak-Margam (Class '60')	Empty steel	10.20 (SO)

Reverse at Stourbridge Junction			*Arr. Stourbridge**
6Z62	Toton (ex-Boston)-Round Oak (Class '56')	Loaded steel	13.45 (WFO-RR)
6Z67	Round Oak-Toton (to Boston) (Class '56')	Empty steel	18.00 (WFO-RR)
6G74	Bescot-Brierley Hill (Class '37')	Loaded steel	09.45 (RR)
6G75	Brierley Hill-Bescot (Class '37')	Empty steel	10.20 (RR)
6G13	Bescot-Round Oak (Class '47')	Loaded steel	18.10 (RR)
6G14	Round Oak-Bescot (Class '47')	Empty steel	21.10 (RR)

* Arrival times are very approximate due to the current temporary closure of Galton Junction requiring all trains to run via Bromsgrove and reverse at Worcester.

Steam Hauled Specials

Early Autumn saw steam once again operating from Stourbridge Junction. On Sunday 24th September, 1995, BR Standard 2-6-4T No. 80079 drew the crowds when it operated a special shuttle service between Stourbridge Junction and Birmingham (Snow Hill) to celebrate the inauguration of the 'Jewellery Line' (Snow Hill Phase 2) linking Smethwick once again with Snow Hill. This is now due to become the main commuter route from Stourbridge into Birmingham continuing through Moor Street and on to Dorridge and Leamington Spa. The £28.5 million line was opened by the Rt Hon. John Prescott MP, and was soon to make the headlines: unfortunately, for the wrong reasons. The timetable relating to the service had inadvertently omitted to show details of the shuttle service (the 'Dodger' as it is still known locally) between the Junction and Town stations. It was subsequently reported in the 3rd October, 1995 edition of the local *Express & Star* that a spokesperson for Centro had said: 'The break-up of the rail industry caused extensive delays in getting the timetable agreed. We are now pulling the right information together and working to make sure passengers have the correct timetables.'

LNER 2-6-0 class 'K4' No. 3442 *Great Marquess* is seen arriving at Stourbridge on 19th September, 1965 with an SLS special. *E.J. Dew*

Another view of No. 3442 *Great Marquess* on the same train . Here it is seen departing Stourbridge Junction heading towards Worcester. *V. Morgan*

Incidentally, the opening of the 'Jewellery Line' was not the first time that No. 80079 has been seen at Stourbridge Junction. On 1st January, 1995 the locomotive, together with ex-LMS No. 46521 and 'King' No. 6024 *King Edward I*, were involved in the movement of empty railtour stock to and from Kidderminster. Some months later, on 19th May, 1995, the Severn Valley Railway's GWR 2-6-0 No. 7325 was utilised on railtour duty between the Junction and Newport. The return leg of this journey saw the train double-headed by No. 7325 and 'Manor' class 4-6-0 No. 7802 *Bradley Manor*, also from the Severn Valley Railway. Unfortunately, No. 7325 failed and was detached at Worcester leaving the 'Manor' to bring the railtour back to Stourbridge Junction alone. Early in November 1995, No. 7325 was again scheduled for railtour duty from Stourbridge Junction. No. 7325 and No. 7802 were earmarked for duty on a Past-time Rail Tour on 20th April, 1997. Booked to work the return steam leg from Stourbridge Junction to Bristol, the tour was cancelled due to the unusually dry weather which resulted in the only too familiar imposition of a steam ban by Railtrack.

On Saturday 3rd February, 1996 the Junction reverberated to the sound of Gresley's 'A4' Pacific No. 60009 *Union of South Africa* on a railtour to Nottingham and Crewe. This was not the first time an ex-LNER locomotive had been seen on railtour duty in the area, as 'K4' No. 3442 *The Great Marquess* had passed through on 19th September, 1965.

GWR 'King' class No. 6024 *King Edward I* made two appearances at Stourbridge Junction during the early Autumn of 1996. The first visit was on 21st September whilst making its way to the Severn Valley Railway at Kidderminster; the second was on 5th October when it was employed on railtour duty taking over the steam leg of Pathfinder Tour's 'The Cities United Express' at Birmingham (Snow Hill), the 'King' initially being attached to the train at Stourbridge Junction.

BR Standard class '4' 2-6-4T No. 80079 leaves Stourbridge Junction for Birmingham (Snow Hill) on 24th September, 1995. *Author*

Ex-LNER class 'A4' class 4-6-2 No. 60009 *Union of South Africa* is seen at Lye on a Pathfinder railtour on 3rd February, 1996.   *Author*

Ex-GWR 'King' class 4-6-0 No. 6024 *King Edward I* is seen on empty railtour stock at Stourbridge Junction on 1st January, 1995.   *E.J. Dew*

Postscript

The Midlands Metro

Plans to construct a Midlands Metro connecting Birmingham, Wolverhampton, Walsall, Dudley and Brierley Hill moved a step closer on 13th July, 1995, when Transport Minister Steven Norris announced that £80 million in grants and borrowing approval would be available to add to the £34 million to be jointly funded by the local Passenger Transport Authority, the Black Country Development Corporation, key Black Country local authorities and the developers Altram. The balance of £31 million to complete the funding of the £145 million Metro Line 1 project was approved by the European Regional Development Fund on 17th July, 1995.

Midland Metro was first launched in September 1987 and a Private Member's Bill went before Parliament during November 1988. Now, after eight years, full Parliamentary and funding approval had been obtained and the contract between Centro and Altram was subsequently signed on 3rd August, 1995. Construction began on Monday 13th November, 1995 when the Rt Hon. George Young MP, Secretary of State for Transport, attended the official opening ceremony. It is hoped that the line will be completed by the beginning of 1999. Line 1 will be 20.14 kilometres of standard gauge track, with 23 stops linking Wolverhampton and Birmingham (Snow Hill) via West Bromwich, Wednesbury and Bilston. With the exception of the last 1.8 km, which will run through the streets of Wolverhampton, the line will follow the former track bed of the Great Western Railway. It is anticipated that 15 electric cars will service the route operating from a 750 volts dc direct contact system and running between 6.30 am and 11.30 pm daily, with a six minute service in each direction between 7.00 am and 7.00 pm. Metro Line 1 is one of three lines that are being promoted. Line 2 is planned to connect Birmingham to the NEC and Birmingham Airport, although it will be Line 3 that will be of most interest to residents in the Dudley/Stourbridge area of the Black Country.

Metro Line 3, as originally proposed, was a Light Railway that would link Brierley Hill, Dudley, Walsall and Wolverhampton. This project has been promoted alongside an earlier plan to provide a heavy rail passenger service between Stourbridge, Dudley and Walsall. Both schemes were to utilise the former freight-only line between Stourbridge and Bescot which had closed beyond Round Oak on 22nd March, 1993, although where the Metro was concerned this would be confined to certain stretches of track bed between Wednesbury and Brierley Hill. The heavy rail option, which proposed stations at Silver End, Round Oak, Shaw Road, Tipton Road, Dudley, Dudley Port, Great Bridge and Wednesbury, first came to the public's attention as early as April 1989. Unfortunately, the announcement was met with a storm of protest from residents occupying the newly-built estate at Withymoor which lay immediately adjacent to the Amblecote embankment. Apparently, the principal objection related to the possibility of trains running round the clock if existing day time freight workings were displaced to vacant late night or early morning paths by the new passenger services. This protest lasted throughout 1989 and was supported by the then Conservative MP for Dudley West, John Blackburn. The idea was resurrected in December 1992, although by now heavy rail was possibly being seen as an interim measure which would only operate until such time as it could be replaced by the Metro Light Railway. For financial reasons this option only applied to a proposed service between Dudley and Walsall, although an extension of services south of Dudley to Stourbridge was to be re-evaluated. However, by February 1996, the problems being experienced with the heavy rail scheme prompted a significant change in local political policy which resulted in the abandonment of support for this proposal in favour of a modified version of Metro Line 3. This version of the line would now leave Metro Line 1 at a spur at Wednesbury and would then continue into Dudley and Brierley Hill as before, although the route would now incorporate a stop at Merry Hill. Included in the plan was an option to continue to Stourbridge at some time in the future. At the time of writing it was not known whether this option would involve a road route or one that utilises the freight-only section from Round Oak to Stourbridge (or a combination of both). Time will tell if the town will eventually become part of this grand scheme of up to 15 planned lines for the Black Country, Birmingham and Coventry.

Despite local political backing for Metro Line 3 the 'Heavy Rail' lobby actively continues to support the proposal to introduce services between Stourbridge and Walsall. In April 1997 the Railway Development Society published its plan for a new 22 mile route between Stourbridge Junction and Lichfield via Walsall which is fully supported by local Rail User Groups. The scheme, which has been costed at up to £15m, envisages the use of three diesel multiple units which should enable a half-hourly service to be maintained over the whole route, each journey taking around 36 minutes to complete. Currently, passengers from Stourbridge wishing to travel to Walsall have to go via Birmingham (New Street), therefore a direct route via Dudley would reduce considerably existing journey times. This proposal followed close on the heels of the new Wolverhampton to Walsall rail service which commenced on 24th May, 1998.

On 27th June, 1997 the *Dudley Chronicle* reported an unexpected development in the debate over 'Light' or 'Heavy' rail for the district. As mentioned above, Dudley Council had last year withdrawn support for the heavy rail option apparently on the grounds that the proposals were for a link between   Dudley and Walsall only; Railtrack was opposed to a track sharing arrangement whereby both the Midland Metro and conventional rail transport would use the same lines; and an additional cost of £250,000 was needed to carry out another feasibility study. However, a change of heart by Railtrack has now resulted in its opposition to track sharing being withdrawn. Consequently, with one of the major obstacles removed, the local Council looks set to revive earlier plans to re-open the Walsall-Dudley-Stourbridge rail link.   This though does not imply that the Council is rethinking its support for the Midland Metro and looking closer at the heavy rail passenger option. Instead, this decision could mean that there is now at least the possibility of freight services running straight through between Walsall and Stourbridge Junction over the stretch of track that has been closed since 1993.

Brierley Hill Steel Terminal

It was announced in the local press on 9th May, 1997 that the English Welsh & Scottish Railway (EWS) depot (formerly Transrail) at Moor Street, Brierley Hill was to be closed and mothballed within the next few months with the loss of seven jobs. The last train of coiled wire had arrived on 26th March and by the end of May, with the stockpile of steel wire almost gone, shutdown was clearly imminent, although the Moor Street site was to be kept on by EWS with a view to the possibility of developing the premises in the future. By the beginning of June the depot had closed down completely, as a result the line's only surviving traffic is the daily steel train between Margam and Round Oak Rail and the occasional Enterprise trip workings between the latter and Bescot. As a matter of interest, Allied Steel & Wire traffic formally handled at Moor Street is now being taken to Burton-on-Trent via the daily Cardiff-Wakefield service which calls as required.

July 1997 witnessed the reopening of Moor Street Depot, but this time the occupiers were not English, Welsh & Scottish Railway. Apparently, EWS has leased the site to Swains of Rochester who are using the depot for deliveries of steel products brought up from Sheerness on the EWS 'Enterprise' service to Mossend. Wagons are detached at Bescot and then 'tripped' to Moor Street on a twice-weekly basis. However, the principal traffic operating over the route continues to be the daily Margam-Round Oak steel trains, the regular services even being supplemented by the odd additional working arriving at Round Oak mid-morning. These extra services may in fact be part of a new flow of steel coil from British Steel's mills at Port Talbot and Llanwern in South Wales that is to be off-loaded at either Round Oak or Wolverhampton. Both of these terminals have recently been earmarked to receive large quantities of South Wales coil to accommodate West Midland industrial requirements. Interestingly, there are indications that Round Oak is also to become the destination for a second new traffic flow involving imported steel from Boston docks in Lincolnshire. This service commenced early in October 1997. It has been forecast that by January 1998 steel traffic arriving at Black Country terminals will have doubled compared to January 1997 - good news indeed! As mentioned elsewhere, the line north of Round Oak has been closed to freight traffic since 22nd March, 1993, as a result all steel trains from Bescot for Moor Street/Round Oak are required to reverse at Stourbridge Junction. The possibility of an increase in goods traffic into the area will undoubtedly add weight to the argument supporting the reinstatement of a heavy rail link from Stourbridge Junction via Dudley to Walsall.

The Parry People Mover

Between 1994 and 1997 J.P.M. Parry & Associates, Centro, British Rail Research, the Department of Transport and HM Railway Inspectorate were involved in moves to develop an Ultra Light Railcar to replace the shuttle service between Stourbridge Town station and Stourbridge Junction, the latter acting as both an interchange for passengers using main line trains and a 'Park and Ride' facility for shoppers not wishing to drive into Stourbridge town centre. The class '153' diesel unit currently employed on the route makes 81 round trips daily, Sundays excluded (as at November 1997), whilst passenger loading is around a maximum of 1,500 per day. The unit is returned to Tyseley MPD at the end of each working day.

In most cases, expensive schemes such as the Midland Metro are the usual alternative to heavy rail operation, although conventional light rail solutions are not necessarily appropriate or justifiable in every situation. In some circumstances, an Ultra Light Rail system may be a more desirable option, consequently, J.P.M. Parry & Associates have developed the 'Parry People Mover', a lightweight rail vehicle that would both reduce costs and be environmentally friendly. By 1996 a change to 'PPM' working over the Stourbridge branch was close to becoming a reality, however, major changes in the Railway industry brought about by privatisation focused attention on other issues. August 1997 saw the 'PPM' programme for Stourbridge suffer a setback when the proposal to run the machine over the branch on a trial basis was rejected by Centro and Central Trains. In the light of this there was a rumour that Glenda Jackson MP, Parliamentary Under Secretary of State at the Department of the Environment, Transport and the Regions, had intervened with the result that discussions with Centro had now been resumed. However, Government sources maintain that it is up to the various parties concerned to come to an agreement regarding the PPM and that it would be inappropriate for Ministers to seek to influence that decision. The Government does recognise the importance to Parry People Movers Ltd, as manufacturers of innovative technology, to be able to test its vehicle properly in a full public service operation, although it is not in a position to press either the train operator, Central Trains Ltd, or Centro, to use a particular form of traction on the Stourbridge Town line.

What then is the 'PPM'? Until recently, the Author knew very little about this vehicle, however, a contribution in the Stourbridge Line User Group's Autumn 1997 Newsletter and technical data from J.P.M. Parry & Associates have now come to the rescue. The vehicle, which has been developed in Cradley Heath as a low cost, pollution free transport system designed for use mainly in town centres, is similar in size to a minibus and would have a carrying capacity of between 30 and 35 passengers. As cost and appearance had ruled out a conventional overhead power supply, it was necessary to develop an on-board energy storage system using either batteries or flywheel. For a number of reasons the battery option was rejected, the company concentrating its research on the development of flywheel power (kinetic energy storage). The resulting system uses an energy input of 70 volts dc to spin the flywheel, power being conveyed to the final drive shaft via a continuously variable transmission. Interestingly, the CVT does not simply transfer power to the rail wheels, it also acts as a speed control. One consequence of this arrangement is that as the vehicle slows the flywheel accelerates thereby reusing energy that would normally be lost through braking. The vehicle can operate at speeds of up to 30 mph and one charge of the flywheel will give an operational range of between 2 and 2½ miles on level track. Recharging the flywheel takes about 90 seconds, although regular 'topping up' can take place at contact points at each stop.

Appendix One

Working of Stourbridge Bank Engines
October 1886

Bank Train No. 1

4.15 am   Leave Stourbridge Engine House for Stourbridge Junction (SJ)

4.45 am   Leave SJ for Lye, Hayes Lane or Corngreaves as required, calling at Homer Hill to put empties in Colliery siding. Return from Corngreaves to SJ, calling as necessary at Lye, Hickman and Timmis' sidings to put off GW empties.

                Leave SJ for Rowley with Halesowen traffic, calling at Cradley and Old Hill for traffic. Make a trip to Oldbury if there are 20 empties to take there. Return from Rowley to SJ calling at Old Hill and Homer Hill for traffic, weigh wagons at Cradley. Arrive SJ at about 11.35 am.

12.15pm   Leave SJ for Lye, Cradley and Corngreaves, clear Homer Hill and Hayes Lane of all traffic for SJ. Finish about 4.15pm.

Bank Train No. 2

5.25 am   Leave Stourbridge Engine House for SJ.

6.15 am   Leave SJ for Stourbridge Basin and clear all traffic, making two or three trips if required. Shunt SJ as required; run to Hayes Lane, Rowley or Dudley as required. Finish at 4.45 pm.

Bank Train No. 3

5.30am   Leave Stourbridge Engine House for Kingswinford taking all traffic for the Kingswinford branch.

7.10 am   Leave the Kingswinford branch for Brettell Lane, shunting as required until 7.50 am. Take empties into Messrs Harrison's, and Bailey & Pegg's sidings if required (not to be kept over 40 minutes at Brettell Lane), return to Kingswinford branch to complete work and put off traffic into Moor Lane sidings.

6.00 pm   Leave Kingswinford branch taking all private empties and coal for Stourbridge Basin & Engine House for No. 2 Bank Train. Finish at 6.15 pm.

Bank Train No. 6

7.20 am   Leave Stourbridge Engine House for SJ, work 7.30 am empty carriages to Stourbridge Town, return with 7.42 am from Stourbridge. Work the 7.56 am Passenger train from SJ to Wolverhampton, return light to Dudley at 8.50am and work the 9.27 am Passenger train from Dudley to Wolverhampton and the 10.20 am Wolverhampton to Dudley.

12 noon   Leave Dudley for Stourbridge Junction, calling at Netherton, Round Oak and Kingswinford Junction, reaching SJ at 1.20 pm. Marshal traffic, run Specials as required and work all traffic to and from Stourbridge Basin, including a trip at 6.25 pm with London traffic for the 4.10pm ex-Victoria Basin. After working the last trip from Stourbridge Basin finish at about 8.15pm.

Bank Train No. 7

4.00 pm   Leave SJ for Corngreaves; run to Cradley and Lye to fetch Brentford, London and Smithfield traffic and work it to SJ in time to meet the 4.10 pm goods from Victoria Basin to London due SJ at 6.40 pm.

6.40 pm   Leave SJ for Lye and Cradley, shunt sidings and put North traffic ready for 7.40 pm ex-Cradley (No. 9 Bank) to pick up. Pilot 9.00 pm Goods ex-SJ from Cradley to Rowley, clear Cradley and Lye of all traffic for SJ, arrive there at 11.00 pm.

11.30 pm   Leave Stourbridge Junction with all Private empties for Cradley, Homer Hill and Hayes Lane Branch; marshal traffic at Lye; clear sidings of all empty GW & Private wagons, take to Hayes Lane branch by 12.30 am and sort. Run to Rowley taking all traffic for Birmingham district; shunt Rowley Colliery Company's siding and clear out Homer Hill and return to SJ. Take Cradley station truck for Gloucester to go forward on 4.45 am ex-SJ.
Finish at 4.00 am.

Bank Train No. 8

6.00 pm   Pilot trains from Stourbridge Junction as required during night, marshal traffic or run Specials as required, finish at 6.30 am.

Bank Train No. 9

1.50 pm   Leave Stourbridge Engine House with van for Hayes Lane to fetch mineral train, returning at 3.00 pm.
4.45 pm   Leave SJ for Dudley.
6.15 pm   Leave Dudley light for Old Hill, pick up Halesowen wagons for the North.
6.35 pm   Leave for Cradley. Shunt and marshal traffic there.
7.40 pm   Leave Cradley and call at Lye for North traffic, arriving SJ at 8.45 pm.
9.20 pm   Leave SJ for Oxley Sidings, call at Brettell Lane and Dudley.
11.40 pm   Leave Oxley Sidings for Stourbridge Junction on Goods train.
           Pick up traffic at Cannock Road Jn for the 1.00 am ex-Victoria Basin to Reading and convey to Priestfield. Finish at 1.45 am. This train will work traffic from stations for the Crewe line and Birkenhead.

Notes

Bank Train No. 4

This was a Wolverhampton turn handling traffic for stations and yards between Victoria Basin and Dudley, as well as an early morning run to Walsall.

Bank Train No. 5

This was a Wolverhampton turn from Victoria Basin to Withymoor Basin, calling at Oxley Sidings and Netherton. The service then worked between Netherton and Withymoor as required. Work was also carried out at Cox's Lane and Rowley before returning to Wolverhampton via Dudley and Oxley Sidings.

Pannier tank No. 2056 is seen with its shunter's truck at Stourbridge Junction *c.* 1922.

Real Photographs

A Summary of Locomotives
Allocated to Stourbridge

January 1948

'1400' 0-4-2T
1410 1414 1438

'1501' 0-6-0PT
1745 1749

'1813' 0-6-0PT
1835

'2021' 0-6-0PT
2090 2092 2107

'2181' 0-6-0PT
2185 2186 2187 2189

'2251' 0-6-0
2246 2270 2279 2281

'Aberdare' 2-6-0
2620 2655

'2700' 0-6-0PT
2706 2712 2771

'2800' 2-8-0
2852

'Bulldog' 4-4-0
3450 *Peacock*

'5700' 0-6-0PT
3649 3667 3740 4638 4687 4696 5719 5726 5754 5794 5795 7705 8704 8742 8791
8792 8797 9613 9636 9741 9767

'5100' 2-6-2T
4104 4146 4148 4149 4150 5101 5105 5107 5122 5131 5134 5136 5138 5141 5146
5147 5155 5160 5165 5167 5170 5180 5189 5191 5193 5196 5197

'5600' 0-6-2T
6617 6646 6665 6667 6674 6677 6678 6684

'7400' 0-6-0PT
7402 7428

'Duke' 4-4-0
9084 *Isle of Jersey*

January 1951

'1400' 0-4-2T
1414 1438 1458

'1600' 0-6-0PT
1621

'2021' 0-6-0PT
2090 2107

'2181' 0-6-0PT
2185 2186 2187

'2251' 0-6-0
2246 2270 2279

'2800' 2-8-0
2852 2856 2857 2885 3821 3827

'5700' 0-6-0PT
3649 3667 3710 3740 4638 4687 4696 5719 5726 5754 5794 5795 7705 8704 8742
8791 8792 8797 9613 9636 9741 9767

'5100' 2-6-2T
4104 4146 4150 4153 4168 4173 5101 5105 5107 5134 5136 5147 5155 5160 5165
5167 5170 5180 5189 5191 5193 5196 5197 5199

'4300' 2-6-0
4337 4375 6327 6332 6354 6391

'5600' 0-6-2T
5606 5651 5658 6617 6646 6667 6674 6677 6678

'Grange' 4-6-0
6828 *Trellech Grange*   6857 *Tudor Grange*

'7400' 0-6-0PT
7402 7428 7429 7430 7432 7435 7448 7449

'9400' 0-6-0PT
8418 8419 9427

January 1954

'1400' 0-4-2T   *'1600' 0-6-0PT*   *'2251' 0-6-0*   *'2800' 2-8-0*
1414   1438   1458   1619   1621   3206   3216   3217   3218   2804   2885   3821   3827

'5700' 0-6-0PT
3649   3658   3667   3710   3743   3751   4646   4687   4696   5719   5754   5794   5795   7705   8704
8742   8791   8792   8797   9613   9636   9719   9767   9782

'5100' 2-6-2T
4104   4173   5101   5105   5107   5160   5165   5167   5180   5189   5191   5199

'4300' 2-6-0
4326   4375   5313   5371   5379   6332   6391

'5600' 0-6-2T
5606   5642   5651   5658   6609   6646   6667   6677   6678   6681   6683   6692   6698

'Grange' 4-6-0
6803 *Bucklebury Grange*   6823 *Oakley Grange*
6828 *Trellech Grange*   6857 *Tudor Grange*

'7400' 0-6-0PT
7428   7429   7430   7432   7435   7441   7448   7449

'9400' 0-6-0PT
8419   8437   8438   9477

January 1957

'1400' 0-4-2T   *'1600' 0-6-0PT*   *'2800' 2-8-0*
1414   1438   1458   1465   1619   1621   2804   2829   2834   2885   3821   3825

'5700' 0-6-0PT
3649   3658   3667   3710   3729   3743   3745   4646   4687   4696   5719   5754   5795   7705   8704
8742   8792   8797   9613   9624   9636   9719   9767   9782

'5100' 2-6-2T
4104   4173   5101   5105   5107   5109   5165   5180   5186   5189   5191   5199

'4300' 2-6-0
4326   4375   5371   6332   6393

'5600' 0-6-2T
5606 5651 5658 6609 6646 6667 6674 6677 6678 6681 6683 6692 6698

'Grange' 4-6-0
6803 *Bucklebury Grange*   6828 *Trellech Grange*

'7400' 0-6-0PT
7420   7428   7429   7430   7432   7435   7441   7447   7448   7449

January 1960
'1600' 0-6-0PT
1619   1621   1663

'2800' 2-8-0
2856   2885   2888   2897   3821   3825   3831   3839   3846

'5700' 0-6-0PT
3649   3658   3667   3710   3729   3743   3745   4646   4687   4696   5754   5795   8704   8742   8792
8797   9613   9624   9636   9719   9767   9782

'5100' 2-6-2T
4104   4110   4140   4161   4168   4173   5176   5199

'4300' 2-6-0
6317   6332   6340   6349   6367

'6400' 0-6-0PT
6403

'5600' 0-6-2T
6604   6609   6646   6667   6677   6678   6683   6692

'Grange' 4-6-0
6803 *Bucklebury Grange*   6879 *Overton Grange*

'7400' 0-6-0PT
7429   7430   7432   7435   7441   7448   7449

January 1963
'5700' 0-6-0PT
3658   4602   4646   4665   4687   4696   9613   9614   9624   9646   9733   9782

'5100' 2-6-2T
4140   4168   5192

'6400' 0-6-0PT
6403   6424

'5600' 0-6-2T
6646   6667   6678   6683   6692

'Grange' 4-6-0
6811 *Cranbourne Grange*   6827 *Llanfrechfa Grange*   6842 *Nunhold Grange*

'7400' 0-6-0PT
7430   7432   7435   7441   7449

Ivatt '2MT' 2-6-0
46506   46517   46526   46527

Stanier '8F' 2-8-0
48330   48402   48410   48415   48417   48424   48430   48450   48459   48460   48474   48475
48478   48724

January 1966
'5700' 0-6-0PT
3607   3619   4646   4696   8718
9608   9614   9641   9724

Stanier '8F' 2-8-0
48121   48410   48412   48417   48424   48450   48459   48460
48468   48526   48531   48550   48757

BR '4MT' 2-6-0
76036   76042

(Data supplied courtesy of Richard Strange, Steam Archive Services.)

Appendix Three

Freight Trains Timetable, Stourbridge Yard, (excluding Sundays), 3rd July, 1939

Code	Time	Day	From	To	Arr. Stb	Dep Stb	Notes
	pm		Down		am	am	
F		MX	Stourbridge Jn	Crewe		1.00	
J		MX	Stourbridge Jn	Bordesley Jn		1.10	BE Cradley
K	1.30 (am)	MX	Hartlebury	Stourbridge Jn	2.27		
F	11.25	MX	Hereford	Bordesley Jn	2.49	3.40	
E	10.15	MO	Cardiff	Bordesley Jn	3.24	3.55	
F		MO	Stourbridge Jn	Crewe		3.30	
J		MX	Stourbridge Jn	Dudley		4.10	
F	8.15	MX	Reading	Oxley Sidings	4.00	4.30	#
C		MXRR	Stourbridge Jn	Kingswinford Sdgs		5.42	Livestock
F	8.15	MO	Worcester Goods (Reading - Sat)	Oxley Sdgs	5.20	5.55	
E	7.20	MX	Landore	Stourbridge Jn	6.18		
F	9.55	MX	Cardiff	Oxley Sdgs	6.45	8.10	
E	9.10	MX	Llandilo Jn	Bordesley Jn	6.56	8.40	
J			Stourbridge Jn	Bordesley Jn		8.45	
J			Stourbridge Jn	Oxley Sdgs		10.30	
	am						
H	4.35		Pontypool Rd	Bilston	11.08	11.36	
J			Stourbridge Jn	Galton Jn		Noon	Colliery empties
					pm	pm	
K		SX	Stourbridge Jn	Cradley Heath		12.30	To Old Hill Goods
H	5.25		Pontypool Rd	Oxley Sdgs	12.29	1.00	
H	4.15	MORR	Alexandra Dock Jn	Stourbridge Jn	1.22		
J		SX	Stourbridge Jn	Bordesley Jn		1.40	
	pm						
C	12.20	RR	Long Marston	Crewe	Pass	3.37	
F	2.20		Worcester Goods	Blower's Green Sdgs	4.17	5.15	
H	9.00 (am)		Pontypool Rd	Stow Heath	4.36	4.58	
C	2.10	SXRR	Littleton & Badsey*	Crewe	Pass	6.08	
E	5.15	MO	Worc. Butts Siding	Stourbridge Jn	6.46		Cattle
C	6.00	SXRR	Worcester Goods†	Crewe	Pass	7.28	Perishables #
E	7.15	Alt. Tu	Kidderminster	Bordesley Jn	7.35	8.00	Cattle
C		WORR	Hereford	Bordesley Jn	7.44	7.59	Cattle
C	8.30	SXRR	Kidderminster	Crewe	Pass	8.46	#
E			Stourbridge Jn	Oxley Sdgs		9.10	
E	8.57	Alt. Tu	Kidderminster††	Stourbridge Jn	9.18		RR/Cattle
C	8.35	SX	Worcester Goods	Crewe	9.45	9.50	BE #
F	8.30	SO	Worcester Goods	Crewe	9.47	10.05	§
H	3.15		Alexandra Dock Jn	Stourbridge Jn	12.14 (am)		
F	8.05		Cradley	Crewe	8.50	10.50	Reverse SJ #
K	6.00		Tenbury	Stourbridge Jn	12.34 (am)		
E	9.45		Worcester Goods	Crewe	11.15	11.20	BE¶ (SO#)
C		RR	Stourbridge Jn	Shrewsbury		11.29	#
J		SORR	Stourbridge Jn	Halesowen		11.45	Reverse Old Hill
						am	
E	10.30	SXRR	Worcester Goods	Crewe	11.58	12.03	BE
					am		
H	5.20	SX	Pontypool Rd	Oxley Sdgs	12.25	1.50	
E/F	11.45	SX	Worcester Goods	Moor Street	1.28	2.30	
J	6.45		Oxford	Stourbridge Jn	3.17		
H	6.20	SO	Pontypool Rd	Oxley Sdgs	1.15	1.50	

Code	Time	Day	From	To	Arr. Stb	Dep. Stb	Notes
	pm		*Up*		*am*	*am*	
C	10.00	MX	Bordesley Jn	Llanelly	12.11	12.30	
C		MX	Stourbridge Jn	Cardiff		1.05	
H	11.35	WORR	Bordesley Jn (Tu)	Hereford	1.30	2.05	Cattle empties
J	12.39 (am)	MX	Dudley	Stourbridge Jn	2.00		
F		MO	Stourbridge Jn	Pontypool Rd		2.35	
F	8.35	MX	Crewe	Stourbridge Jn	3.20		
F	11.30	MX	Bordesley Jn	Pontypool Rd	1.41	2.35	
H	2.00 (am)	MO	Bilston	Pontypool Rd	Pass	3.05	
E	9.35	MX	Crewe	Worcester Goods	2.28	3.15	#
	am						
F	1.00	MX	Bordesley Jn	Gloucester	2.41	4.00	
F	2.00	MO	Bordesley Jn	Gloucester	3.07	4.10	
J	3.05	MX	Bordesley Jn	Stourbridge Jn	4.30		
H	3.55	MO	Bordesley Jn	Stourbridge Jn	5.25		
F	3.15	MX	Moor Street	Worcester Goods	5.26	6.00	
E/F	12.50	MX	Crewe	Worcester Goods	6.30	7.07	#
F			Stourbridge Jn	Tenbury Wells		8.36	
J	3.45	MX	Oxley Sidings	Stourbridge Jn	8.40		Dept. 4.30 am (MO)***
F	4.50	MX	Crewe	Kidderminster	8.53	9.50	Dept. 4.30 am (MO)#
H		SX	Stourbridge Jn	Pontypool Rd		9.25	Dept. 2.20 pm (SO)
H		MX	Stourbridge Jn	Pontypool Rd		10.30	RR Monday
J	7.22		Bordesley Jn	Stourbridge Jn	11.26		
					pm	*pm*	
H	11.50		Bilston	Pontypool Rd	12.45	1.35	
	pm						
H	1.45	RR	Dudley	Stourbridge Jn	2.55		
J	11.30 (am)	SX	Bordesley Jn	Stourbridge Jn	3.07		
E	1.00	Alt. Tu	Bordesley Jn	Kidderminster	Pass	2.55	Cattle empties
K	2.45		Galton Jn	Stourbridge Jn	3.25		
J	4.30		Cradley Heath	Stourbridge Jn	4.50		Starts Old Hill Gds
J	3.45		Dudley	Stourbridge Jn	4.52		
J	5.20		Oxley Sdgs	Stourbridge Jn	6.49		#
F	6.18		Blower's Green	Worcester Goods	8.20	9.30	
J	9.05	SX	Oldbury & L. Green	Stourbridge Jn	9.50		
J	7.53	SX	Bordesley Jn	Stourbridge Jn	10.47		
J	8.25	SO	Prince's End Goods	Stourbridge Jn	11.00		
J	7.30	SO	Bordesley Jn	Stourbridge Jn	11.05		
F	7.50		Cannock Rd Jn	Reading	10.05	10.35	
F	8.45	SO	Priestfield	Pontypool Rd	10.53	11.30	
J	9.50	SX	Tipton	Stourbridge Jn	m/nt		
J	9.15		Oxley Sdgs	Worcester Goods	10.15	11.00	#
H		SX	Stourbridge Jn	Pontypool Rd		11.30	
						am	
E	9.50		Victoria Basin	Cardiff	11.40	1.33	
					am		
F	11.20	SX	Priestfield	Pontypool Rd	1.25	1.55	

Notes
*   This train is marshalled at Worcester GW goods yard, departure at 5.30 pm.
**   Runs via Handsworth.
†   Attach passenger train-rated traffic put off 3.30 pm freight from Bromyard.
††   Ex-Tenbury Wells.
¶   Diverted over the Wombourn branch when 10.30 pm Worcester to Oxley Sidings is running. (Both 9.45 and 10.30 ran via Wolverhampton unless former re-routed.)
#   Via Wombourn.
§   Via Wolverhampton.
BE   Attach bank engine, e.g. change engine.
O   On that day only, e.g. MO Monday only.
X   Not on that day, e.g. SX Saturday excepted.
RR   Run as required.

Appendix Four

Freight Trains Timetable, Kingswinford Sidings (including Sundays), 10th September, 1951

Code	Time	Day	From	Arr.	Dep.	To	Notes
	pm		*Down*	*am*	*am*		
H	5.25	MTX	Swindon	1.08		Kingswinford	
H		MX+Su	Kingswinford		1.55	Crewe	Via Wombourn
F	10.20	MX	Morris Cowley	2.25		Kingswinford†	Via Wombourn
H	8.15	MX+Su	Scours Lane	4.00		Kingswinford	
K		MX	Kingswinford		4.45	Oxley Sdgs	
H			Kingswinford		6.45	Birkenhead	Via Wombourn
	am						
F	2.25	MX	Didcot	7.28		Kingswinford	
H			Kingswinford		10.55	Crewe	
H	2.45	MO	Swindon	11.14		Kingswinford	
				pm	*pm*		
H	5.00	MX	Basingstoke	12.56		Kingswinford	
H	6.25	MO	Scours Lane	12.56		Kingswinford	
H	5.45	MX	Swindon	2.15	2.30	Oxley Sdgs	
H	12.15	MO	Tavistock Jn	2.33		Kingswinford	
H			Kingswinford		3.15	Crewe	Via Wombourn
	pm						
K	6.45	SO	Engine Shed Sdgs	6.50	7.15	Dudley	
K	7.15	SX	Engine Shed Sdgs	7.20	7.45	Tipton (5 Ways)	
					am		
H	10.50		Stourbridge Jn	11.00	12.14	Crewe	Via Wombourn
				am			
H	5.25	Su	Swindon (Sat.)	1.07		Kingswinford	
K		Su	Kingswinford North		4.45	Oxley Sdgs	

Code	Time	Day	From	Arr.	Dep.	To	Notes
	pm		*Up*	*am*	*am*		
H	11.20	MX+Su	Priestfield	12.57	1.29	Pontypool Rd	
	am						
K	12.45	MX	Dudley	1.22	1.47	Stourbridge Jn	
K	12.20	MX+Su (i)	Cannock Rd Jn	2.37	3.05	Stourbridge Jn	
D	11.10 (pm)	MX+Su(ii)	Welshpool	1.38	2.00	Cradley	Reverse Stourbr.
F	9.35 (pm)	MX+Su	Crewe	2.11	2.30	Worcester Goods	Via Wombourn
H	1.05	MX	Hollinswood	2.39		Kingswinford	Via Wombourn
H	3.17	MSX	Great Bridge	4.47		Kingswinford	From LMR
K	6.05	MX	Dudley	7.02	7.30	Stourbridge Jn	
H	5.15	MX	Oxley Sdgs	5.50	6.22	Worcester Goods	Via Wombourn
H	5.35	MO	Hollinswood	6.58	7.18	Stourbridge Jn*	Via Wombourn
H	4.50		Crewe	8.44	9.15	Worcester Goods	Via Wombourn
	pm			*pm*	*pm*		
K	12.15		Cannock Rd Jn	1.07	1.30	Stourbridge Jn	
H	1.45	RR	Dudley	2.34	2.45	Stourbridge Jn	
H	5.10		Hollinswood	6.37	7.00	Stourbridge Jn	Via Wombourn
H	6.18		Blower's Green	7.41	8.00	Worcester Goods	
K	8.25	SO	Dudley	9.17	10.00	Stourbridge Jn	
F	3.32		Stanlow	9.31	10.05	Rowley Regis	Reverse Stourbr.
K	9.45	SX	Tipton (5 Ways)	11.03	11.50	Stourbridge Jn	

Code	Time	Day	From	Arr.	Dep.	To	Notes
	pm	*Up*		*am*	*am*		
K	11.20	SO	Dudley	12.07	12.25	Stourbridge Jn	
	am						
F	1.15	Su	Hollinswood	2.30		Kingswinford	Via Wombourn
H	4.20	Su	Oxley Sdgs	5.11	5.25	Worcester Goods	

Key
RR   Runs as required.
O   On that day only, e.g. MO Monday only.
X   Not on that day, e.g. SX Saturday excepted.
*   Will run to Worcester if necessary.
†   Will run to Birkenhead depart 2.55 am if necessary.
(i)   Arrives at 2.27 am Sundays.
(ii)   Arrives at 1.46 am Sundays.

Annex to Appendices Three and Four

Key to GWR Train Codes

C   Parcels, Fish, Meat, Fruit, Milk, Horse, Cattle or Perishable Train, composed entirely of Vacuum-fitted Stock, vacuum pipe connected to engine.
      Express Freight, Livestock, Perishable or Ballast Train partly Vacuum-fitted, with not less than one-third vacuum-braked vehicles connected by vacuum pipe to engine.
D   Express Freight or Ballast Train conveying not less than four vacuum-braked vehicles connected by vacuum pipe to engine and authorised to run at a maximum speed of 35 mph.
E   Express Freight, Fish, Meat, Cattle or Ballast Train, not running under 'C' or 'D' Head Lamp conditions.
F   Through Fast Freight not running under 'C', 'D' or 'E' Head Lamp conditions, conveying Through load.
H   Freight, Mineral or Ballast Train, or Train of Empties carrying Through load to destination.
J   Through Freight, Mineral or Ballast Train stopping at intermediate stations.
K   Ordinary Freight, Mineral or Ballast Train stopping at local stations.
      Branch Freight.

Key to BR Train Codes (1950-1962)
C   Parcels , Fish, Fruit, Horse, Livestock, Meat, Milk, Pigeon or Perishable Train composed entirely of vehicles conforming to coaching stock requirements.
      Express Freight, Livestock, Perishable or Ballast Train piped throughout with the automatic brake operative on not less than 50 per cent of the vehicles.
D   Express Freight, Livestock, Perishable or Ballast Train partly fitted with the automatic brake operative on at least 33 per cent of the vehicles.
E   Express Freight, Livestock, Perishable or Ballast Train partly fitted with at least four braked vehicles connected to the engine by the vacuum pipe.
F   Unfitted Express Freight, Livestock, Perishable or Ballast Train.
H   Through Freight or Ballast Train not running under 'C', 'D', 'E' or 'F' Head Lamp conditions.
J   Mineral or Train conveying empty wagons.
K   Freight, Mineral or Ballast Train stopping at intermediate stations.
      Branch Freight.

List of Signal Boxes (1939)

	Times during which boxes are open			
	Weekdays		Sundays	
	Opened	Closed	Opened	Closed
Stourbridge Junction to Dudley				
Stourbridge Junction South	5.00 am		5.00 am *	
		6.00 am	10.30 pm	
Stourbridge Junction Middle	Open continuously			
Stourbridge Junction North	Open continuously			
Stourbridge Junction Engine House	Open continuously			
Stourbridge Goods Branch	Signal box closed down			
Brettell Lane	6.15 am	12.15 am	12.15 am *	
Kingswinford Junction South	4.30 am		See below	(1)
Kingswinford Junction North	6.00 am		See below	(2)
Round Oak South	6.00 am		6.30 am *	
		10.00 am	4.00 pm	
Round Oak North	6.00 am		4.00 am *	
Blower's Green Sidings	6.00 am		4.00 am *	
Blower's Green Junction	5.30 am		4.00 am *	
		8.00 pm	11.00 pm	
Dudley South	Open continuously			
Dudley North	5.00 am		6.00 am *	(3)
Stourbridge Junction to Old Hill				
Timmis' Siding	Opened as required for traffic for sidings only			
Lye	5.00 am		4.00 am	
		8.00 pm	10.30 pm	(4)
Cradley West	5.30 am	12.00 midnight		(5)
Cradley East	Open continuously			
Old Hill Junction	4.15 am		6.00 am *	
		7.45 am	9.30 am	
		8.00 pm	10.30 pm	(4)
Windmill End Branch - Old Hill Junction to Blower's Green Junction				
Cox's Lane	6.00 am		2.00 am	(6)
Windmill End	6.00 am		2.00 am	(6)
Windmill End Junction	6.00 am	10.00 pm		
Halesowen Branch-Old Hill Junction				
Halesowen Station	4.45 am		6.00 am	(6)
Kingswinford Branch - Kingswinford Junction to Baggeridge Junction				
Bromley Basin	10.15 am	1.30 pm		
	4.45 pm	7.00 pm		
Pensnett	9.00 am	5.00 pm		(7)
Baggeridge Junction	6.00 am		2.00 am *	

| | Times during which boxes are open | | | |
| | Weekdays | | Sundays | |
	Opened	Closed	Opened	Closed
Stourbridge Junction to Kidderminster				
Hagley	6.00 am			3.00 am
			8.00 am	11.30 am
			7.00 pm	10.20 pm (8)
Churchill	4.00 am			10.20 pm (8)
Kidderminster Station	4.30 am			5.30 am
			8.00 am	10.15 pm (8)

Notes

*   Or as ordered by Control.

(1)   Closed after 10.15 am Bordesley Junction to Kingswinford Pig Special arrived. This 'ran as required' Sundays only.

(2)   Closed 4.00 am or after 3.25 am Oxley Sidings had left.

(3)   Provided all booked trains had passed.

(4)   Or after 10.25 pm Stourbridge Junction to Birmingham Snow Hill Passenger Service has passed.

(5)   During the time box is switched out Up Distant signals to be left at Caution.

(6)   Or after last train.

(7)   Or after passing of last booked Local Branch Goods Train.

(8)   Or after 9.25 pm Passenger from Great Malvern to Birmingham Snow Hill clears section.

Class '3600' 2-4-2T No. 3624 accelerates a Birmingham (Snow Hill) service out of Stourbridge Junction past Middle signal box during the early 1920s. By March 1925 six of these locomotives had been allocated to Stourbridge, however, by the end of the decade all had been displaced by 2-6-2 tank engines.   *Real Photographs*

Appendix Six

Stourbridge Junction Yards

The sidings situated between North and Middle signal boxes were known as follows:

Down Yard

No. of siding	Description of traffic	Holding wagon capacity
Front Yard		
No. 1	Down goods line (next to down main line)	50 *
No. 2	Down good reception line	45 *
No. 3	Traffic transferred from up yard	38
No. 4	Stourbridge Town branch traffic	37
No. 5	Storage and marshalling sidings	45
No. 6	Storage and marshalling sidings	44
No. 7	Storage and marshalling sidings	40
No. 8	Storage and marshalling sidings	37
No. 9	Storage and marshalling sidings	33
No. 10	Storage and marshalling sidings	30
No. 11	Storage and marshalling sidings	27
Back Yard		
No. 1	Storage and marshalling sidings	43
No. 2	Storage and marshalling sidings	40
No. 3	Storage and marshalling sidings	25
No. 4	Storage and marshalling sidings	12
No. 5	Storage and marshalling sidings	10
No. 6	Storage and marshalling sidings	9
No. 7	Storage and marshalling sidings	8
No. 8	Cripple sidings	36
No. 9	Cripple sidings	36
No. 10	Cripple sidings	36
No. 11	Brake van siding	9 brake vans
No. 12	Civil Engineer's siding	8

Up Yard

No. of siding	Description of traffic	Holding wagon capacity
Middle Yard		
No. 1	Up goods line (next to up main line)	45 *
No. 2	Storage and marshalling sidings	41
No. 3	Storage and marshalling sidings	40
No. 4	Storage and marshalling sidings	33
No. 5	Storage and marshalling sidings	22
No. 6	Up goods reception line	44 *
Back Yard		
No. 7	Situated north of No. 6 up to a dead end. To be used for traffic blocked back.	20
No. 8	Coal yard sidings	22
No. 9	Coal yard sidings	18
No. 10	Storage and marshalling sidings	60
No. 11	Storage and marshalling sidings	58
No. 12	Storage and marshalling sidings	52
No. 13	Storage and marshalling sidings	49
No. 14	Storage and marshalling sidings	44
No. 15	Storage and marshalling sidings	42

* In addition to tender engine and brake van.

Chronology

Original Stourbridge station opened   1st May, 1852
  (opened to regular traffic on Monday 3rd May, 1852)
OWWR from Stourbridge to Dudley opened(freight)   16th November, 1852
OWWR from Stourbridge to Dudley opened(passenger)   20th December, 1852
OWWR from Dudley to LNWR at Tipton Junction opened   1st December, 1853
Through services between Wolverhampton (LNWR) and London (Euston)
  over the Tipton Curve via Tipton Junction began   1st April, 1854
OWWR from Tipton to Cannock Road Junction, Wolverhampton   completed during April 1854
OWWR from Cannock Road Junction to Bushbury opened (freight)   July 1854
OWWR from Tipton to Wolverhampton Low Level opened (passenger)   1st July, 1854
LNWR Through service between Kidderminster, Stourbridge Jn,
  Dudley & Birmingham(New Street) via Sedgeley Loop began   1st March, 1856
Brierley Hill station opened   1st December, 1858
Through services between Wolverhampton(LNWR) and London (Euston)
  over the Tipton curve via Tipton Junction withdrawn   1st October, 1861
Stourbridge Railway from Stourbridge to Cradley opened   1st April, 1863
Stourbridge Railway from Cradley to Old Hill opened   1st January, 1866
Stourbridge Extension Railway from Old Hill to LNWR at
  Galton Junction & GWR at Handsworth Junction opened   1st April, 1867
LNWR Through service between Hereford/Worcester, Kidderminster
  Stourbridge Jn & Birmingham (New St) via Stourbridge Extension commenced   1st April, 1867
LNWR Through service between Kidderminster, Stourbridge Jn,
  Dudley & Birmingham(New Street) via Sedgeley Loop ended   *c.* August 1867
Stourbridge station renamed Stourbridge Junction   1st October, 1879
New Stambermill viaduct opened to traffic   10th May, 1882
Harts Hill & Woodside station opened on OWWR   1st April, 1895
Original Stourbridge Junction station closed   1st October, 1901
New Stourbridge Junction station opened   1st October, 1901
New connection to the Town branch opened   1st October, 1901
Original branch disconnected   1st October, 1901
Harts Hill & Woodside station closed   1st January, 1917
LNWR Through service between Hereford/Worcester, Kidderminster
  Stourbridge Junction & Birmingham(New St) via
  Stourbridge Extension withdrawn   1st January, 1917
Stourbridge Jn-Wolverhampton LL passenger service withdrawn   30th July, 1962
Amblecote deviation built and removed   *c.* 1972-74
Stourbridge South signal box closed   30th December, 1973
Stourbridge North signal box closed   29th July, 1978
Cradley station rebuilt during   January 1984
Former OWWR main line closed north of Round Oak   22nd March, 1993
Jewellery line opened   24th September, 1995

Stourbridge Town Station and Branch

Original Stourbridge Branch from Amblecote opened   30th July, 1859
Branch from Amblecote closed   *c.* 1879
Branch from Stourbridge Jn opened for passenger traffic   1st October, 1879
Branch from Stourbridge Jn opened for freight traffic   1st January, 1880
Passenger services to the Town station suspended   1st April, 1915
Passenger services to the Town reintroduced   28th February, 1919
New arrangements begun for operating up and down goods and
  passenger traffic; closure of Town signal box   25th August, 1935

Stourbridge Town Station and Branch (Continued)

Siding to Turney & Co. closed	1960
Gas works siding closed	31st May, 1963
Siding to Bradley & Co. closed from level crossing	March 1965
Last Freight train to use branch	30th April, 1965
Siding to DF Fellows closed	May 1965
Single goods line closed	20th September, 1965
Goods line lifted by	22nd October, 1967
Town station buildings demolished & platforms cutback	February 1979
Remains of original Town station completely removed	February 1994
New Town station opened to passenger traffic	25th April, 1994
Single passenger line	Still Operational

Stourbridge Junction Engine Sheds

Original engine shed opened	1870
Original engine shed closed	8th February, 1926
New engine shed opened	8th February, 1926
Original shed re-opened	1944
Both sheds closed to steam traction	11th July, 1966
Motive Power Depots demolished	by June 1969

Branches and Sidings

The OWWR Main Line

Woodside branch built	1852
Kingswinford branch opened	14th November, 1858
Rufford's siding opened	23rd August, 1882
John Hall's siding built	*c.* 1900
Marsh & Baxter's siding at Kingswinford Junction built	February 1916
Moor Lane Goods branch and Mileage Depot opened	14th August, 1922
Kingswinford branch opened as Through route via Wombourn for freight traffic	11th January, 1925
Kingswinford branch opened as Through route via Wombourn for passenger traffic	11th May, 1925
Passenger traffic via the Wombourn branch withdrawn	31st October, 1932
Rufford's siding taken out of use	7th December, 1949
John Hall's siding taken out of use	March 1961
Kingswinford Marshalling Yard closed	16th September, 1963
Wombourn branch ceased as a Through route, reverted to original Kingswinford branch	1st March, 1965
Parkhead sidings taken out of use	23rd May, 1965
Moor Lane Concentration Depot opened	31st May, 1965
Marsh & Baxter's siding taken out of use	13th March, 1967
Kingswinford branch reduced to Pensnett Trading Estate	1st April, 1968
Blower's Green sidings taken out of use	*c.* 1969
Round Oak crossing repositioned	January 1971
Kingswinford branch 'mothballed'	1994
Moor Street Steel Terminal 'mothballed'	June 1997
Moor Street Steel Terminal brought back into use	July 1997

The Stourbridge Railway Main Line

Corngreaves Branch opened	1st April, 1863
Cradley Park Branch (Hayes Branch) opened	June 1863
Homer Hill sidings brought into operation	April 1867
Netherend Reception sidings brought into operation	*c.* 1867
Timmis' siding & siding to Regina Works opened	*c.* 1882
Mineral Railway from Witley Colliery to Corngreaves opened	*c.* 1885
Spinners End Branch opened	1st July, 1907
Netherend Reception & Homer Hill sidings taken out of use by	1919
Mineral Railway from Witley Colliery to Corngreaves closed	*c.* 1921
Regina Works siding taken out of use	during 1951
Timmis' siding taken out of use	during 1964
Cradley Park Branch closed	10th August, 1964
Spinners End Branch closed	10th August, 1964
Corngreaves Branch closed	12th April, 1965

The Netherton & Halesowen Branch

Dudley (South Side) and Netherton to Old Hill/Old Hill to Halesowen opened	1st March, 1878
Withymoor Basin (Netherton Goods) branch opened	10th March, 1879
Halesowen Railway to Northfield via Halesowen Junction opened	10th September, 1883
Halesowen Basin branch opened	2nd April, 1902
Workmen's Services from Old Hill & Halesowen to Longbridge commenced	18th April, 1917
Halesowen to Old Hill closed to public passenger traffic	5th December, 1927
Workmen's services to/from Halesowen operated by steam railmotor ceased	31st March, 1928
Workmen's services between Old Hill & Longbridge ceased	1st September, 1958
Old Hill to Dudley (Blower's Green Junction) closed to passenger traffic	15th June, 1964
Netherton Goods Branch and Windmill End Junction closed	5th July, 1965
Old Hill to Dudley (Blower's Green Junction) closed	1st January, 1968
Halesowen Goods Yard closed	9th September, 1968
Halesowen Basin branch closed	1st October, 1969
Halesowen to Old Hill section closed	1st October, 1969

'14XX' class 0-4-2T No. 1438 takes water at Old Hill on 8th April, 1957.   *H.C. Casserley*

Bibliography

'Railways to Stourbridge' by John Marshall (Journal of the Railway and Canal Historical Society Vol. 29, part 1, No. 135, March 1987)
Atlas of the Great Western Railway 1947 by R.A. Cooke (Wild Swan Publications)
The West Midland Lines of the GWR by Keith M. Beck (Ian Allan Ltd)
The Birmingham & Gloucester Railway by P.J. Long & The Revd W.V. Awdry (A. Sutton)
The Oxford, Worcester & Wolverhampton Railway by S.C. Jenkins & H.I. Quayle (Oakwood Press)
Complete British Railways Maps and Gazetteer 1825 to 1985 by C.J. Wignall (OPC)
Railways of the Black Country Vol. 1 The Byways by N. Williams (Urailia Press)
A Historical Survey of Selected Great Western Stations Vol. 4 by C.R. Potts (OPC)
The Stourbridge Scene 1851 to 1951 by H.J. Haden
The Railway to Wombourn by N. Williams (Urailia Press)
A Regional History of the Railways of Great Britain Vol. 7 The West Midlands by R. Christiansen (David & Charles)
By Rail to Halesowen by M. Hale and N. Williams (M. Hale and Urailia Press)
Forgotten Railways of the West Midlands by R. Christiansen (David and Charles)
History of the Great Western Railway Vols. 1 & 2 by E.T. MacDermot (Ian Allan Ltd)
Rail Centres: Wolverhampton by Paul Collins (Ian Allan Ltd)
A Historical Survey of Great Western Engine Sheds 1947 by E. Lyons (OPC)
Great Western Engine Sheds 1837 to 1947 by E. Lyons and E. Mountford (OPC)
Steam at Round Oak by G.L. Chatham (Halmar Publications)
History of the Pensnett Railway by W.K.V. Gale
Timetable of the Great Western Railway 1902 - reprinted by Ian Allan
Great Western Railway Time Tables 6th October, 1947 - reprinted by OPC
A Regional History of the Railways of Great Britain, Vol. 12 South Wales by D.S.M. Barrie revised by P. Baughan (David St John Thomas)
Locomotives of the LNER Part 5 - RCTS
BR Steam Motive Power Depots (WR) by Paul Bolger (Ian Allan Ltd)
British Railway Locomotives 1948 by Chris Banks (OPC)
Industrial Locomotives of West Midlands - Industrial Railway Society
A selection of Public and Working Timetables 1876-1994
The *Wolverhampton Chronicle/ Brierley Hill Advertiser/ County Express* various, between 1844 and 1990
The Blackcountryman Vol. 10, Nos. 2 and 3; Vol. 12 No. 4 (Articles by M. Hale)
Dudley Chronicle, 6th August, 1995, 9th May, 1997 & 27th June, 1997
Centro Information 1995
Railway Magazine September 1995
Trains Illustrated/Modern Railways: Various 1951 to 1964
Freightmaster-Power Handle Productions Autumn 1995 & Spring 1996
BR Steam Shed Allocations Pt Two Western Region Sheds by P.Hands (Defiant Pub)
Track Layout Diagrams of the GWR & BR WR Section 31 West Midlands by R.A. Cooke
Railways of the West Midlands: A Chronology 1808 to 1954 - SLS
Railways in Wales by Herbert Williams (Christopher Davies, Swansea)
The Economic Emergence of the Black Country by T.J. Raybould (David & Charles)
The Great Western Railway by Avon Anglia Publications & Services
'Stourbridge and its Historic Locomotives' - edited by Paul Collins (Dudley MBC)
Report of the Railway Department of the Board of Trade - 28th February, 1845
Britain's Rail Super Centres: Birmingham by Paul Collins (Ian Allan Publishing)
The Heyday of GWR Train Services by P.W.B. Semmens (David & Charles)
GWR Locomotive Allocations 1921 by I. Harrison (Wild Swan Publications)
GWR Locomotive Allocations 1934 by Revd N. Pocock & I. Harrison (Wild Swan)
Locomotives of the GWR Parts 3 to 9 - RCTS
Railway Development Society Leaflet, April 1997
The *Journal* of the Stephenson Locomotive Society 1942-51
British Steam Railcars by R.W. Rush (Oakwood Press)
The GWR Registers of Locomotives at PRO Kew
British Railway History 1830-1876 by C. Hamilton Ellis (Allen & Unwin)
Red for Danger by L.T.C. Rolt (David & Charles)
The Canals of the West Midlands by Charles Hadfield (David and Charles)
The Dudley and Stourbridge Canals - Dudley Canal Trust and the Staffs & Worcs Canal Society (Lapal Publications)
Stourbridge Canal by J. Ian Langford (Lapal Publications)

Index